FOR WOOD RIVER OR BUST

THE IDAHO LEGACY SERIES

The Idaho Legacy Series is copublished by the University of Idaho
Press and the Idaho State Historical Society. Monographs in the series
focus on Idaho history and offer regional perspectives. The Idaho Legacy
Series is supported by funding initially provided by the Idaho Centen-
nial Commission.

THE IDAHO LEGACY SERIES

CLARK C. SPENCE

FOR WOOD RIVER OR BUST

IDAHO'S SILVER BOOM OF THE 1880s

UNIVERSITY OF IDAHO PRESS
Moscow, Idaho

IDAHO STATE HISTORICAL SOCIETY
Boise, Idaho
1999

2003
2002
2001
2000
1999
5
4
3
2
1

Library of Congress Cataloging-in-Publication Data
Spence, Clark C.
For Wood River or bust : Idaho's silver boom of the 1880s / by Clark C. Spence.
p.   cm. — (The Idaho legacy series)
Includes bibliographical references and index.
Summary: Chronicles the history of the silver rush in the Wood River area of
Idaho during the late nineteenth century, describing the mining companies, settle-
ments, and prospectors.
ISBN 0-89301-215-7
I. Big Wood River (Idaho)—History—Juvenile literature.   2. Frontier and pio-
neer life—Idaho—Big Wood River—Juvenile literature.   3. Silver mines and
mining—Idaho—Big Wood River—History—19th century—Juvenile literature.
[1. Big Wood River (Idaho)—History.   2. Idaho—History.   3. Frontier and
pioneer life—Idaho—Big Wood River.   4. Silver mines and mining—Idaho—
Big Wood River—History—19th century.]   I. Title.   II. Series.
E752.B55   1998
979.6'3—dc21   98-10145
CIP
AC

Cover photograph: Rupert's Drug Store and the Nevada Chop House
in Hailey, 1884. Courtesy of the Idaho State Historical Society.

TO MERLE W. WELLS

CONTENTS

ILLUSTRATIONS

FOR MINING COMMUNITIES as well as mortals, there is a time to be born and a time to die. A few, like Butte, Montana, enjoyed a prosperous longevity; most lived fleetingly, a brief and intense blaze of glory across the pages of history, then lapsed, either to perish completely or to survive with much altered economic bases or their province diminished. The moment of brilliance of the Wood River mining towns spanned roughly the decade of the 1880s, when silver-lead ores dictated both the rise and decline of such Idaho centers as Bellevue, Hailey, Bullion, Broadford, Ketchum, and Muldoon—though a wider definition of Wood River would include areas as far north as Galena and as far west as Vienna. In its day, Wood River's boom and its production record were common enough knowledge. But even though it was not comparable in the long run to Leadville, Colorado, or the Coeur d'Alenes, Wood River has never been given its due—in its heyday by contemporaries or by later historians. "For Wood River or Bust" tries to capture a bit of the flavor of these early camps and to pay tribute to those who made them what they were: the average people, in settlements typical of the mineral West in general. They were not unique, but part of a larger whole.

Today only three of the old boom towns remain: Ketchum, Hailey, and Bellevue. None of them are dependent upon mining anymore; instead all three serve the surrounding areas as commercial centers and jump-off points to the Sawtooth National Recreational Area to the north. Each is a little different.

Since the 1930s Ketchum has been closely tied to nearby Sun Valley and the skiing industry. In recent years, it has emerged as an expensive, upscale community where business tycoons and celebrities like Ernest Hemingway built luxurious ski lodges and summer homes, but which still has a core of well-to-do, year-round residents. Hailey has become an affordable family town for those working in Ketchum and Sun Valley, and Bellevue, four miles south of Hailey, serves the same function. But all three communities are quick to remind visitors of their nineteenth century silver-lead heritage through local museums, guided tours of historic districts, and special annual celebrations, such as Ketchum's "Wagon Days" and "Days of the West" in Hailey.

This book draws on the ideas and cooperation of a number of individuals and institutions, but its errors are mine alone. I owe a debt of gratitude to a disparate group of people. Everett Sanders, principal of Glenns Ferry High School, chose Ketchum and Hailey for the Class of 1941 Senior Sneak and first introduced me to the Wood River country. Much later, Judith Austin pointed me in the direction of the historical Wood River. She has generously shared her expertise and has gone far beyond the call of duty in making materials available from the Idaho State Historical Society. Wallace D. Farnham has made fruitful suggestions and provided contacts, especially with Alan Virta, who furnished copies of documents from the Special Collections Department at Boise State University. Paul Link of Idaho State University also supplied helpful information. At the Montana Historical Society Archives, Ellie Arguimbau and her staff made research both pleasant and productive. I am also grateful to Peter Blodgett and Jenny Watts of the Henry E. Huntington Library for their cheerful and persistent searching on my behalf.

For Wood River or Bust

For financial support I am indebted to the Department of History and the Research Board of the University of Illinois.

CLARK C. SPENCE
Champaign
April 1997

CHAPTER ONE

THEY GATHERED AT THE RIVER

IF MINING DISCOVERIES were sometimes the result of chance, more often they were the product of stamina, patience, and persistence on the part of a hardy and resourceful group of prospectors—men and a few women—who carried out the dictates of the basic commandment of the mineral world: "first find your mine." The successful prospector, it was said, was born, not made, and required special attributes: restlessness, endurance, a hopeful temperament, an easygoing disposition, a quick eye not only for mineral indications but also for danger, and an indifference to luxury or even comfort. Prospectors were self-taught, endowed with a tough ability to survive, and usually grubstaked by some local speculator or businessman. The "lonely, unkempt professional prospector, with his furtive attempts to conceal his journeyings, became a central and often romanticized figure in Western folklore," says historian Rodman Paul.[1] With bare essentials and with the sky and the stars as his roof, he spent weeks or even months in the wilderness accompanied only by his faithful burro and sustained by a diet of salt bacon, beans, and daydreams of undiscovered wealth. Often scruffy, smelly, profane, and always on the pry, his aspiration to hit it big kept him going. Rarely did he dig a hole more than a dozen feet deep: his object was to discover and sell, not to work an actual mine. Occasionally, he was successful enough to attract a host of amateurs and to inspire the rise of a boisterous new mining camp.[2]

Whether lured by the siren call of gold, or heading home after abandoning the search in some recent rush, these veterans continually panned the streams as they ambled along, more than once washing colors enough to start a new stampede. Thus parties returning from British Columbia's Fraser River in 1860 hit gold on the Clearwater River in what became Idaho. Two years later, eager Coloradans heading for the north Idaho diggings found gold on Grasshopper Creek and touched off a new rush to the area that became Montana. Wood River might have shared that fate, but the conditions were slightly different and the pay dirt was silver, not gold.

Silver was rarely, if ever, found in placer deposits; it almost invariably occurred in veins, often in carbonate form or in combination with lead, as was the case in Wood River, where most deposits were of silver-bearing galena ores. A few were in chalcopyrite, a sulfide of copper and iron, and a few were of gold-bearing pyrite, chalcopyrite, or arsenopyrite.[3]

In whatever form, silver often went unrecognized by single-minded prospectors suffering from gold fever. At the Comstock Lode in Nevada and at Leadville, Colorado, placer miners swore at the "damned blue stuff" that clogged their equipment, unaware that the blue stuff and the dirty rocks from which it had decomposed were fabulously rich in silver. In Wood River prospectors recognized the silver metal, but times were not yet ripe for its exploitation.

Like many new mineral areas, the Wood River country was isolated and desolate. Artist and author Mary Hallock Foote called it "the darkest part of darkest Idaho" when her husband went there to manage a mine in 1882.[4] Originating in the northern extremities of the Smoky and Boulder Mountains at an altitude of 8,500 feet, Wood River itself sweeps across 95 miles and eventually drains some 3,800 square miles into the Snake River by several different routes.[5]

Geologists place the Wood River region near the southern border of the great mountain mass of central Idaho and describe it as "a rugged region of marked relief, in which the only level tracts are the terraces and alluvial flats along a few of the larger streams, such as the Big Wood River and the Big Lost River." From Bellevue on the lowest fringe north to the vicinity of Ketchum, peaks range up to eight thousand feet with valleys about two thousand feet lower. Farther north, the relief is greater with summits along the main divide three or four thousand feet above the major streams. Some peaks rise above ten thousand feet and culminate in the Pioneer Range at Hyndman Peak, 12,078 feet above sea level.

Away from the divide, the valleys are comparatively open, especially in the south and southwest toward the Snake River plains, but they narrow and become more gorge-like nearer the divide. Many open out at their heads into glacial cirques with precipitous walls. The lower, less rugged sections, the valley bottoms, and the lower slopes of hills are mainly treeless and covered with grass and sagebrush. The streams are lined with willows, while trees become more abundant at middle altitudes. Patches of aspen are common up to eight or nine thousand feet, and evergreens predominate up to the timber line about a thousand feet higher. About two-thirds of the area was ultimately included in the Sawtooth National Forest and the Lemhi National Forest.[6]

Within these broad perimeters the mineral boom of the 1880s took place, from the Sawtooth Mountain camps of Vienna and Sawtooth City in the north to the major centers on the Big Wood itself—Bellevue, Hailey, and Ketchum—along with the discoveries on the Little Smoky to the west and the Little Wood River to the east. Overlapping the heyday of Leadville in Colorado, Wood River was the preeminent silver rush in Idaho until it was eclipsed by the Coeur d'Alene excitement in the late 1880s.

Prospectors from farther west had tried their hand on Wood River as early as 1863, but no actual mining occurred. In 1864, one of those restless souls, Pennsylvania-born Warren P. Callahan, was moseying from the Boise Basin to Montana, working the streams flowing into the Wood River, when he found promising silver-lead indications near Goodale's Cutoff on the road from Boise to Salmon City. But gold interested him, not galena ore, so Callahan moved on. Later that same year, M. H. Williams, W. H. Spencer, Ross Smith, and David Whitmer located the Big Camas Mine, which showed free gold as well as silver, about nine miles west of the future site of Bellevue. Over the next year and a half, the quartet drove a tunnel and tapped the ledge, which proved a good one. But they were forced to cease work because of the high cost of labor and materials. Nine years later, either Callahan or his brother John, or perhaps both, returned with packhorses and tools to locate the Galena and the Keystone Mines, both high-grade galena and carbonate silver producers. Back, too, were M. H. Williams and W. H. Spencer, along with Matthew Graham, to stake out the Antelope and the Phoenix.[7]

Despite all this activity, development was still in the future. Silver-lead ores were far less exciting than Everyman's dream: free-milling gold. The techniques for handling these ores had already been worked out in Colorado and Nevada, especially at Eureka, but they required expensive furnaces. Lead was a commercially valuable base metal only if smelting and rail transportation were available. Wood River had neither. It could either raise substantial amounts of capital to build its own plants or ship its ores to the nearest facilities. Unfortunately, the closest smelting plants were in Montana or Utah—and a railroad was only an aspiration.[8]

The Wood River pioneers liked to blame hostile Indians for delaying the opening of the area, and some historians have lent credence to this point of view by arguing that not until the successful completion of the so-called Bannock War in the late 1870s was the way clear to unlock Wood River's hidden wealth. Old-timer John Hailey wrote that the Indian troubles made it unsafe for small parties to prospect in isolated areas and gave mining "quite a setback."[9] To be sure, sporadic harassment by roving Sheepeaters (a small band of Shoshone Indians) and the threat of the Bannock were at times deterrents to prospectors. These Indians were relatively few in number, however, and by no means powerful tribes. Besides, mere hardship and danger never hindered prospectors for long. Rarely in the West had Indians, even the superb Plains warriors, prevented mining rushes when their time had come; the Sioux, among the best fighters on the continent, were unable to stem the tide of miners pouring into the Black Hills.

All was quiet by the end of the 1870s with the Bannock and the Nez Perce farther north crushed, and mining men saw glimmerings of hope for branch rail lines to complete the links between mines and smelters and to facilitate the attraction of capital. There was talk of a railroad to link the Utah and Northern to Oregon. It would pass near the Wood River galena belts, and that was a vital factor that stimulated prospectors at the end of the 1870s.[10] In all likelihood, if the rich ores had been discovered years earlier, and if transportation and technical smelting know-how had been readily available, Wood River would have blossomed then—Indians or no Indians.

Idaho Territory had already seen its share of mining rushes, beginning with Pierce and Orofino in the Nez Perce country in 1860 and 1861, and continuing at Florence and Warrens on tributaries of the Salmon River not long afterward. But in the long run, the Boise Basin, some thirty miles northeast of the present city of Boise, proved to be more important. The first discoveries there came in 1862 and spawned Idaho City, Placerville, Centerville, and other boom towns. Next came gold discoveries farther east on the Middle Fork of the Boise River at Atlanta and at Rocky Bar, located on a tributary of the South Fork.

All of these had been primarily gold camps, as were the Owyhee diggings on Jordan Creek in 1863. But within a year or two, placer gold deposits had given way to newly discovered veins rich in silver. In the Owyhee boom, which contemporaries compared to the Comstock Lode, such centers as Ruby City, Silver City, and DeLamar flourished. By 1875, the area had reputedly produced $30 million in mineral wealth.[11]

Meanwhile, prospectors in the Stanley Basin and Bear Valley found enough precious metal to whip up new excitement along the Salmon. Some of them located galena outcroppings on Wood River and copper prospects on Lost River, although in 1864 these minerals were ignored. New finds in the Atlanta area included silver in paying quantities, and in the mid-1860s a number of mining districts developed around Leesburg, Gibbonsville, Shoup, and Ulysses. A brief silver boom erupted in 1869 at Black Pine, in southeast Idaho, north of Kelton and the Utah line, but it soon fizzled out. Major silver discoveries also came on the Salmon at Yankee Fork, Bay Horse, and Clayton—all products of the 1870s.

The movement of Chief Joseph and the Nez Perce across Idaho in 1877 may have caused apprehension, but this threat was too far north to be critical. In the spring of 1878 while heading from Challis to the upper Salmon, Levi Smiley and a party of prospectors found a rich quartz outcrop, but potential trouble with the Bannock prompted them to retreat.

Returning the following year, another Smiley group staked promising gold and silver properties in the Sawtooth region lying between the Salmon and the Wood River basin. The activity brought an influx to such new camps as Vienna and Sawtooth City, and the stage was set for the opening of a much larger silver-lead region.[12]

At the same time, prospectors fanning out from the Sawtooth mines, Rocky Bar, Yankee Fork, and other Salmon River centers in the summer of 1879 made rich strikes on the Wood River. The first important finds came at Galena at the mouth of Gladiator Creek followed by a number on the lower Wood, where veins reportedly two-and-a-half-feet thick ran forty to sixty percent lead and assayed $80 to $250 a ton in silver.[13] These new discoveries, the easier and better smelting techniques, and the rail facilities on the horizon (rather than the defeat of the Bannock or the Sheepeaters) were the major ingredients in the forthcoming rush.

In the late 1870s, two Salt Lake City men, Frank W. Jacobs and a partner named Kennedy, built a blacksmith shop near the old emigrant road to Oregon and Washington in the lower part of the district. They prospected on the side, and some say that Jacobs located the first mines in the area as early as 1877; certainly his most important discovery, the Queen of the Hills, turned out to be a valuable producer. A small settlement grew up at Jacobs City (which was renamed Broadford in 1880 and later became Bradford) on an easy crossing of the Wood River about a mile west of the future town of Bellevue, which eventually absorbed it. Six miles above Jacobs City another camp clustered around Warren Callahan's mines, especially the Keystone and one that bore his own name, to provide the nucleus for what later became Hailey. Locations were also being made on Warm Springs Creek in the Middle Wood River District, where Ketchum would eventually evolve, and at Galena, the oldest town on the river, where miners organized a new sweeping Wood River Mining District.[14]

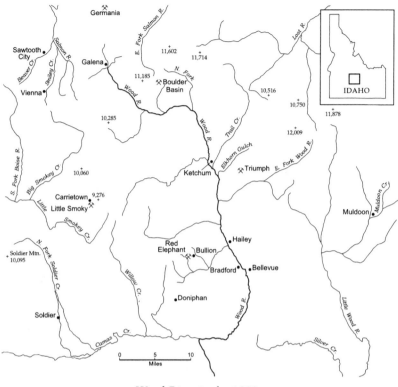

Wood River in the 1880s

The flood gates were open. By late September, it was reported that 233 claims had been located or relocated and filed in the district. No doubt some of these were by optimists driven by the eternal hope of striking gold, but the word was out that silver was the prize and Wood River was the place. Already there were a dozen or so dwellings, prospects for a railroad connection were openly discussed, and those in the know were certain that the area would control future Idaho trade.[15]

While some onlookers thought the climate "particularly advantageous" for year-round activity, it was clear to most that cold and snow would curtail winter activity and that most prospectors would winter elsewhere, though a hardy contingent did remain. "That great and good man and Christian muleskinner, Dave Ketchum," whose name lingers on, had found some fair-looking silver lodes near the juncture of Warm Springs Creek and Wood River. He built a cabin and stored supplies, but spent the cold months in Nevada.[16]

Twenty-seven people, including Commodore Perry Croy and part of his family, and at least one woman, Mrs. James Loving, remained after the winter exodus to experience some unpleasant times, although a food shortage was averted when Owen Riley, who would erect the first building in Hailey, brought in a load of provisions. When Frank Myers drove the first stage in from Blackfoot in early May, traveling the last leg by sleigh over two feet of snow, he found all hands in good shape, but with minimal food supplies.[17]

Not far behind Myers came the return of many of the seventy-niners, along with an army of new stampeders, three thousand strong, swarming in like field mice to scour the district "as if in search of that which was lost," as one mining editor put it.[18] A whisper had grown to a shout: Silver! Like other mining rushes, they came on foot, on horseback, by wagon, or by stagecoach. From Boise to Bellevue by stage took three and a half days, by horseback or team took nearly twice that; the Blackfoot stage, soon running on a daily basis, was comparable to the Boise run and cost twenty-five dollars, with meals a dollar each and lodging seventy-five cents a night to share the floor of a log cabin with a dozen others. From the railhead at Kelton, Utah, the Goose Creek and Wood River coach came in four times a week over an arduous route.[19]

Newcomers found a whole new world. The hustle and bustle was punctuated by the braying of pack animals and genuine frontier language, loudly and impiously spoken. A self-described "nomad of the pick and canteen" reported:

"All day long, and far into the night, men from every quarter of the globe, bronzed and bearded miners, merchants, professional men, uncouth bullwhackers, profane mule skinners, quartz experts, stock sharps, gamblers and desperados crowd the side-walks and throng the saloons."[20]

One of those reaching the new diggings that spring was Isaac I. Lewis, a Montanan of ten years standing who had been involved in mining around Helena and Clancy and who had close ties with Samuel Hauser's banking and ore-buying operations. Lewis became one of the "stayers" who settled permanently and became one of the leading citizens of the area. In the fall of 1877, he and a small party had passed through part of the Wood River country while on a grueling sixty-five-day, 1,200-mile round trip to examine a copper prospect in the Seven Devils area of the Snake River on the Idaho-Oregon border, 120 miles north and west of Boise.[21] Back in Montana, after talking with miners returned from the new diggings in the winter of 1879–80, Lewis contracted Wood River fever. "I felt it in my bones that I must go there," he wrote. Consequently, he took a sixty-day leave of absence. With two companions, John H. Lewis and Charles Swan, both with mining experience, he outfitted a wagon with camping gear and prospecting equipment—including his assaying materials and surveying instruments—and headed south over Lemhi Pass in the spring of 1880. Joined by Albert Griffith along the way, the little band retraced the first part of Lewis's route of three years earlier and met other emigrants also heading for the silver fields—including William H. Greenhow, Jim Kellogg, and A. R. French.[22]

After a tough month-long wagon trip, Isaac Lewis came upon a camp of "prospectors, merchants and all sorts" near Broadford, where Boisean Jim Hart had a covered wagon and a tent with some merchandise and a barrel of whiskey handy with spigot and tin cup. Lewis resisted Hart's efforts to get him to locate there and help lay out a town, took a quick pull at the cup, and proceeded on to Quigley's Gulch, opposite where Hailey would soon stand. There, he saw his first cabin, one just completed. He found several cabins at Broadford and eventually pitched his tent along with a number of others in a cottonwood grove on Trail Creek bottom near where Ketchum would develop. Lewis staked himself four lots, commenced the task of surveying the new town site (called Leadville until the U.S. postal officials refused to sanction the name because there was already a famous Leadville in the West), and prepared to open the first assay office in the Wood River country. The "Keystone City," as Ketchum was sometimes called, was starting to thrive. Apart from Jim Kellogg's new saloon and other canvas structures, Lewis's building was the second one completed; T. E. Clohecy & Company had opened their store, bringing in goods by pack animals from Blackfoot; Pinkham & Leonard were about to start a second store on Main Street; and others were flocking in, although they had to shovel the snow away to clear the ground for construction.[23]

Arriving in May after "a long contest with bad roads, high water and unfavorable weather," J. B. Foster, a correspondent for the *Boise Statesman*, was impressed with Bellevue. With its four saloons, two restaurants, two stores, blacksmith shop, livery stable, meat market, and Chinese wash houses, "besides several other buildings" and fifteen houses going up, this was "the live town of the valley." Bellevue was reminiscent of early California or the Boise Basin in the summer of 1863: "Tents, wagons and willow shanties are scattered along the margin of the stream for half a mile; and as soon as some restless prospector folds his tent and leaves for the scene of some new excitement his place is promptly filled by some newcomer."[24]

While an ancient forty-niner beguiled an attentive flock of tenderfeet with salty stories of the old days, across the street another group carefully inspected a pile of ore specimens brought down the mountain by a canny prospector:

Just at this juncture the man who owns the oldest restaurant in town (which by the way was opened a full week ago) comes to the door and using an old rusty frying pan for a gong, frightens the horses which are hitched to the Meat Market which was only opened today and carried on in a wagon. Then down street go the horses at full speed, scattering beef among the dwellers in tents and finally run over a wagon which is used as a residence and brought up against a post.[25]

Foster reported again a few days later from a novel vantage point: "Seated on a box of giant-powder by the flickering light of a tallow candle, within the walls of a newly built log store house with the wind whistling through the unchinked walls, surrounded by some thirty miners and prospectors." With 125 lots recorded, thirteen houses complete, twenty more under construction, and Alexander Toponce's stage running on a regular basis from Blackfoot, Foster wrote:

. . . [T]aken all together we begin to feel that the genial rays of civilization are rapidly penetrating this land, which only two short years ago was a waste and howling wilderness, almost unknown except as the hiding place of hostile savages.[26]

"Day after day," he continued later, "the stream of bonanza hunters continues to pour through our little town, each armed with pick, pan and shovel and such articles as are necessary for the simple culinary department of the prospector." In the wings, capitalists waited for the roads to clear, eagerly anticipating the opportunity to make millions.[27]

Carrie and Robert Strahorn arrived from Montana that same summer of 1880, coming up by coach from Blackfoot via the lava beds, Arco, Deadman's Flat, Fish Creek, and Little Wood River, then over the hills to Silver Creek and up the Big Wood, a distance of some one hundred fifty miles. Strahorn, a newspaperman who had covered Crook's campaigns against the Sioux and the Cheyenne, was head of the Union Pacific Railroad's "literary bureau"—his job was to publicize the line and to prepare a series of guidebooks for prospective settlers along the route. His wife, Carrie, a graduate of the University of Michigan who invariably accompanied her beloved husband on his travels, eventually became what Judith Austin calls "a hostess to the West"—an unofficial Welcome Wagon-greeter for newcomers moving into areas she and her husband had visited earlier.[28] The Strahorns were impressed with the beautiful meadows and sparkling mountain streams of the area. They found Bellevue—then the hub of the Wood River rush—interesting, if below their usual standards of comfort. They were fortunate to find even primitive room assignments in the log hotel; most buildings were of cloth or canvas and some had no roofs at all.[29]

Other camps blossomed along with Bellevue and Ketchum.

Robert E. Strahorn, railroad and town builder, made his mark on both Ketchum and Hailey. *Idaho State Historical Society*

Carrie Strahorn, Wood River booster, at the time of her marriage in 1877.
Idaho State Historical Society

Entrepreneur-politician John Hailey gave his name to one of the most important of the Wood River towns. *Idaho State Historical Society*

To the north, at the mouth of Gladiator Creek and the Big Wood, Galena had a short but lively season, and would soon have an active population of at least seven hundred. Over the divide and west of Galena, Sawtooth City was laid out in Beaver Canyon, and soon grew to six hundred people, with a post office, three general stores, assay office, livery stable, three restaurants, four saloons, and a stage line to Ketchum—not to mention a link by pack trail over the mountains to Atlanta.

Only eight miles away, on Smiley Creek, the town of Vienna was a fierce competitor and enjoyed a busy second year.[30] Late in 1880, stagecoach operator John Hailey and several others filed on government land between Ketchum and Bellevue and located a town site at an elevation of 5,328 feet. Near the end of November, Hailey was laying out the new town. It was reported that about fifty lots had been taken up by Boise businessmen, the First National Bank of Boise would move its branch from Idaho City, and Hailey would put a line of stages on a new cut-off route from the capital, which "will leave Bellevue out in the cold." The following spring, the new metropolis of Hailey completed its first permanent building. Seven miles west, Bullion City cropped up to serve a number of producing mines and developed into a bustling little community.[31]

Since mining was the reason for it all, one of the first actions taken by Wood River prospectors was to follow what previous stampeders had done everywhere else since the California gold rush: they held impromptu meetings to define the boundaries of mining districts and lay out the rules for recording and regulating claims. Galena City miners had done the same in the fall of 1879, electing James Fulton recorder and creating a district of nearly six hundred square miles. Isaac Lewis presided over a meeting at Cottonwood on Trail Creek in May of 1880, where the Warm Springs Creek Mining District was defined and guidelines for its governance laid out. Men near "Cetchem's" camp met later that fall to select a recorder and agreed to apply the U.S. mining laws, which by now had superseded local regulations.[32]

On the horizon, local optimists saw a future development "hardly second to the carbonate camp of Colorado," but in terms of actual ore production, 1880 was more a season of prospecting, locating, and attempting to sell. Those with the most luck prospecting, it was said, were not those with a previous knowledge of California or Nevada ores, but those who had familiarized themselves with other rich finds in the Wood River area. "Most of the prospecting so far has been done on horseback," one observer noted late in the year, "and many of the finds have been purely accidental."[33] By late November an estimated two thousand mineral locations had been made, including some that would prove outstanding. Commodore Perry Croy discovered the Bullion Mine, after which the town would be named. A. P. Turner and Thomas Edgington located the Idahoan, and the Lewis brothers located the Jay Gould Mine. Postmaster John Moore of Salt Lake City and ten postal employees from Washington had grubstaked a prospector, Daniel W. Scribner, who arrived with a burro, a dog, and high hopes. According to tradition, Touser had chased a rabbit into a badger hole and was digging away at him when Scribner noticed glittering silver particles in the dirt.[34] This story is probably as apocryphal as that of Noah Kellogg's jackass leading him to rich silver in the Coeur d'Alenes a few years later. Either that or Scribner's dog and Kellogg's burro knew what they were doing and, like Roy Rogers' horse, Trigger, were among the smartest animals in the West. Scribner went on to name the mine the Minnie Moore after the daughter of the man who had grubstaked him.

The 1880 season saw a good deal of speculative activity and some actual mining. One problem, "the bane of this country," according to J. B. Foster, was "the large numbers of barefoot capitalists who come loaded down with letters of recommendation, but without a cent of money." Taking options on mining ground, they wrote "bushels of letters" trying to sell the properties, but succeeded only in tying them up for months.[35]

What Foster was complaining about was a common western institution: mine promoters. But these much-maligned men played a crucial role in the industry's success. Promoters were not always popular: many people viewed them as parasites in the same light as three-card monte sharps and traveling snake oil salesmen. Promoters worked their claims or those of someone else "with their jaw instead of their picks"; they were often short on both capital and character, the critics charged. One common definition of a promoter was: "A man who has unlimited capital behind him, but not any in front of him; his watch is in soak [in hock]."[36]

Promoters come, promoters go,
But mostly, soon or late,
They leave a load of waste and woe,
A heritage of hate.[37]

At the same time, as responsible editors pointed out, legitimate promoters were vital to the advance of the western mineral industry. They were the imaginative and persistent midwives in the transfer of property from an owner without funds to a corporation with development capital.[38] The standard approach to mine sales everywhere was for promoters to "bond" property: they took an option to buy at a set price within a prescribed time period, then scurried around, trying to find capitalists to purchase at a higher price or to organize an operating company.

At Wood River, as in all new mining camps, active promoters who came from all walks of life abounded. One former Episcopal minister greeted Alexander Toponce in the winter of 1879 with a lowered voice: "Don't call me Parson. Someone might hear you. I'm a mining promoter up here." Colonel Edmund Green, the California-Philadelphia entrepreneur, had organized a total of twenty-six mining companies by 1884, many of them on the river. Charles H. Moore, one-time keeper of the Alturas Hotel and several restaurants in Hailey, had crossed the Atlantic eight times to sell mining property during his thirteen years on Wood River.[39]

Clearly there was a good deal of such activity going on in 1880 and mines were changing hands. Isaac Lewis wanted "nothing to do with adventurers wanting to bond mines," although he was not adverse to bonding property himself; he attempted to sell the Star Mountain group at a 500 percent markup in a two-month period. The Edgington brothers of Ogden had discovered the Mayflower and had bonded it at a high price ($35,000) to Richard MacIntosh of Salt Lake City, a veteran of the Comstock who had an ore sampling business in Utah and who also had options on the Jay Gould, the War Eagle, and other properties. Croy's

Bullion was already in the hands of the Wood River Company, a Salt Lake outfit that also owned the adjoining Ophir.[40] Several mines were reported to be under option to New York companies. Colonel Green, the seasoned promoter from the California scene, had control of the Pilgrim Mine, while Colonel W. H. Broadhead—"another capitalist" from Montana—was waiting for the roads to clear in late May so he could begin a lengthy career of buying and selling silver properties.[41]

It was obvious that capital was required before Wood River could prosper. Limited ore shipment to smelters in Salt Lake City, Omaha, or elsewhere was no substitute for plants erected locally. If the district was going to live up to its expectations as "one of the best," smelters were vital. But they did not come the first season. Meanwhile, Wood Riverites awaited transportation improvement and contemplated rumors: Denver capitalists were shipping in a smelter that could handle thirty tons a day; Omaha parties were going to erect another and Ogdenites still a third; the Salt Lake owners of the Bullion planned to put in a reduction works of their own.[42]

Only a restricted amount of development and actual mining went on. Nineteen different mines shipped an aggregate of six to seven hundred tons of ore from Wood River to Salt Lake City that year. Isaac Lewis owned a quarter interest in the Elkhorn, a promising lode on the creek of the same name, a few miles east of Ketchum. He had quickly seen the potential and had urged his Helena friends to invest in Wood River mines at reasonable prices, "with a fair prospect of making from three to five for one," and was successful in lining up three absentee partners: Samuel T. Hauser, one of Montana's "Big Four" business and political entrepreneurs; Anton M. Holter, already a Helena lumber, hardware, and mining tycoon; and Robert S. Hale, also of Helena, who was busy amassing a fortune from real estate, drug stores, and mines.[43]

For $12,000, Lewis and his associates had acquired the property from John Keeler, "a Dutchman" (German), and "Uncle John" Rassmussen, a Norwegian who had followed the sea for twenty years before turning to prospecting. Traveling to Helena to get the funds from Sam Hauser and his cohorts, Lewis sewed the money—half in cash and half in "sight exchange" (a draft authorizing payment)—into the collar and wrist bands of a new red flannel miner's shirt and wore it back to Wood River. He also shipped down a load of equipment—including ore scales, jig irons, a new assay furnace, and ore sacks—built a road about three-quarters of a mile long to his property, and set men to work erecting a log house and a blacksmith shop. With Albert Griffith as foreman, work on the mine went ahead and on August 2, 1880, Lewis shipped off his first ten-ton lot of ore to Walker Brothers in Salt Lake City by way of wagon freight to Kelton, then by rail. Much of this was surface ore, including a soft carbonate powder around the mine "that looks like the dust in a well traveled road in August" and could be shoveled up without sorting. Despite a strike by most of his miners for higher wages, by the time Lewis closed down operations for the winter at the end of October, he had shipped $13,000 worth of ore and had another $5,000 worth sacked, but he believed that no other mines were producing that season. Another four and a half tons of Lewis's ore spent the winter in a wagon bogged down by weather halfway to the Kelton railhead, abandoned by its driver until spring.[44]

But this was not all profit. Lewis shipped eighty-eight tons which assayed one hundred forty-one ounces of silver and 65 percent lead, worth $141 a ton and $15 a ton for the lead in Salt Lake City. The cost of ore sacks, wagon haulage, rail shipment, and sampling and smelting fees amounted to $31 a ton, apart from the expense of mining itself. Clearly, in Lewis's thinking, these figures bore out the need for both a railroad and a local smelter, and Hauser was just the man to finance the latter, if he could only be persuaded.[45]

Other mine owners were scurrying "in good earnest" to take

out ore and sought advances to meet working expenses. At least some Ketchum merchants were willing to provide them with needed supplies in exchange for ore hauled down to their stores by packtrain. Teams bringing merchandise to their stores from the railheads at Kelton or Blackfoot then picked up the ore for the return journey, giving store owners an edge in transport.[46]

The season ended on a note of optimism and expectation for a big rush the following spring. "We are going to have a *Boom* here, as well as you in Montana," Isaac Lewis wrote Sam Hauser. "But *the Mines* are in this Country." When the snow brought activity to a halt, some two hundred families and a thousand single men decided to winter in the area. Save for an occasional log hotel or saloon, most were in tents. Bellevue was the hub: here Pinkham & Leonard had a store, Fletcher and Walling had a restaurant of a sort, Nichols had a general blacksmith shop, and J. O. Smith had a saloon. At times, supplies dwindled and food costs were high. Eggs went to $1.50 a dozen, and meat and flour were expensive because of the $.06 cents a pound added by freight charges. But with silver at $1.50 an ounce, why worry? One forward-looking migrant had driven in some dairy stock that summer and a fellow named Buckley is supposed to have made a killing by bringing in one hundred fifty cats to be sold at $5 a head.[47]

At least once, supply lines were cut by heavy snow and the communities found themselves isolated: "no traveling—no roads open," one citizen put it. As the *Statesman's* Bellevue correspondent said, with three feet of snow on the ground and no mail for more than two weeks, "the miner, the merchant and the lover, each and all, are in the same category—hemmed in, housed up, holed up like a bear, with no chance to send a letter out or to receive one from abroad." But nobody went hungry. "Everybody in town has a good supply of fine, fat venison." Indeed, as many as fifteen to forty deer had been killed at one time. "Snow-shoeing [skiing] by day and dancing by night constitute the principal amusements of our citizens, and are indulged in by almost every one, without regard to age or sex," Foster reported.[48]

The sinking of prospect holes and the construction of buildings went on at a reduced pace during the winter, although Ketchum had two shingle factories and three blacksmith shops at work. Bellevue residents lamented that they had not laid in a greater supply of hay and grain the previous fall. Lacking feed, they had sent out many of their teams to the Snake for winter pasture, leaving themselves without enough horses to keep the roads open or to supply timber and facilitate construction.[49] Thus ended the first season of the Wood River rush.

CHAPTER ONE NOTES

1. Rodman Wilson Paul, *Mining Frontiers of the Far West 1848–1880* (New York: Holt, Rinehart & Winston, 1963), p. 98.

2. For editorial acclaim of the common prospector in America, see *Mining and Scientific Press* (San Francisco), XLVIII (June 14, 1884): 398; LI (August 29, 1885): 149; *The Mining Industry and Tradesman* (Denver), c. 1892, quoted in Lawrence I. Berklove, ed., *The Fighting Horse of the Stanislaus: Stories & Essays by Dan De Quille* (Iowa City: University of Iowa Press, 1990), pp. 40–41.

3. Joseph B. Umpleby, Lewis G. Westgate, and Clyde P. Ross, "Geology and Ore Deposits of the Wood River Region, Idaho" ("With a Description of the Minnie Moore and Near-by Mines," by D. F. Hewett), U.S. Geological Survey *Bulletin* No. 814 (Washington: Government Printing Office, 1930), p. 245.

4. Paul, ed., *A Victorian Gentlewoman in the Far West: The Reminiscences of Mary Hallock Foote* (San Marino: Huntington Library, 1972), p. 263.

5. Vardis Fisher, comp., *The Idaho Encyclopedia* (Caldwell: Caxton Printers, 1938), p. 61.

6. Umpleby, et al., pp. 6–8.

7. Merle W. Wells, *Gold Camps & Silver Cities: Nineteenth Century Mining in Central and Southern Idaho*, 2d ed. (Moscow: Idaho Bureau of Mines & Geology *Bulletin* No. 22, 1983), p. 63; *Mining and Scientific Press* (San Francisco), XLII (June 18, 1881): 406; *Wood River Times* (Hailey) (weekly), June 15, 1881; *Wood River Times*, August 17, 1882; *Hailey Times*, June 18, 1931; Umpleby, et al., p. 81; "The Works of Hubert Howe Bancroft," XXXI (*History of Washington, Idaho, and Montana 1845–1889*) (San Francisco: The History Company, 1890), pp. 229–30.

8. See Paul, *Mining Frontiers of the Far West*, pp. 102–105.

9. *Wood River Times* (weekly), June 15, 1881; *Mining and Scientific Press*, XLII (June 18, 1881): 406; August C. Bolino, "The Role of Mining in the Economic Development of Idaho Territory," Idaho Bureau of Mines and Geology, Information Circular No. 6 (Moscow: the Bureau, August, 1960), p. 6; John Hailey, *The History of Idaho* (Boise: Press of Syms-York Co., 1910), p. 255.

10. *Mining and Scientific Press*, XXXIX (December 13, 1879): 370.

11. William S. Greever, *The Bonanza West: The Story of the Western Mining Rushes, 1848–1900* (Norman: University of Oklahoma Press, 1963, reprint, Moscow: University of Idaho Press, 1993), p. 272.

12. The best description of Idaho's early mining history is in Wells, *Gold Camps & Silver Cities*.

13. *Yankee Fork Herald* (Bonanza City), August 14, 1879; *Mining and Scientific Press*, XXXIX (December 13, 1879): 370; George A. McLeod, *History of Alturas and Blaine Counties Idaho* (Hailey: *Hailey Times*, 1938), pp. 5–6.

14. *Yankee Fork Herald*, August 4 and November 22, 1879; *Wood River Times* (weekly), June 15, 1881; *Mining and Scientific Press*, XXXIX (December 13, 1879): 370.

15. *Idaho Tri-Weekly Statesman* (Boise), September 23 and October 18, 1879.

16. *Ketchum Keystone* (weekly), December 29, 1882; *Mining and Scientific Press*, XXXIX (December 13, 1879): 370; *State Preservation Plan, Idaho* (Boise: Idaho State Historical Society, 1974), I, p. 52.

17. *Hailey Times*, June 18, 1931; McLeod, p. 52.

18. *Mining and Scientific Press*, XLII (June 18, 1881): 406.

19. *Idaho Tri-Weekly Statesman*, May 27, 1880; Carrie Adell Strahorn, *Fifteen Thousand Miles by Stage* (New York and London: G. P. Putnam's Sons, 1911; reprint Lincoln and London: University of Nebraska Press, 1988), p. 292.

20. *Idaho Tri-Weekly Statesman*, April 13, 1880.

21. Isaac I. Lewis, "Reminiscences" (Ketchum, March 28, 1892), typescript, pp. 160–63, American Heritage Center, University of Wyoming.

22. Ibid., pp. 163, 165, 167–68.

23. Isaac I. Lewis to Samuel T. Hauser (Ketchum, June 8, 1880), Samuel T. Hauser Papers, Montana Historical Society Archives, Helena; Lewis, "Reminiscences," pp. 167–71. Thomas E. Clohency had lived in Utah, where he had been a charter member of the Alta Club in Salt Lake City, a group with many mining men. O. N. Malmquist, *The Alta Club 1883–1974* (Salt Lake City: The Alta Club, 1974), p. 130.

24. "F" (J. B. Foster) to editor (Bellevue, May 15, 1880), *Idaho Tri-Weekly Statesman*, May 27, 1880.

25. Ibid.

26. "F" to editor (Bellevue, May 20, 1880), *Idaho Tri-Weekly Statesman*, May 29, 1880.

27. "F" to editor (Bellevue, May 29, 1880), *Idaho Tri-Weekly Statesman*, June 1, 1880.

28. Judith Austin, "Introduction," in C. Strahorn, pp. ix–x. For Robert Strahorn, see *The National Cyclopaedia of American Biography* (New York: James T. White & Co., 1930), Vol. C, pp. 445–46, and Oliver Knight, "Robert E. Strahorn, Propagandist for the West," *Pacific Northwest Quarterly*, LIX (January, 1969): 33–45.

29. Lewis, "Reminiscences," p. 181; C. Strahorn, pp. 292–94.

30. *Idaho Tri-Weekly Statesman*, September 25, 1879; *Wood River*

Times (weekly), June 15, 1881; Nancy Miller, "Mining in the Sawtooths," *Idaho Yesterdays*, IX (Spring, 1965): 11; Wayne C. Sparling, *Southern Idaho Ghost Towns* (Caldwell: Caxton Printers, 1974), pp. 83–84; Fisher, p. 111.

31. The Tennessee-born Hailey had crossed the plains to Oregon in 1853, had participated in the Rogue River Indian war, then had followed the rush to the Idaho mines in 1862. A popular figure, he had engaged in mining, ranching, and stagecoaching and served twice as territorial delegate to Congress. *Biographical Directory of the American Congress 1774–1949* (Washington: Government Printing Office, 1950), p. 1248; Howard Lamar, ed., *The Reader's Encyclopedia of the American West* (New York: Thomas Y. Crowell Company, 1977), p. 480; McLeod, pp. 55, 57; Lewis to Hauser (Ketchum, November 26, 1880), Hauser Papers, Box 5; Donald C. Miller, *Ghost Towns of Idaho* (Boulder: Pruett Publishing Co., 1976), pp. 2, 3, 4, 5; Sparling, pp. 79, 80; *Wood River Times* (weekly), June 15, 1881.

32. *Yankee Fork Herald*, September 25 and October 2, 1880; *Mining and Scientific Press*, XXXIX (December 13, 1879): 370; D. Miller, p. 4; Lewis, "Reminiscences," p. 171.

33. G. L. Lucas (December 25, 1880, Albion, Idaho), quoted in *Mining and Scientific Press*, XLI (August 7, 1880): 86; XLII (January 15, 1881): 38.

34. *Hailey Times*, June 18, 1931. Alexander Toponce, who made the arrangements with Scribner, makes no mention of a canine collabora-tor at the discovery site. See *Reminiscences of Alexander Toponce* (Norman: University of Oklahoma Press, 1971), p. 183. Stories of ani-mal involvement in locating subsequent riches were not uncommon. John Boyle stumbled over rich outcroppings of the Ornament in 1881 while hunting a strayed horse. Two partners on the East Fork of the Wood River made their strike from small pieces of float traced to a gopher hole; and in Elkhorn Gulch in 1883 Eugene Gillenwater locat-ed the rich Parker mine from ore fragments around a badger hole. *Mining and Scientific Press*, XLII (April 23, 1881): 268; XLVIII (May 17, 1884): 359; Umpleby, et al., p. 185.

35. "F" to editor (Ketchum, September 20, 1880), *Idaho Tri-Weekly Statesman*, September 30, 1880.

36. Charles Howard Shinn, *The Story of the Mine* (New York: D. Appleton & Co., 1901), p. 137; *Mining and Scientific Press,* LXXIX (September 2, 1899): 257.

37. J. C. Murray, "Promoters," in Eugene Louis Chicanot, comp. and ed., *Rhymes of the Miner: An Anthology of Canadian Mining Verse* (Gardenvale, Quebec: Federal Publications, Ltd., n.d.), p. 129.

38. For positive comment on the mine promoter as a middle man, see *Mining and Scientific Press,* LV (November 5, 1887): 292.

39. Toponce, p. 182; *Wood River Times,* July 26, 1884 and March 20, 1894.

40. Lewis to Hauser (Ketchum, July 9 and October 20, 1880); Lewis to Hauser, Anton Holter and Robert S. Hale (December 22, 1880), all in Hauser Papers, Box 5; *Salt Lake Daily Tribune,* July 13, 1880; "F" to editor (Bellevue, May 29, 1880), *Idaho Tri-Weekly Statesman,* June 1, 1880; Malmquist, pp. 134–35. "F" to editor (Bellevue, May 29, 1880), *Idaho Tri-Weekly Statesman,* June 1880.

41. "F" to editor (Bellevue, May 29, 1880), *Idaho-Tri-Weekly Statesman,* June 1, 1880.

42. *Idaho Tri-Weekly Statesman,* December 4, 1880.

43. Lewis to Hauser (Ketchum, July 9, 1880), Hauser Papers, Box 5.

44. *Wood River Times* (weekly), June 15, 1881; *Mining and Scientific Press,* XLII (January 29, 1881): 77; Lewis to Hauser (Helena, July 2, 14 and 19, 1880), Hauser Papers, Box 5; Lewis, "Reminiscences," pp. 170, 171–73, 174.

45. Lewis to Hauser (Ketchum, July 9 and 26, and August 23, 1880); Lewis "Statement of Ore Mined out of Elkhorn Mine in 23 Days, ending August 7th, 1880," in Hauser Papers, Box 5.

46. Lewis to Hauser (Ketchum, July 26 and September 1, 1880), Hauser Papers, Box 5.

47. Lewis to Hauser (Ketchum, November 26, 1880), Hauser Papers, Box 5; "F" to editor (Bellevue, May 29, 1880), *Idaho Tri-Weekly Statesman,* June 1, 1880; *Hailey Times,* June 18, 1931.

48. Lewis to Hauser and Granville Stuart (Ketchum, December 9,

1880), Hauser Papers, Box 5; "F" to editor (Bellevue, December 14, 1880), *Idaho Tri-Weekly Statesman,* December 28, 1880.

49. "F" to editor (Bellevue, March 11, 1881), *Idaho Tri-Weekly Statesman,* March 17, 1881; *Mining and Scientific Press,* XLII (March 19, 1881): 181.

CHAPTER TWO

"IT WAS A TOUGH
TRIP YOU BET"

FROM THE BEGINNING, Wood River was an isolated district. Poet Ezra Pound was born there, but after visiting Paris, he referred to it as being 5,000 feet above sea level "and five million or thousand miles from ANYwhere, let alone from civilisation. . . ."[1] Initially, it was 150 miles from the railroad at Kelton, and its transportation ties were slender, tenuous, and expensive. Hard enough to get to at any time of the year, it was periodically impossible to reach during the inhospitable winter months, especially in the days of horse-drawn vehicles. Many fair-weather residents spent the cold season elsewhere, and often those who remained were snowed in for a week or two at a time.

Winter communications proved chancy. Alturas County, where the district was located, had been created in 1864 and contained 19,000 square miles—an area larger than Connecticut, Delaware, Maryland, and Rhode Island combined. Size and isolation of this "Empire of Alturas" made for primitive transportation.[2] Through the territorial legislature, Wood Riverites petitioned the federal postmaster general early in 1881 for improvements in the tri-weekly mail service that ran from Arco to Bellevue, then up Wood River via Ketchum to Galena. The problem, they argued, was that deep snow had prevented the delivery of any mail over the Arco-Bellevue route between December 1 and 15 of 1880, and from Bellevue to Boise between mid-December to New Year's Day 1881. The 1,500 people in the Wood River mineral fields—"the richest and most extensive now known on this Continent"—deserved "a liberal system of mail facilities" over an all-season route unhampered by deep snow: down Wood River to the Malad, then via the Snake to Salmon Falls, across Camas Prairie to Mountain Home and Boise.[3]

Riding the stagecoach was always uncomfortable and frequently unpredictable as well. When Carrie and Robert Strahorn came up from Blackfoot in 1880, they had to spend the night with fourteen other travelers at Fish Creek in a two-room cabin with a dirt floor. There was one bed in the kitchen and two in the living room, draped with calico curtains for privacy. (Two years later, when they again stopped at Fish Creek, the living room held six beds, the curtains were gone, and the chinks between the boards "were large enough for a cat to crawl through.") When they tried to leave Bellevue in 1880, they found that the stage had been taken off the route to Boise because of limited business and the coming of winter. The idea of being stranded on Wood River "made us feel pretty frosty," Carrie related, but they were rescued by a Boisean named Riddle, who had brought in a covered wagon full of fruit, and who agreed (for a fee) to carry them to Boise. With a fine bay team pulling the vehicle and an extra one tied behind, Riddle and the Strahorns took four days to travel the 150 miles to Boise and the civilized haven of the Overland Hotel.[4]

As the boom developed, several coach lines were involved. The Blackfoot & Wood River Stage Company was running tri-weekly service in early December 1880, but planned soon to be on a daily basis. A year later, reorganized as the Blackfoot, Bonanza and Wood River Stage Company, the firm used second-rate equipment to carry passengers, mail, express, and freight on daily runs from the Utah and Northern Railway at Blackfoot to Hailey, Bellevue, Ketchum, and Galena. Early in 1881, the Goose Creek & Wood River branch of the Kelton and Dallas line was also active, although there was still enough snow in the spring to make the schedules of both erratic. The Blackfoot sleigh was "coming in when it could get in," which was about once a week, and the Goose Creek stage was "making the riffle" about four times a week. The first issue of the weekly *Wood River Times* advertised the Utah, Idaho, and Oregon Stage Company, John Hailey's outfit, with daily connections between Hailey's new town and Kelton, Boise, Silver City, and Winnemucca. The fare to Boise was $22.50. In August 1881 the driver of the Boise stage faced armed robbers near Soul's Rest, but whipped up his team and escaped with two bullets through his hat. On several other occasions, passengers were startled by the cry "Stand and deliver!" and subsequently found themselves relieved of their wallets and watches.[5]

Early in April 1881, while Hailey's town site was still being surveyed, Wells Fargo & Company established offices at Bellevue, Ketchum, Galena, Bonanza City, and Challis. The Pacific Express Company, with C. B. Fox as agent, provided the main competition until early 1883, when, with the railroad nearing completion, Wells Fargo threw in the towel. They sent a special agent to close down the company offices in Hailey, Bellevue, and Ketchum. Wood River Freight also carried passengers from Hailey to Kelton for a fare of $12. Freight charges were $.04 a pound; in either case the trip took three days.[6]

If 1880 was a year of prospecting, locating and transferring property, planning for the future, and poor transportation, 1881 involved more of the same, plus some solid advances in the realm of town building and actual mining and smelting. The winter was merely an interlude in the stampede, which resumed again as soon as the weather permitted. Editors in Boise saw the need to give frequent warnings against migrating too early. Two to three feet of snow was still on the ground in early April, they cautioned, and roads would be too soft for any real hauling before June 1. Thawing brought high water and impassable roads in mid-April 1881 and left over a hundred people stranded in Blackfoot. Emigrants should go "tolerably well heeled," with "grub enough to last them two or three months," since travel and living costs were expensive.[7]

The journey from Carson City, Nevada, to Bellevue, for example, came to a total of $66.76, including rail and stagecoach fare, meals of $1 each, and $.75 a night for sleeping space on the floor of a log cabin. A man might travel on his own for less, but it would not be easy nor would it be cheap. Station keepers and ferry operators had "a good many axes to grind" and so did Mother Nature. An old California miner wrote of his eight-day trek between Kelton and Bellevue,

> . . . [I]t was a rough trip you bet, walking and pushing a horse over the 45 miles between Little Wood river and this place. We had to wade in mud and water belly deep in some places. Meals on the road are miserable and cost a dollar apiece. There is very little food on the table and it is dirty at that.[8]

On the River, hay was $45 a ton and barley unavailable; potatoes cost $8 a hundred weight and flour $7; board ran $7 to $8 a week, with no beef to be had and not much bacon or beans. Employment in building construction might normally be a possibility, but early in the year both lumber and jobs were in short supply.[9]

The *Statesman's* man on the scene noticed numerous strangers looking for places to set up businesses in Bellevue, and estimated that at least fifty thousand board feet could be sold readily at eighty to a hundred dollars per thousand. The town was a little short on flour, he reported, but Ketchum had good supplies; the new town of Hailey (which a correspondent of a rival paper had dubbed "Yip Yap") was looking good, while Galena, still under five feet of snow, ordinarily did not awaken until mid-June.[10]

The first issue of Hailey's *Wood River News,* which was widely parroted by western editors, warned that prospecting was not easy and that only experienced miners or skilled artisans were likely to find work in the sprawling new silver fields. "It is well to think of this before grabbing up your gunny sack full of threadbare clothing, old letters and faded photographs, to seek employment at big wages of a poor people in an unexplored though evidently rich mineral region 150 miles from the railroad ties." Those ignoring such advice, the editor cautioned, might soon find themselves "hoofing it" for the railroad "on scant rations—cussing your luck and the country." Those expecting "to be dependent upon capital for daily labor, had better linger in more congenial climes, and where 'spuds' and 'hamfat' are cheaper."[11]

Despite such admonitions, the rush resumed. "This country is *Booming* this spring," Isaac Lewis wrote one of his partners in Montana in May. "Cities are springing up, like '*Jonah's* Gourd.'" As soon as the roads were open in the spring, stagecoaches lumbered in, struggling through the mud and snow, "fairly groaning under their load of live freight," many of them ill-prepared and unemployed and not likely to be until business picked up and construction materials became available. In Bellevue, it was reported in mid-April that "there are not a thousand dollars in circulation in the town."[12]

According to the *Statesman* editor (a romantic if there ever was one) many of the newcomers were "hardy, iron-fisted miners," of the kind that made the difficult discoveries elsewhere in the West, but died poor, leaving behind "greater legacies to the rest of mankind than all of the bonanza kings that have ever lived." They neither gambled in stocks nor cheated widows and children out of their savings; rather, they traveled on foot over all terrain and with pick, shovel, and the sweat of their brow uncovered "the hidden treasures which have blessed us as a people and a nation beyond all calculation."[13]

A more realistic assessment would show that as in the previous season the strangers pouring in at a rate of fifteen to thirty per day were from all walks of life. An occasional minister concerned with saving souls was among them, but the bulk were there to make their fortunes, either from mining the earth or mining the miners. Along with a sprinkling of doctors and lawyers stepping down from the sleighs or coaches were numerous others with high aspirations:

. . . [C]apitalists in quest of good prospects for sale at bedrock figures; drummers for mercantile houses in the east and San Francisco, anxious to secure a share of the trade of this vast and soon to be prosperous country; hotel keepers looking out for a good point at which to locate; smelter men seeking the best sites for the erection of reduction works; miners seeking employment in the mines; prospectors anxious to discover new ledges, and last, but not least in number, is the professional gambler, with the tools of his craft.[14]

The first immigrant waves also brought in an indolent class of men "even too lazy to gamble" who were labeled by San Francisco labor agitator Dennis Kearney as "honorable bilks," whose creed was: "never miss a meal nor pay a cent." By the second or third year, one Wood River editor pointed out, this element would be "pretty well weeded out." "So long as the honey is plenty they can feed, but when it gets short the working bees sting the drones out of the hive."[15]

As the coaches continued to rattle in, the seasonal bustle accelerated. At peak seventy-five to a hundred newcomers were arriving each day, with prospecting "in full blast" and the hills full of "anxious seekers for hidden treasure." As was frequently pointed out, Leadville was a highly compact silver area, but the Wood River mineral belt sprawled over a much larger region extending perhaps sixty by ninety or a hundred miles, enough space to absorb thousands of miners and prospectors in what was possibly "the greatest belt of rich mining ground on the coast."[16]

The new arrivals dispersed, many of them pushing on through the "Gate City," as Bellevue called itself, to Galena, Ketchum, Bullion or the new boom town of Hailey. One man who had been in the area the previous autumn returned in 1881 and was amazed at the changes he found. On his prior trip he saw only one small log cabin in the sixteen miles between Bellevue and Ketchum; now he estimated ten thousand people lived in the region, no doubt a greatly inflated figure, with tremendous activity and excitement in the expanding towns.[17]

But at the beginning of the 1881 season, none of these camps were large; nor did they have adequate supplies and facilities to handle the hordes thronging in. According to one observer, Bellevue might soon "take rank with Leadville or Tombstone," but currently contained about three hundred inhabitants, mainly prospectors and miners, and "most of them broke." He counted seven stores, five saloons, three restaurants, two barber shops, one lodging house, one tin shop, two stables, "and two meat markets, but no beef." A correspondent of an Ogden newspaper, however, thought that "Bellevue has all the town and no business, while Hailey has all the business and no town." Another visitor judged that Bellevue's population had ballooned to fifteen hundred by late August.[18]

The terminus of both the major stage lines, the new Hailey town site was filling up. By early April, eighty-six lots had been sold, with stipulations that buildings be put on them within sixty days, and twenty houses were already under construction. At that time "two twenty-five cent saloons" were "in full blast, and one 4-bit restaurant." Three weeks later, the same observer recorded seventy-five buildings up or going up—many of picket, stockade, or solid cottonwood log construction. In addition there were at least a hundred sheeting or tent houses and "five first-class saloons, or saloons where first-class liquor is sold at two bits a drink." Hailey had established a graveyard close to the city limits, lest Bellevue claim it as their own, and it had two weekly newspapers. The *Wood River News* was established in June by Canadian-born Theodore E. Picotte, a roving printer and editor who initially set up shop in a tent before moving to a log cabin with a dirt floor. Picotte had learned his trade in New York and practiced it in Colorado and Nevada before he arrived on the River. The first 1,000 copies of his new *Wood River Times* had been "gobbled up like hot cakes," according to the editor. "The infant town of Hailey is two months old to-day," another onlooker wrote early in June, "and is already a bouncer." By autumn, according to a correspondent of the *Salt Lake Tribune*, it was a "lively village of 1,500 people."[19]

Bullion City, a tributary to Hailey, was smaller but well located for growth in an area of potentially rich mines. It was described as "a very pretty little town. It lays in a semi-circle in a narrow gulch, and is composed of 25 houses"—among them a store, three boarding places, a few saloons, several lodging houses, and a number of tents.[20]

Crash building programs went ahead to meet the needs of the influx of 1881. A continuing problem was the dearth of lumber, which for a time meant construction with hewn cottonwood logs. Smelting machinery, useless until lumber was available, lay along the road in Bellevue that spring. When the season commenced, the only sawmill was at Ketchum, but the "rattle-trap affair" was not working. This was probably the Corbett and Quantrell Mill, which had started up on Warm Springs Creek in June of the previous year. A month into the new season, in the wave of activity that gripped the area, the situation had much improved. The "rattle-trap affair" was turning out boards, a Boisean named Robinson had brought in a sawmill that was about ready to start up below Ketchum, and Oscar Lewis was building another one two miles above the same town. By autumn, according to a visitor, "sawmills, last year only hoped for, are now buzzing in the shadows of forests that afford abundant timber and upon swift streams that furnish cheap and unfailing water-power."[21] Even so, a shortage of lumber was ongoing and the Wood River towns would wear many of their canvas tops even into the next season.

The most important part of the economy, however, were the mines, which were the lifeblood of the community. In 1881, a good deal was happening in Wood River mining. Ground was transferring to outside capitalists and companies, and reduction works and smelters were being built, but such activity proceeded slowly. Between three and five thousand people were on the river, perhaps half of them in the towns and the rest scattered throughout the mineral belt, and a goodly number had mining locations for sale. One observer noted that the hills around Bullion were staked out for miles with posts and monuments "so that they now resemble Lone Mountain Cemetery."[22]

Some soreheads had returned home disgruntled and spread the word that Wood River was "a grand humbug," that paying mines were in short supply, and that the majority of the stampeders were there to speculate. The editor of the *Statesman* would not go that far, but he acknowledged that many of those at Wood River had in mind profits from "whisky mills, stores, shops, or some easy kind of speculating business," when it was capital for development of mills, smelters, and mining that was needed. Nor were the miners much better: "most of them intend to strike a lead and sell out at big figures."[23] Of course, they did; how else would a poor miner without capital make his pile? Discover and sell: that was the dream on which the prospector's world was founded. Typical were Garrard and Campbell, discoverers of the Guy Mine on Rock Creek, who sold to an Ohio company for

$13,000 cash in 1881, and were soon prospecting again "out Snake river way."[24]

Despite the somewhat confused Boise editor who lauded the mineral belt as ground par excellence for the poor prospector ("the ore can be sold by the bushel or ton as readily as the farmer sells his wheat or oats")[25] lode mining was a much more complex kind of business than that. To begin with, a discovery might or might not develop into a full-fledged producing mine, and the original locator had to make a critical decision early on. If indications were promising, he was torn:

> To sink or not to sink? That is the question;
> Whether 'tis fitter in the prospector to sell
> The highly metalliferous croppings for a song,
> Or, using muscle, to dig down,
> And thus, by perseverance, strike it rich.[26]

But muscle and perseverance were usually not enough. For many, the "sure thing of the sale" was preferable to the "doubtful thing of working the mine."[27] Even though the Wood River veins were relatively close to the surface, shafting, tunneling, and hoisting were required before the ore could be removed. Once on the surface it had to be smelted to separate the silver and lead from other elements. In short, like deep-level lode mining elsewhere, it became a capital-intensive industry. Rarely did individual prospectors have the wherewithal or the stamina to develop their own properties; most sold out for relatively low prices to entrepreneurs who knew how to organize both capital and manpower—and who reaped the highest rewards from the mines. Recognizing from experience that extremely rich ores would have to be available to return a profit after shipment to Salt Lake City or Omaha, Boise merchant David Falk was one of the first to see the possibilities for smelting at Wood River.[28]

Bavarian-born Falk and his brother Nathan had been in the mercantile business in the Idaho capital since 1868. Together with Alonzo Wolters, assayer in charge of the U.S. Assay Office in Boise, and Lieutenant Patten, on detached duty from the 21st Infantry, David Falk built a smelter at the mouth of Indian Creek, a few miles north of Hailey. The smelter used a Fraser & Chalmers four-tuyère furnace with a daily capacity of fifteen tons of heavy galena or twenty-five tons of carbonate ores. The blast was furnished by a Root blower and the machinery run by a Leffel turbine having a twenty-four-foot head of water. Local sources provided lime and red oxide of iron for flux, as well as charcoal, which cost from $.20 to $.22 per bushel delivered.[29]

On June 25, Falk's pioneer smelter exhibited its first bar of Wood River bullion—an ingot weighing 105 pounds and assaying 240 ounces of silver and 60 percent lead. When this enterprise, the Wood River Smelting Company, started up, Falk, the "coming bloated monopolist of Wood River," was asked how long it would run. "Forever, sir," was his response. The smelter worked ten to fifteen tons a day for the next few months. During one week in August, it shipped 150 tons of base bullion and high-grade ore to Utah—some of it routed by way of Blackfoot because no teams were available for the road to Kelton. In mid-October, Wolters thought there was enough ore in area dumps to last three months. Unfortunately, before the end of the month, the company's plant was attached by a Salt Lake City creditor. His Boise business was not doing well, and Falk had overextended himself and become insolvent. In 1882, Falk was offering a half interest in the plant, fifteen acres of land with water rights, and half interest in "a good iron mine" thrown in—all for $8,000. Eventually the smelter was acquired by a Wood River mining man, Jabez Chase, who converted it into a custom concentrating works.[30]

Other smelters were being erected. The largest and most successful was that of the Philadelphia Mining and Smelting

Company at the mouth of Warm Springs Creek near Ketchum. The first unit produced its initial ingot on October 13, 1881, in a forty-ton furnace brought in from Colorado. Two weeks later, Hailey residents saw half a dozen wagons loaded with bullion from the Philadelphia smelter pass through their streets heading for Blackfoot, and eventually east by rail. Another small plant was erected by the Senate Mining and Smelting Company at Galena some distance to the north. But interminable delays, including a breakdown of negotiations with charcoal burners, deferred blowing in the furnace.[31] In July 1881, the Avon smelter was being put up near Bellevue by Joseph H. Douglas, who was described as a shrewd Comstock millionaire who "never let go of a dollar unless he has three in sight." Apparently, in this instance Douglas suffered from severe myopia, as well as misplaced faith in his builder, E. A. Martin, who put cost-cutting foremost. After only three weeks of operation, during which it turned out $2,000, his "crude, old-fashioned and imperfect" works had to shut down. Martin subsequently bought out Douglas, but the smelter soon went out of business for good.[32]

In mid-July the Granger Mining Investment Company, a group of New York capitalists that owned five claims at Bullion, had a man in Hailey, who was also superintendent of the New York Sampling and Smelting Company, contract for ore and arrange for the erection of several smelting and sampling works, none of which seem to have materialized.[33]

But even though times were considered dull in August, optimists saw better days ahead. Expecting four smelters and two concentrating mills to be in operation within a month and a half, they noted that the mines were opening up well and that men of means were coming in and buying.[34]

As sharp operators sought to move quickly, readers grew accustomed to such headlines in the *Wood River Times* as: "Californians Coming In" or "San Franciscans Taking Hold." "Buy in a *calm* and sell in a typhoon if you want to make money," one told an expert whom he asked to examine a mine near Galena. But Pacific Coast investors were not the only financiers involved. Boiseans and Utahans were well represented, and promoters were working hard to attract eastern funds in markets that were risky at best and at worst might be termed "a system of robbery on rock representations." Entrepreneurs were "looking around for bargains," but they were serious about it. "Bare-footed capitalists have to take a back seat this year," the *Statesman* reported.[35] A fair number of mining properties changed hands in 1880 and 1881, but it wasn't the original discoverers who reaped most of the benefit.

In the summer of 1881 the California triumvirate of George Hearst, James Ben Ali Haggin, and Lloyd Tevis were reported to be interested. These major investors employed top experts and had a Midas touch. Eventually, they would be involved in more than a hundred mines, including the rich Ontario in Utah, the Homestake in South Dakota (which is still producing) and Butte's fabulous Anaconda. The rough and tough George Hearst was in Wood River in June when Isaac Lewis (who, the year before, had acquired the Elkhorn for himself and Montana backers for $12,000, and the Star Mountain group for a quarter of that) was trying to sell either property for whatever the market would bear. Hearst did not bite at this time, but a Boston group seemed about to take the Star Mountain mines at $18,000 until Lewis's partners upped the price to $44,000 and scared off the buyers. At the same time, Lewis reported that he had Governor John B. Neil of Idaho "on the string at $40,000" for the same property. A few months later, he was dickering with British capitalists, first over the Star Mountain, and then over the Elkhorn.[36] Unfortunately for Lewis, no transactions took place.

Another entrepreneur-promoter, "Colonel" Enos A. Wall of Salt Lake City (his title was conferred by his friends), did much better. Wall had mined in Colorado and Montana in the early 1860s, then engaged in freighting between Montana and Utah after 1868. Wall and former U.S. Marshal M. M. Shaughnessy, also of Salt Lake City, bought several Wood River mines at bargain-basement prices in 1881, sold some off, and organized an operating company to work others, including the Eureka, the Ophir, the Bullion, and the Mayflower, all in Bullion Gulch. A lengthy lawsuit ensued over the Eureka after its original owners sought to regain possession by charging that shortly before purchase, Wall and Shaughnessy had discovered a rich vein on the property, but had deliberately undervalued it.[37] Later that year, it was rumored that Wall and Shaughnessy had sold the May-flower, the Eureka, and another property to Horace A. W. Tabor and other Coloradans for $450,000, but that proved false. Next, word on the grapevine was that the Mayflower and the Jay Gould had been peddled to George Roberts, "the great mining manipulator" of New York and California who had waxed fat on Comstock and Leadville mine stock. That, too, proved unfounded. But early in 1882, the Mayflower, which Wall and Shaughnessy had acquired from the discoverer for $25,000, was indeed sold—for $375,000—to a group headed by John V. Farwell, who was described by the *Wood River Times* as "one of the brainiest, most energetic and 'solidist' citizens of Chicago."[38]

The original owners of the Bullion were said to have sold for $1,500. The property was incorporated by Salt Lake City parties, presumably organized by Wall and Shaughnessy, and developed into "a real bonanza" under the auspices of the Wood River Gold & Silver Mining Company. Wall was reported to have added the Bullion to his other holdings at a cost of $200,000 and to have shipped out well over six hundred thousand dollars in ore between November 1 and December 10, 1882.[39] Wall and Shaughnessy hung onto the Eureka, for which they had paid $2,300, and developed it under the agency of the Wood River Gold & Silver Mining Company (of which Wall was a major shareholder and superintendent). In 1882, the estimated worth of the property was around half a million dollars. A strong supporter of his miners and well liked by his fellow citizens, Wall was sent to the Twelfth Session of the Idaho Territorial Legislature in 1882–83. After he left the company in 1885, he spent two years perfecting new corrugated ore crushing rolls, then returned to Utah, where he became one of the early owners and promoters of low-grade copper property at Bingham.[40]

Another of the promoters active on an ongoing basis at Wood River was the veteran Californian Colonel Edmund Green, who had been in on the ground floor in 1880. Isaac Lewis had tried to interest him in handling the Elkhorn and the Star Mountain, but Green was too busy bonding other properties, including the Pilgrim, the Hot Springs group, the Idahoan, and the Muldoon (named for a popular wrestler), which was located in the drainage basin of the Little Wood River about twenty-four miles due east of Hailey by wagon road. The Muldoon now passed from J. O. Swift and Company for $50,000 to the Little Wood River Mining and Smelting Company, a Philadelphia concern, to whom Colonel Green was both midwife and general manager.[41]

Five miles below Hailey, near Broadford, the Minnie Moore would eventually become the show mine of the area. The Old Girl, as it was affectionately known locally, was originally owned by its locator, Daniel Scribner, former Salt Lake City Postmaster John M. Moore, and others who had grubstaked him. But in 1881, after the shaft had been sunk forty-five feet, Moore sold half his interest to Henry E. Miller for $10,000. That same summer, when the property was said to be "opening up magnificently," it was bonded to George W. Grayson of San Francisco for $40,000, but apparently was not sold at that time. Eventually, in 1882, F. H. Meyers and M. M. Shaughnessy, both of Salt Lake City, each acquired a one-quarter interest. Shaughnessy paid Moore $100,000 for his share.[42]

The Jay Gould Mine adjoined the Mayflower. In 1881, it was sold for $30,000 to a group that included Salt Lake banker Warren Hussey, Judge Volney "Stamps" Anderson, formerly of

Rocky Bar and Boise, and S. V. White and S. R. Inhain, both of
New York. A year later, its owners supposedly turned down an
offer of $150,000 for it.[43] At the same time, the Idahoan, also in
Bullion Gulch, was retained by the original locators, who included
W. H. Nye and Judge A. P. Turner of Boise, Thomas J. Edgington
of Ogden, and Stamps Anderson. Several times they were on the
verge of selling, but the sale was never completed. Colonel
Green had options on it in the spring of 1882 and hoped to interest California capitalists. Once, its bonders, Green or others,
were unable to produce the required $200,000 at the deadline
and asked for an extension. Since new ore had been discovered
in the interim, the price was now raised to $300,000, and the
locators refused $350,000 for it in mid-1882.[44]

In general, the early pattern at Wood River was the same as
in other western mining camps. Every camp had it rags to riches
success stories, but it had far more examples of discoverers who
sold out for a pittance to men who subsequently made millions
out of the property, just as Henry T. P. Comstock had earlier sold
his share of the lode in Nevada that bore his name for $11,000
and two jackasses, critters which in terms of later yield cost him
about $1.5 million each.[45]

At the same time, in 1881, buying and selling were not the
only mining activities under way. Individuals were trying to develop their property either to sell or, that failing, to work it themselves. Most of the major mines that had changed hands had
development work being pushed on them.

As a new hoisting works was being installed at the Bullion,
Enos Wall exercised ingenuity in the absence of proper materials: When sawed timbers were unavailable for a foundation and
gallows frame, Wall had red fir trees hewed to the required size;
he had no commercial pig lead for soldering his anchor bolts, so
he used 400-ounce bullion instead. As soon as this was completed,
the Wood River Gold & Silver Mining Company would resume
sinking the shaft and open a number of levels and stopes from

the surface. They expected to ship about four tons of ore per day.[46] Shortly before the first snowfall was expected, the Idahoan Mine, also at Bullion, had driven its tunnel to 200 feet. Already it had taken out 150 tons and expected to extract another 500 tons before the season ended, for an anticipated yield of $148,750, with that much more again in sight.[47]

The largest operation at that time, the Minnie Moore, was pushing development work as well. In one three-month period late in the 1881 season it produced 231 tons of ore, which sold for $140 to $160 a ton, and paid operating expenses, plus another $5,000 for working capital for the next year and a dividend of $12,000. Near Bellevue, one of the first locations made, the Queen of the Hills was taking out good ore, as were the Overland, the Clipper, the Jay Gould, the Penobscot and the Mayflower. As the season ended, the *Times* reported incomplete figures of ore shipped out from Wood River that included the Homestake (12 tons), the Eureka (38 tons), the Jay Gould (150 tons), the Mayflower (725 tons), and the Wood River Gold & Silver Company (436 tons).[48] It was clear that industrial mining, as well as prospecting and speculating, was getting under way.

In the early Wood River years, a cyclical pattern prevailed. Most mining activity did not go through the winter. By about December 1, when the chill winds and blowing snows came, the working season was closed and the towns on the river quieted down until spring made the roads passable. Estimates on the amount of lead and silver shipped out in ore and bullion between May 1 and December 1, 1881, ranged from six hundred thousand dollars to more than a million dollars. The Idahoan, the year's largest producer, was supposed to have sent out over two hundred thousand dollars worth of rich ores, while Falk's smelter at Hailey had produced about seventy-five thousand dollars in bullion and the Philadelphia smelter near Ketchum some thirty-two thousand dollars worth.[49]

When the season ended, mining men had to make another decision: they could stay, or, as many did, leave the area for the winter and travel to California or the East to try to raise capital. A lucky prospector might even find a buyer for his claim and spend a few months in luxury.

> *The miner bold his claim has sold,*
> *And will winter in the "Hub;"*
> *The miner meek will wait and seek*
> *A job for his winter's grub.*
> *The miner tough has had enough*
> *Prospecting, for this year.*
> *He'll read of mines in the* Daily Times
> *Until spring does again appear.*[50]

Off-season employment in Wood River was limited, although an estimated two thousand people wintered in the region in 1881–82. A number of the larger mines employed a reduced number of men doing development work through the winter. The Queen of the Hills employed six, the Overland kept only three, and the Minnie Moore retained ten. At Hailey, some two hundred miners remained at work and another hundred cut lumber or ties for the railroad, which was on its way. The "remainder of the able bodied men played 'slough' for beer and d----d the weather."[51]

If New Year's Eve was a time of celebration for many Americans, it signaled something else for wintering Wood River miners: At the stroke of midnight, literally hundreds of abandoned claims—and some that were not abandoned—were relocated by prospectors who camped with tents, blankets, and provisions on pre-selected sites where they believed the necessary improvement work had not been completed by the original owners. Every sleigh and team in town was engaged in advance for

December 31 as the interlopers jockeyed for position. A typical New Year's Day "witnessed fully 350 re-locations and a hundred newly created prospective millionaires."[52]

CHAPTER TWO NOTES

1. Ezra Pound, *Indiscretions; or, Une Revue de Deux Mondes* (Paris: Three Mountains Press, 1923), p. 38.

2. Vardis Fisher, comp., *The Idaho Encyclopedia* (Caldwell: Caxton Printers, 1938), p. 229.

3. Memorial of January 7, 1881, *Journal of the House of Representatives of the Eleventh Legislative Assembly of the Territory of Idaho, Convened on the Thirteenth Day of December, A. D., and Adjourned on the Tenth Day of February, A.D. 1881, at Boise City* (Boise: A. J. Boyakin, Territorial Printer, 1881), pp. 286–288.

4. Carrie Adell Strahorn, *Fifteen Thousand Miles by Stage* (New York and London: G. P. Putnam's Sons, 1911, reprint, Lincoln and London: University of Nebraska Press, 1988), pp. 292, 294, 296, 452.

5. *Idaho Tri-Weekly Statesman* (Boise), December 4, 1880; "H" to editor (Hailey, April 9, 1881), *Idaho Tri-Weekly Statesman*, April 19, 1881; Betty M. Madsen and Brigham D. Madsen, *North to Montana!* (Salt Lake City: University of Utah Press, 1980), p. 245; *State Preservation Plan, Idaho* (Boise: Idaho State Historical Society, 1974), I, p. 52; George A. McLeod, *History of Blaine and Alturas Counties Idaho* (Hailey: Hailey Times, 1938), pp. 17, 19; *Wood River Times* (Hailey) (weekly), August 3, 1881 and July 26, 1882.

6. McLeod, pp. 16, 19; *Wood River Times* (weekly), September 6, 1882; W. Turrentine Jackson, "Wells Fargo & Co. in Idaho Territory: The 1870's and Beyond," *Idaho Yesterdays*, XXVII (Spring, 1983): 29.

7. *Mining and Scientific Press* (San Francisco), XLII (April 16, 1881): 245, 248, 252; *Idaho Tri-Weekly Statesman*, April 5, 1881. For fur-

ther comments on impassable roads in mid-April, see Isaac I. Lewis to Samuel T. Hauser, April 17, 1881, Hauser Papers, Box 6, Montana Historical Society Archives, Helena.

8. G. W. Hobart to H. A. Lord, quoted in *Mining and Scientific Press*, XLII (April 23, 1881): 268.

9. Ibid., XLII (April 16 and 23, May 7, 1881): 248, 268, 295.

10. "F" to editor (Bellevue, March 27, 1881), *Idaho Tri-Weekly Statesman*, April 5, 1881.

11. Quoted in *Mining and Scientific Press*, XLII (May 28, 1881): 342.

12. Lewis to Hauser (Ketchum, May 4, 1881), Hauser Papers, Box 6; "F" to editor (Bellevue, April 11, 1881), *Idaho Tri-Weekly Statesman*, April 21, 1881; *Mining and Scientific Press*, XLII (April 16, 1881): 248.

13. *Idaho Tri-Weekly Statesman*, May 7, 1881.

14. "F" to editor (Bellevue, April 11, 1881), *Idaho Tri-Weekly Statesman*, April 21, 1881.

15. *Idaho Tri-Weekly Statesman*, November 1, 1881.

16. *Idaho Tri-Weekly Statesman*, May 7, 1881; "F" to editor (Wood River, May 8, 1881), *Idaho Tri-Weekly Statesman*, May 17, 1881; "F" to editor (Wood River, May 22, 1881), *Idaho Tri-Weekly Statesman*, May 28, 1881; *Mining and Scientific Press*, XLII (April 16, 1881): 268.

17. *Engineering and Mining Journal* (New York), XXXII (August 27, 1881): 141.

18. *Mining and Scientific Press*, XLII (April 16, 1881): 248, 268; *Wood River Times* (weekly), June 22, 1881; *Engineering and Mining Journal*, XXXII (August 27, 1881): 141.

19. "H" to editor (Hailey, April 9, 1881), *Idaho Tri-Weekly Statesman*, April 19, 1881; "H" to editor (Hailey, April 29, 1881), *Idaho Tri-Weekly Statesman*, May 7, 1881; A. L. M. to editor (Hailey, June 7, 1881), *Idaho Tri-Weekly Statesman*, June 16, 1881; James H. Hawley, ed., *History of Idaho: The Gem of the Mountains* (Chicago: S. J. Clarke Publishing Co., 1920), I, p. 373; McLeod, p. 25; Strahorn, p. 422; *Wood River Times* (weekly), June 22 and July 27, 1881; *Engineering and Mining Journal*, XXXII (August 27, 1881): 141.

20. James H. Hart to Judge Kelly (Hailey, May 30, 1881), *Idaho Tri-Weekly Statesman*, June 4, 1881; *Wood River Times* (weekly), June 15, 1881.

21. *Idaho Tri-Weekly Statesman*, April 5, 1881; "H" to editor (Hailey, April 9, 1881), *Idaho Tri-Weekly Statesman*, April 19, 1881; "F" to editor (Wood River, May 8, 1881), *Idaho Tri-Weekly Statesman*, May 17, 1881; *Mining and Scientific Press*, XLII (May 7, 1881): 293; *Engineering and Mining Journal*, XXXII (August 27, 1881): 141.

22. "A. L. M." in *Mining and Scientific Press*, XLII (June 25, 1881): 422.

23. From the Willamette, Oregon, newspapers, cited by *Wood River Times* (weekly), June 22, 1881; *Idaho Tri-Weekly Statesman*, June 21, 1881. Local editors disagreed and believed that the *Statesman* had "given the Wood River country a paralyzing kick." *Idaho Tri-Weekly Statesman*, June 28, 1881.

24. *Mining and Scientific Press*, XLIV (January 7, 1882): 5.

25. *Idaho Tri-Weekly Statesman*, May 7, 1881.

26. Captain Jack Crawford, "The Prospector's Soliloquy," *The Poet Scout* (New York: Funk & Wagnalls, 1886), p. 123.

27. *Mining and Scientific Press*, XLII (March 19, 1881): 177.

28. Falk and two others were owners of the Star Mine, located west of the river, a few miles below Hailey. The mine had shipped a little over five tons of ore to Salt Lake City smelters in 1880 only to be disappointed by the high cost of handling, transportation, and commissions. Smelters at Wood River would reduce expenses by one-third, he estimated. *Mining and Scientific Press*, XLI (December 18, 1880): 389; XLII (June 25, 1881): 422.

29. *Mining and Scientific Press*, XLII (June 25, 1881): 422. A tuyère or tweer was a pipe inserted in the side of the furnace through which the blast was forced.

30. *Engineering and Mining Journal*, XXXII (July 16, September 10, and October 15, 1881): 49, 172, 257; *Wood River Times*, June 15, July 6 and 27, September 28, October 26, 1881 and October 2, 1893; McLeod, p. 13; *Mining and Scientific Press*, XLIII (August 13 and 20, October 8, 1881): 101, 117, 237; XLVIII (May 17, 1884): 338; Lewis to Hauser (Ketchum, August 5, 1882), Hauser Papers, Box 7.

31. Lewis to Hauser (Ketchum, November 26, 1880), Hauser Papers, Box 5; Lewis to Hauser (Ketchum, September 10, 1881), Hauser Papers, Box 6; McLeod, pp. 13–14; *Engineering and Mining Journal,* XXXII (October 22, 1881): 272; *Mining and Scientific Press,* XLIII (August 20, 1881): 117; XLVI (February 17, 1883): 109; XLVIII (May 24, 1884): 353; *Wood River Times* (weekly), September 21 and October 26, 1881; *Wood River Times,* August 1, 1885.

32. *Wood River Times* (weekly), July 27 and October 19, 1881; *Idaho Tri-Weekly Statesman,* December 6, 1881; *Mining and Scientific Press,* XLIII (October 29, 1881): 285; XLIV (June 3, 1882): 357.

33. *Wood River Times* (weekly), July 20, 1881; *Idaho Tri-Weekly Statesman,* July 23, 1881.

34. *Wood River Times* (weekly), August 24, 1881.

35. Stephen Roberts to George Clark (San Francisco, February 5, 1881), letterpress book I, Bancroft Library; *Mining World* (Las Vegas, New Mexico), II (September 1, 1881), p. 3; "F" to editor (Wood River, May 22, 1881), *Idaho Tri-Weekly Statesman,* May 28, 1881.

36. *Wood River Times* (weekly), June 22 and 29, 1881; Lewis to Hauser (Ketchum, June 1, 19, and 24, August 3, October 19, December 28, 1881), all in Hauser Papers, Box 6. The Star Mountain mines were listed in Elkhorn records as costing $3,303. Trial Balance, Elkhorn Mine Books, Nov. 15, 1881, Hauser Papers, Box 6.

37. Thomas A. Rickard, *A History of American Mining* (New York and London: McGraw-Hill Book Co., 1932), p. 191; *Synnott v. Shaughnessy,* 2 *Idaho Reports* (March 2, 1885), pp. 124–25.

38. Rickard, p. 191; *Wood River Times* (weekly), July 13 and 20, September 28, October 26, December 28, 1881; January 11, May 24 and 26, August 23, 1882; *Idaho Tri-Weekly Statesman,* July 21 and 23, 1881; *Engineering and Mining Journal,* XXXIII (January 7, 1882): 8.

39. *Wood River Times* (weekly), July 13, 1881 and August 23, 1882; *State Preservation Plan, Idaho,* I, p. 52.

40. *Wood River Times* (weekly), August 23, 1882; G. W. Barrett, "Colonel E. A. Wall: Mines, Miners, and Mormons," *Idaho Yesterdays,* XIV (Summer, 1970): 3, 6–11; G. W. Barrett, "Enos Andrew Wall; Mine Superintendent and Inventor," *Idaho Yesterdays,* XV (Spring, 1971):

24–25; Leonard J. Arrington and Gary B. Hansen, *"The Richest Hole on Earth": A History of the Bingham Copper Mine* (Monograph Series, Vol. XI, Logan: Utah State University Press, 1963), pp. 15–16.

41. Lewis to Hauser (Ketchum, December 22, 1880; April 17, May 11 and 27, August 16, October 19, 1881), all in Hauser Papers, Box 6; *Ketchum Keystone*, January 26, 1882; "F" to editor (Bellevue, May 29, 1880), *Idaho Tri-Weekly Statesman*, June 1, 1880; "J. B. F." to editor (Gimlet, March 3, 1882), *Idaho Tri-Weekly Statesman*, March 11, 1882; Elmer B. Fitch, "Muldoon District," in Joseph B. Umpleby, *Geology and Ore Deposits of the Mackay Region, Idaho, USGS Professional Paper* No. 97 (Washington: Government Printing Office, 1917), p. 106.

42. Lucille Hathaway Hall, *Memories of Old Alturas County, Idaho* (Denver: Big Mountain Press, 1956), p. 36; *Wood River Times* (weekly), July 27 and November 16, 1881; *Engineering and Mining Journal*, XXXI-II (February 11 and June 10, 1882): 83, 306; Umpleby, et al., p. 220. Both Miller and Shaughnessy had been among the original organizers of the Alta Club in Utah. See Malmquist, pp. 2, 5, 135.

43. *Wood River Times* (weekly), July 13, 1881 and August 23, 1882; Thomas B. Donaldson, *Idaho of Yesterday* (Caldwell: Caxton Printers, 1941), p. 134.

44. *Wood River Times* (weekly), September 28, 1881 and August 23, 1882.

45. The discoverer of the Homestake Mine in White Oaks, New Mexico, one editor wrote in 1882, "sold it for an old revolver, a few dollars of gold washings, and two sheep skins. To-day he is a poor man, while the buyer is a millionaire." See *Mining World*, II (April 20, 1882): 193.

46. *Mining and Scientific Press*, XLIII (August 13, 1881): 101; *Engineering and Mining Journal*, XXXII (July 23, 1881): 59.

47. *Engineering and Mining Journal*, XXXII (October 15, 1881): 257.

48. *Engineering and Mining Journal*, XXXII (October 1 and 22, 1881): 226, 272; XXXIII (February 11, 1882): 83.

49. *Idaho Tri-Weekly Statesman*, December 6, 1881; *Wood River Times* (weekly), December 7, 1881; *Engineering and Mining Journal*, XXXII (December 24, 1881): 420.

50. *Wood River Times*, October 2, 1882.

51. *Engineering and Mining Journal*, XXXIII (February 11, 1882): 83; "One of Them" to editor (Hailey, December 1, 1881), *Idaho Tri-Weekly Statesman*, December 6, 1881; "H" to editor (Hailey, March 28, 1882), *Idaho Tri-Weekly Statesman*, April 4, 1882. Slough (pronounced "sluff") is a card game of the Euchre group.

52. *Wood River Times*, January 3, 1883.

CHAPTER THREE

"THE RICHEST SILVER-LEAD PRODUCING COUNTRY IN THE WORLD"

THE NEXT FEW seasons solidified the trend toward the expansion, consolidation, and development of industrial mining and smelting, not only on the Lower Wood River, but in the fringe areas as well. The year 1883 brought an over-arching advance that touched the lives of all residents and business interests on the River: the coming of the railroad. Wood River passed from lusty infancy into a more orderly adolescence.

Those on the scene reported a good deal of construction activity during the winter of 1881–82 along with a shortage of grain, as snowstorms and snowslides isolated the towns even more than usual. By the end of March, three stages were running which linked Ketchum and Blackfoot, Hailey and Boise, and Hailey and the railroad at Kelton. Demand for seats was so great that coach passengers from Blackfoot and Kelton needed reservations several days in advance. Once they had arrived, they needed deep pockets to meet the stiff commodity prices that still prevailed. Fresh beef, when available, ran from $.15 to $.20 a pound; butter, $.62½; sugar, $.25; and whiskey and beer, "a mining camp's chief staple," were $.12½ and $.25 a glass.[1]

The shortage of lumber continued. Although dealers had laid in a supply of over two hundred thousand board feet the previous fall, and area sawmills had turned out an additional three hundred thousand feet, all the wood was gone. Demands for more were strong at $60 per thousand. Nor was there a vacant dwelling house of any kind to be had in Hailey, and "as high as $50 a month is offered for houses of three or four rooms."[2]

This situation, along with a dearth of all kinds of goods, was worsened by a scarcity of teams to bring freight wagons from the railroad. With the Oregon Short Line building across southern Idaho, Blackfoot had now become the closest connecting point. Since railroad contractors were willing to pay more for horses than forwarding agents and business houses were, freight rates were up and supplies piled up in the Blackfoot rail yard causing a shortage of goods.[3] The *Times* lamented:

No butter, no limes, no lemons, no eggs, no vegetables. Things are getting decidedly scarce, and if freight does not begin coming in soon, we will have to fall back on canned goods.[4]

As strangers continued to pour in, filling every available sleeping space in hotels, boardinghouses, sheds, and corrals, the pinch continued. In October a flour famine struck. Some families and several mining boardinghouses ran completely out. But by November the shortage was over; the price had dropped and flour was coming in from all directions.[5] But late in October the work force of the Jay Gould Mine—forty-five to fifty men—was laid off. The owners could not get transport for the ore in the dumps and decided to lease the property for the winter and market its ore in the spring.[6] When no postage stamps or stamped envelopes were available at the post offices in Hailey, Bellevue, Ketchum, and Blackfoot, citizens did not condemn the transportation system; like good Americans, they blamed the government in Washington.[7]

Local boosters noted that the region had plenty of miners and ore, but a shortage of men of capital and ability to invest in transportation *and* mining, milling, and smelting. At the same time, it behooved Wood River mine owners to proceed warily when dealing with outsiders, because "on the flanks of the real prospector there always hang a species of parasite, who hope as middle-men and promoters to get their fingers in, and make thrift of the labors of the men of the industry."[8]

During the summer of 1882, a business depression in the East was apparent. "Financially there is nothing doing in New York," a knowledgeable observer reported. Earnings were down, stocks were sagging, railroads were expanding too rapidly, and the public showed its skepticism by not buying. During the lull, Wood River prospect owners found their galena veins narrowing with depth. In fear that the veins might vanish and prove worthless, many of them eased up on development work and stepped up efforts to sell. Isaac Lewis was typical. When the Elkhorn vein "pinched down to almost nothing" in mid-July, he cut his crew in half and concentrated on making the mine look good. "The stopes may open up again," he said, "& if they do I propose to hold the showing in sight for a sale." Editors complained that this was retarding the local economy and admonished owners to "stop loafing and go to work" on their claims if they hoped to succeed. When undeveloped property proved a drug on the market, many took this advice and tapped the veins lower down, and found them opened-up again and full of promise. At this point, a number of major mines changed hands and prosperity seemed assured.[9]

An estimated $1.5 million had been invested in the Wood River mines in 1882 and over $1 million taken out. About one-fifth of the ore was handled by the Philadelphia Mining and Smelting Company, which expanded its facilities, although most ore still went outside the territory. There were at least fourteen major sales of mining property in 1882. The Mayflower went for $375,000, and Enos Wall added the Bullion to his other holdings at a cost of $200,000. But the investment proved sound; the Bullion shipped out almost $700,000 in ore between November 1 and December 10.[10]

The Elkhorn was shipping ore regularly to the Philadelphia smelter as its superintendent walked the slippery line between taking out ore to provide operating capital and the need to show value to a potential purchaser. The Morning Star, owned by the Warm Spring Consolidated Mining Company, struck a four-foot vein of rich ore. By mid-1882, the Bullion was down about two hundred twenty-five feet, with numerous drifts and crosscuts. On the same ledge, work was being pushed on the Jay Gould and the Mayflower. Meanwhile, according to its superintendent, a man not without imagination, the Minnie Moore had hit galena assaying 2,600 ounces to the ton—"one of the finest ore bodies ever discovered," one with "no waste at all."[11]

Even before the 1883 season opened, it was evident that a fair number of shabby hangers-on were wintering in Hailey—a situation not viewed lightly by some residents, including editor Picotte. In the spring, before the jobs had opened up, the number of newcomers swelled and included more of the down-and-outers. Some predicted that an even more "frightful class of people," including disorderly "opium fiends and prostitutes," were likely to follow in the wake of the railroad, as was the case on the new Oregon Short Line farther south.[12]

Given high freight rates, Wood River mine owners were hardly concerned about any undesirable impact of rail transportation and understandably exerted pressure to draw railroad lines into their midst to ease the cost of shipping ore. Indeed, the fact that high Union Pacific officials were seriously discussing building through Idaho soon undoubtedly had something to do with men like Warren Callahan and the other early prospectors deciding to move ahead with their galena discoveries in 1879.[13] It was not unusual for railroad companies to respond to mine operators' persuasion to build branch lines, which in turn fostered improved transportation, gave extra incentive to the growth of agriculture, including the livestock industry, and helped set capitalistic machinery into motion.

In 1870, the Utah Northern Railroad had commenced building north from Ogden heading for Butte, but by 1878 they had only reached the town of Franklin, barely across the Idaho border. The railroad pushed on. In 1883 it reached its northern terminus, linking with the Northern Pacific at Garrison, Montana. From 1879 to 1883, Blackfoot was the nearest stagecoach and railroad connection to Wood River. Near the end of 1880, even before any branch line into Wood River was under way, the Union Pacific Railroad Company had a large group of workers improving the wagon road between Bellevue and Blackfoot with the intent of shortening the route to about a hundred thirty miles. Shortly after that, it was reliably reported that the Utah Northern and the Northern Pacific both had crews making field surveys for a route to the head of the River.[14]

But when Wood River finally received a rail line, it came from a different direction. In 1881 the Union Pacific commenced building the Oregon Short Line, a route across southern Idaho to link the main line in Wyoming with Oregon. Bellevue spokesmen immediately inaugurated a campaign for a branch connection.[15] By the end of 1882, 321 miles had been completed from Granger Junction to Shoshone, and a branch line was pushed 70 miles north to Wood River.

Robert Strahorn's role in this is not clear. As vice president of one of Union Pacific's subsidiaries, the Idaho and Oregon Land Improvement Company (which did advance work laying out town sites, reserving land for stations, and promoting towns), Strahorn had his own investments in Hailey and had piqued his company's interest. In the summer of 1882, according to Picotte, there had occurred the "most important transaction in the history of Hailey and Wood River" when John Hailey, W. T. Riley, J. H. Boomer, and E. S. Chase—the original town site locators— sold the four sections comprising and surrounding the Hailey town site to the Idaho and Oregon Land Improvement Company.[16]

Strahorn had long been a publicist for the Union Pacific and had visited Wood River a number of times, always emphasizing the positive features of the area and predicting that a rail line would bring thousands of settlers. Because he touted Hailey specifically, Strahorn was anathema to Ketchum, whose major editor belittled the "few little hammerings" of Strahorn "and other wildcat capitalists." The Union Pacific and its chief cheerleader were so closely involved with boosting the Idaho diggings that the *Denver Republican* labeled it "the much-lauded Wood River Country" "the biggest mining fraud of the age . . . a mining boom inaugurated by a railroad corporation." Not true, replied Wood River stalwarts. If the Union Pacific and the Oregon Short Line had encouraged migration, they did so on facts and on "the MERIT of our mines."[17]

In Hailey, late in April 1883, Picotte chortled with glee at the imminence of the "Iron Horse": "He is Snorting and Cavorting within Eight Miles of this Metropolis."[18] Picotte reported that the first passenger train, a special, pulled into town on May 18— fourteen hours and 300 miles out of Ogden. Carrie Strahorn gave the date as May 23, and went on to describe the scene. The Strahorns were aboard, along with Fred Willard of the *St. Louis Times*, Miss Louise Skinner of Denver, and Alexander Caldwell, former United States senator from Kansas and now president of the Idaho and Oregon Land Improvement Company. The train was met "with a brass band and all the enthusiasm of a Fourth of July." Eighteen months later, the railroad was extended to Ketchum, whose citizens welcomed its coming with a sixteen-piece band and a gala festival at the big Metropolitan Saloon with dancing in the huge upstairs ballroom and in another large chamber on the ground floor. Drinks were at a premium that night.[19]

Located under the so-called "ten-dollar-lot law" (an act of Congress allowing each inhabitant two lots at the minimum price of ten dollars each), the Ketchum town site included 1,600 lots, all of them taken up by settlers and improved. Thus, with the town lots all occupied, the railroad had to establish its depot, terminal, engine house, machine shop, and siding on lands of the Alturas Land Improvement and Manufacturing Company, a group which held title to property in the valley north of Ketchum.[20]

So the braying of the jackass and the coarse maledictions of the muleskinner gave way to the whistle of the locomotive on Wood River. Salt Lake City was now only twelve hours away and Wood River seemed assured of prosperity "unsurpassed by either Leadville or Butte." Along with the railroad came the telegraph and optimistic visions of the future, although it was quickly apparent that freight outfits and stagecoaches were not going to share the benefits of this advancing technology. Stages still ran to the higher places like Sawtooth and Galena, and in 1884 a new toll road opened up Trail Creek to Lost River and Bayhorse, over which Horace Lewis's big ore wagons would travel regularly.[21]

The railroad lowered the cost of goods coming in and going out. It meant a savings of twenty dollars a ton over hauling by wagon, and it made it possible to bring Pennsylvania coke to Wood River to be used in roasting the galena ore before shipping it to smelters elsewhere.[22] As it did everywhere, the coming of the railroad expedited the flow of capital and the exploitation of a region's resources. It was a slow process, but it made an enduring imprint.

In 1883 it was calculated that as many as ten thousand people had been in the Wood River country the previous season, about three thousand of them in the towns. Optimists expected at least twenty thousand for the 1883 season, but as of late May, Hailey was not crowded. Of an estimated one thousand arriving there by that time, roughly eight hundred had stopped long enough to repack and strike out as prospectors or as day miners. A few, James Blackwood among them, thought prospecting too chancy, and sought "a sure thing"—preferably a contract to deliver timber, charcoal, or ties. With the coming of the railroad, the towns continued to grow, despite another lumber shortage in the autumn.[23]

According to the *Times,* Wood River produced $3 million in ores in 1883, $500,000 more than in the previous year—and twice as much as later estimates by U.S. Geological Survey experts. Most ores were still sent elsewhere for smelting, but as the Hailey Sampling Works discovered early in the year, only ores worth $100 or more per ton were profitable to ship: sampling, transport, smelting, and other costs totaled over $90 on a ton sent to Omaha.[24]

Although they were off to a shaky start, the Hailey Sampling Works was one of several important agencies that tested ores and expedited their transfer to the smelter, whether in Wood River or out of the territory. Jabez Chase, who converted the old Falk smelter north of Hailey into a custom concentrating plant using a process to handle certain types of low-grade ores, also emphasized sampling. Salt Lake City entrepreneurs installed machinery made by the Colorado Iron Works in the new Ketchum Sampling Works, located near the depot, in 1884. More than 30 percent of the more than fifteen million pounds of ore received by the Philadelphia Smelter in 1883 came from the Sampling works of Conkling & Mouton at Hailey; five years later, the Hailey and Bellevue Sampling Mills handled 6,033,423 pounds.[25]

Part of the success recorded in 1883 was due to the expansion of the Philadelphia smelter, under the watchful eye of Colonel Edmund Green, who supervised at Ketchum during the warmer months and promoted Wood River mines on either coast during the winter. Located near Ketchum in 1881, convenient for power, timber, and lime and iron ore deposits for flux, the original plant had two large smelting furnaces. During the summer of 1883 the company added several large new buildings and two state-of-the-art, 50-ton furnaces patterned after those of the Grant Works in Denver. This expansion gave a total capacity of 120 to 180 tons a day and enabled the company to "compete with the world," according to a spokesman, although it failed to reach its maximum potential that season. Even so, it worked 100 tons of ore per day, drawn from fifty-two different mines, and was one of the major reasons Ketchum was regarded by some as "probably the most healthy mining town on Wood River." Before the year was over, it was estimated that the smelter would produce seven million pounds of "base bullion," worth about $1.3 million although this crude argentiferous lead had to be further refined elsewhere.[26]

But the route of the Philadelphia Mining and Smelting Company was not always smooth. It owned several mines, including especially the North Star group on the East Fork, where the company built a modern concentrating mill to eliminate much of the base and refractory materials and leave relatively clean concentrates for the smelter. It installed a clever arrangement for a steady flow of heated water from Guyer Hot Springs to protect its water supply for its two forty-horsepower waterwheels in cold weather. But it had to do a good deal of experimenting in its treatment of ores before it settled on a winning combination. Silver ores that were high in lead usually contained sulfur, some zinc, arsenic, and other base metals that proved difficult to handle and added seven to ten dollars per ton to the cost of smelting. A special oxidizing charge had to be used to remove antimony. The smelter refused to buy ores with 50 percent or more of lead content, which meant that the Mayflower, the Jay Gould, the Narrow Gauge and other important mines had to make arrangements to ship to Omaha, Denver, Salt Lake City, or elsewhere. After much trial and error, and some embarrassment,

The Philadelphia Smelter at Ketchum. From H. N. Elliott, *History of the Territory of Idaho. Idaho State Historical Society*

the company erected five roasting furnaces to treat the high-grade lead ores and eliminate impurities before smelting.[27]

In Wood River, the smelting of average ore required about .6 ton of iron flux, .2 ton of lime and forty-two bushels of charcoal. The iron ore cost $6 a ton, the lime $4 a ton, and the charcoal $.14 a bushel. Thus the expense of smelting in a forty-ton furnace was estimated at $11.53 per ton, although the actual figures may have been higher.[28] After the coming of the railroad, coke was imported from Pennsylvania, but from the beginning, the company contracted out for charcoal and for lime, both used as fluxes. In 1884, former California turkey grower Frank Gooding was handling these contracts for the smelter and supervising as many as fifteen men who rafted timber down the river to the company's twenty charcoal kilns near the plant. From his profits,

Gooding bought sheep and went on to be one of Idaho's large wool-growers and a United States senator.[29]

Lime was acquired locally, although early lime burners were sometimes distracted. E. D. Browne, for example, was getting out smelting lime in Greenhorn Gulch when he hit galena ore assaying 190 ounces of silver per ton and decided that owning a silver mine had many advantages. Initially, the iron ore needed for flux came from Wood River owners, especially magnetite from the Iron Clad and the P. K. Mines, both in the Mascot group on the East Fork of the Big Wood River. It was sent down the tramway used for Paymaster ore, then by wagon to Hailey, a total distance of about twenty miles. Eventually, however, when manipulators cornered the supply and boosted prices, the smelter was forced to import iron in substantial amounts from Rawlins, Wyoming and Tintic, Utah. At one point in 1885, after the Union Pacific failed to live up to its contract to supply twenty tons of iron ore per day, the smelter had to close down for two weeks until a new agreement could be put into effect, one which required the railroad to deliver two cars of coke and two of iron each day for a specified period, and obligated the smelter to ship two cars of lead bullion daily.[30]

At the time of the Philadelphia Company's plant expansion in 1883–84, other smelters were considered. The Little Wood River Mining and Smelting Company installed a forty-ton Rankin and Brayton-type copper matting furnace at Muldoon. It was also announced that the copper smelter of Brunner, Hennicke & Cranston at Hailey would be operating soon. Its stack would handle three furnaces, but only one was to be built that year. It was expected that the company's two mines—one on Deadman's Flat and one on Lost River—would keep the smelter going. Later that year, the *Times* noted that a new smelter at Bellevue would be completed in the near future.[31] In the end, most of these ventures never got off the ground. The few that did, like the original Falk furnace and the Muldoon smelter, were short-lived and unprofitable.

Meanwhile, the show mines—among them the Bullion, the Mayflower, the Jay Gould, the Eureka, the Idahoan, and the

The Bullion Mine was operated by the Wood River Gold & Silver Mining Company near Bullion. From H. N. Elliott, *History of the Territory of Idaho* (1884). *Idaho State Historical Society*

Minnie Moore—were all beginning to come into their own as producers. In September, the Bullion had just completed a new concentration mill, which would concentrate fifty tons of crude or undressed ore per day and make five to fifteen tons of shipping ore, depending on the character of the ore. The Bullion was employing a hundred men and was shipping a dozen tons of first-class ore daily. But three months later, having finished much "dead work," the company laid off three-quarters of its labor force for the winter.

The Jay Gould was also building a new concentrator and had stockpiled 3,000 tons of ore to be processed when it opened. The upper tunnel of the Idahoan was 525 feet down on a rich body of ore, 4 feet thick, and 1,500 tons of first-class ore were in the dumps, ready for shipping to the Hailey Sampling Works and for sale to the smelter in Ketchum or in Salt Lake City. The Queen of the Hills was taking out bright galena ore—about 75 percent lead and 104 ounces of silver a ton from new strikes near the Minnie Moore. The Mayflower managers had sold 100 tons of ore to Salt Lake Smelters, then concluded a deal to ship all their ores to the Kansas City Reduction Works.[32]

Even more modest mines received high acclaim. Near the end of 1883, the Elkhorn, owned by Isaac Lewis and his Montana partners, was regularly sending twelve tons of ore per day to the Philadelphia Smelter, with average net receipts of $165 a ton after transportation and reduction costs.[33]

Owners of the Elkhorn had flirted with various promising buyers: Salt Lake banker Warren Hussey (in the end, his financial "friends" were "a little shy"); W. C. Tatro, who had in mind a company in which General Ulysses S. Grant was interested; and especially the California mining genius, George Hearst, who sent his experts to look at the property several times (see chart opposite). (Two of them were offered kickbacks of $5,000 each in 1883 by the mine's superintendent to report favorably.)[35] Although Hearst's geologist, Walter P. Jenny, thought the mine overpriced at $300,000, Hearst's renewed presence was in itself an endorsement of Wood River. "When a district gets good enough for Hearst, they say, it is good enough for any mining man," the *Times* editor trumpeted. How much investment Hearst and his partner, James Ben Ali Haggin, had in the district is not clear. Their negotiations for the Elkhorn and the Mayflower fell through, but in 1883 Haggin acquired the Solace Mine near Vienna.[36]

By the end of 1884, the Elkhorn had paid a total of $260,900 in dividends. As early as mid-1883, Lewis must have realized that the long-range prospects of the property were speculative and stepped up his efforts to present the best face of the mine to would-be buyers. "My whole work from now on, will be to make it look its best & close up & hide places I don't want them to see," he wrote Samuel Hauser. After 1884, the Elkhorn's production fell off sharply. The vein fizzled out at about three hundred feet and it paid only $6,000 in dividends in 1885, and none after that. Part of the mine had been leased to three partners, but lengthy litigation followed after Lewis charged that $10,000

PROFIT AND EXPENSE, ELKHORN MINE,
DECEMBER 7, 1882-NOVEMBER 7, 1883[34]

Labor, salaries, board	$24,536.23
Incidentals, taxes, assay, &c.	505.91
Tools, iron, candles, &c.	2,480.72
Hauling ore, &c.	5,102.18
Timber for mine houses, &c.	2,595.29
Incidentals	152.00
Total	35,375.53
Ore sold	161,841.22
Net profit	126,467.69

worth of ore had been removed from unleased ground on the property. In the end, Lewis and his partners won the case. "The whole thing was & is a black mailing scheme backed up by some cut throat schalawags [sic] at Hailey," including a "red headed cuss" named Jack Ervin.[37] This was one of a relatively few cases of litigation in Wood River mines in the boom period. Owners of the Elkhorn also clashed over disputed ground with the Noon Day Company, whose people were "a set of thieves & intended to steal from the word go," according to Lewis, who believed the sole intent of the intrusion was to sell Noon Day claims for $60,000.[38]

At the same time, more property was changing hands and more eastern firms were getting involved. An Ohio company was being organized to develop mines in Narrow Gauge Gulch. A Maryland group, the Carrollton Mining Company of Baltimore, bought the St. Patrick Mine near Bellevue. The Morton Mine, five miles from Hailey, was sold for $20,000, and the Baltimore group, in the Elkhorn mineral belt, went for $30,000; the Baltimore and Victoria Mining Company was organized in Salt Lake City, with capital stock of $1.5 million to work the property. David Falk and Alonzo Wolters sold part of the Star group, a mile and a half southwest of Hailey, to another Salt Lake combine, while the Point Lookout Mine (near the Mayflower) was taken over by a third Utah group, who sold an interest to New York capitalists.[39]

Although production may not have been as high as the local estimate of $5 million for the combined Wood River-Sawtooth region, 1883 was a good year despite a momentary scarcity of rail cars in Hailey in November, which slowed the movement of ores and bullion. The crisis was deemed "alarming and is seriously interfering with the yield of the mines," but the threat was brief.[40]

The new year loomed even more promising. Silver-lead properties continued to sell well and to attract outside capital. Experts predicted that by the summer of 1884, Wood River would have more than a hundred and ten paying mines.[41] The biggest mining news that season, however, was the sale of the Minnie Moore to English investors. For several years British capitalists had nibbled at the expensive bait set out by Wood River promoters. They had shown an interest in the Elkhorn in 1881, when it had been in the $25,000 category, and again early in 1884, when the price had skyrocketed to $400,000, but had backed off when the owners demanded cash.[42]

In the same year it was rumored that the Mayflower, the Bullion, the Jay Gould, and other mines had been marketed to a British outfit whose experts had visited Wood River and were impressed. The rumor proved unfounded, but three months later John V. Farwell was in London trying to negotiate the sale of the Bullion, the Ophir, and other property of the Wood River Gold & Silver Mining Company for $2 million—another transaction which remained uncompleted at that time.[43]

In January of the following year, American entrepreneurs James S. Leeds and Dr. Buna Newton signed a contract with a spokesman of a British joint stock company to be formed to acquire the Bullion Mine for £137,000 cash and £73,000 in shares. Incorporated ten days later, the Bullion Mining Company, Ltd., issued an impressive prospectus designed to raise capital of £220,000 in shares of £1 each. With the typical "guinea pig" board of directors—men of some stature who lent their names to the enterprise in return for payment of one guinea per meeting— the prospectus listed Enos Wall as general manager and quoted statements by Warren Hussey, Walter P. Jenney, and experts of the London engineering firm of John Taylor & Sons lauding the mine and estimating £182,000 to £400,000 of ore in sight.[44] Although Wood Riverites hailed the news as the beginning of a new era, at least one English journal was sarcastically skeptical:

It might be supposed that the worthy citizen of Idaho, who is the vendor, is selling his mine at a somewhat dear figure. This, however, is a mistake. He is simply reckless in his desire to benefit investors on this side of the Atlantic.[45]

In the end, as Colonel Wall had to report late in April, the deal fell through. The Bullion did not pass into British hands; too few shares were sold, and although the company was carried officially on the rolls for another ten years, it remained inactive.[46]

About the time the Bullion transaction went on the rocks, rumors surfaced that the Idahoan Mine was to be sold to "a Strong English Syndicate" headed by Count de Barranca of London. But by the end of 1884, no action had been taken, according to the Hailey editor, because the transfer papers had been mislaid.[47] Nothing ever did transpire.

The Minnie Moore was another matter. Reports early in 1884 had that mine, along with the Queen of the Hills and the Monday, being sold for $500,000 to Scottish capitalists.[48] The reports proved to be partially true. Working through the New York agency of Dr. John Walsh, the Minnie Moore's American owners, John Moore, Henry E. Miller, Fred Myers, and M. M. Shaughnessy, sold the property to Dent, Palmer & Company, a well-established London financial firm, at a price of $500,000. Handling the matter in England was one of the directors of the Bank of England, Cecil Brook Palmer. No separate joint stock company was organized to handle the mine, but British sources called it "one of the best properties of the West," and thought it promising for investors that there was so much British capital in Wood River holdings.[49]

When it changed hands, the Minnie Moore's main works was an inclined shaft, 160 feet deep, two levels running to the east a maximum of 205 feet and three to the west a distance of 80 feet. Most of the work had been exploratory, but at the time of the sale, with the price of silver at $1.14 an ounce and lead at

$100 a ton, the gross value of reserves was set at $673,329—hence the substantial price.[50]

The end of 1884 closed an especially active, profitable season on Wood River. In the month of March alone, the Hailey Sampling-Works had handled a total of 697,470 pounds, of which three cars were of base bullion, three were of concentrates sent to Aurora, Illinois, and thirty went to Kansas City for smelting. About the same time it was reported that the Germania Smelting Company of Utah was about to reenter the Wood River market to buy all classes of ore. During the spring, the $20 per ton rate on ores between Hailey and Omaha was replaced with a uniform rate of $25 a ton on all classes and grades of ore, base bullion, matte, and lead from Hailey to Salt Lake City, San Francisco, Denver, Omaha, and Council Bluffs, while the cost to Kansas City was $26 a ton.[51] Many of the mines and smelters still shut down or cut back operations severely during the winter months. So did the Miners' Hospital, but Dr. Brown pledged to reopen it as soon as the work force was sufficiently increased in the spring.[52]

When territorial Governor William M. Bunn made his annual report for 1884, he noted that Wood River "is now generally conceded to be the richest silver-lead producing country in the world." At the same time, Bunn perpetuated the old mining myth: "In all cases the ores have steadily increased in value as depth has been obtained,"[53] an axiom certainly not borne out by future developments in this area of relatively shallow and interrupted ore bodies.

The years 1885 and 1886 were also good for Wood River mining, although success chose its mines carefully and some of the early producers ceased to pay, especially if the price of silver slipped. The Minnie Moore had shipped more than $364,271 in ore from April 1 to October 31, 1886, after deducting railroad and smelting costs, and was reported as "doing splendidly" as 1887 commenced—months before it struck a 4-foot ledge of high-grade ore at the 750-foot level. The Minnie Moore and the Queen of the Hills were labeled the two main operating properties in the Broadford area that summer, with the Queen employing about a hundred and fifteen men, although elsewhere other mines continued to be productive. The Idahoan had hit a good vein at 400 feet and was still turning out rich ore and paying dividends. The once rich Parker Brothers Group was doing poorly; both the Mayflower and the Bullion were in the hands of lessees and not producing much. In the winter of 1886–87, the Mayflower had forty to fifty leasers working its ground, plus ten miners of its own prospecting for ore bodies, apparently without luck. The New York owners of the King of the Hills Mine near Bullion expressed delight with their property's promise, and the Philadelphia Smelter Company thought its Silver Star and North Star on the East Fork of the Wood River were also real comers.[54]

Even with mixed success, with some properties doing well and others playing out, optimism flourished. In the generally good years of the mid-1880s, countless new promotions were made, properties were bonded, changed hands, and companies formed, especially in Salt Lake City. The Hailey Hill Company, for example, was incorporated in the Mormon capital in late 1885, with a nominal capital of $1.5 million, to develop the Japan, the Way Up, and other claims. A few months later, the Northern Belle Company, another Utah outfit, was organized with a stated capital of $1 million to develop the Old Judge and Belle claims in the Warm Springs Mining District.[55]

The Anglo-Idaho Mining Company, also a Salt Lake venture (with capital of $1 million), was organized in mid-1887 to develop the Lookout, Good Hope, and Florence claims in the Little Wood River Mining District to the east. Still later that year, S. S. Wilson discovered the Black Spar on Bear Gulch in the same district, thus reviving an interest in the Muldoon area. Wilson sold part of his interest to a St. Louis group, the Black Spar Mining and Milling Company, who began developing the mine, only to be stymied by low silver and lead prices.[56]

Meanwhile, Shaughnessy and Groesbeck, both experienced Utah entrepreneurs on Wood River, bonded the property bordering the Tip Top and were at work trying to organize a New York company to develop it. Ores of the Croesus Mine in Scorpion Gulch contained both gold and silver, plus heavy iron sulfites. When its owners went heavily in debt to Isaac Lewis's First Bank of Ketchum, Lewis forced its sale and took it over. At one point, he thought it had been taken up by eastern capitalists for $75,000, but that was not to be. The King of the West in the Smoky District, northwest of Hailey, was bonded to James Ben Ali Haggin of San Francisco for $40,000, and the Carrie Leonard group, located in the same area, changed hands after debt forced its owner to sell. After yielding $70,000 in 1886 and paying dividends of $30,000 (after the erection of a new concentrator and ore-house) the Carrie Leonard sold to Salt Lake City people for $105,000.[57]

Optimism was also reflected in June 1886 when a new sampling works was installed at Ketchum. Owned by lawyer William McKay and insurance agent Hugh Anderson of Salt Lake City, and managed by Charles Weaver, the plant had a capacity of thirty tons a day and charged four dollars a ton for sampling, except for special contracts. A little later in the same year, the Idaho Sampling Milling Company was organized by G. L. Havens, J. C. Conklin, J. O. Swift, Walter P. Jenney, and others to incorporate the sampling works owned by Swift and Conklin in Hailey and to build a new mill at Bellevue. They made arrangements with a number of large mines and ore shippers, many of whom were shareholders in the new corporation, for sampling their ores.[58]

Ore had to be rich to meet the high overhead costs and still pay a profit. For example, between October 1, 1884, and December 1, 1885, the Bellevue Idaho Company, which owned the Queen of the Hills, handled ores worth $464,078.98 in its concentrating plant and paid transportation and freight charges of

$134,540.63, leaving net receipts of $329,538.35. The cost of $37 a ton for freight and smelting took almost one-third the value of the ore. The cost of concentration ran about $10 a ton and other expenses included mine timber, $.05 a running foot; coal, $10 per car; and labor, $3.50 per person per ten-hour shift. Ore shipped from Hailey in February, 1886, amounted to 1,014,200 pounds, some 110,000 pounds more than for the previous February.[59]

Part of the ore handled by Hailey and Ketchum in the good years came from the outlying districts, which meant additional costs of transportation. In the upper Wood River country, for example, ore from the Parnell Mine in Germania Basin due north of Galena in the mid-1880s had to be carried by packtrain to Galena, then shipped by wagon over the turnpike to the smelter at Ketchum. From the Blue Jacket Mine in rugged Boulder Basin, just north of Boulder Peak and the Wood River, W. A. Broadhead was sending "a pack train load per day" of ore to the Philadelphia smelter in Ketchum in 1884.[60]

Of more importance was the output from the mines in Sawtooth, Vienna, and Galena, much of which came to the Lower Wood, although some moved laboriously to Atlanta. Ores from these districts were generally not galena, but quartz carrying black sulfurets and ruby or antimonial silver, along with some gold, and could be treated by roasting or chlorination. By the summer of 1881, these upper camps had been linked to Ketchum by toll road, although its use was sorely limited to good weather. The opening of mines in Sawtooth went ahead—including the Pilgrim in Beaver Canyon, the Silver King nearby, and the properties of the New York-owned Columbia and Beaver Company. But progress was slow: it took time and great effort to move heavy mill machinery into the district; litigation and fire took their toll; management difficulties hampered the Columbia and Beaver Company and retarded its output for several years. Reorganized as the Sawtooth Milling and Mining Company, it eventually expanded its holdings, erected a concentrating mill at the Silver King Mine, and by 1885 it was sending concentrates worth $500 to $800 a ton to Ketchum for smelting. In the following year some two hundred men were employed in the Sawtooth mines, but after that production fell off.

In Smiley's Canyon near the bustling camp of Vienna, the Vienna Consolidated Mining Company, a Wisconsin outfit, pushed the opening of the Vienna Mine, the most important in the area. While the town flourished with a population of eight hundred and even for a time had its own newspaper, the company erected an expensive mill at a cost of over $200,000, but winter snows isolated both Vienna and Sawtooth and a lack of supplies delayed milling until the summer of 1883. After nearly a year of operation, by June of 1884, the total output of the Vienna mill was reported at 150 bars of bullion worth $250,000. Although the company continued during 1885, 1883–84 was the peak of its production.[61]

Galena, the thriving town at the mouth of Gladiator Creek, served a number of promising mines, especially the Senate group, owned by the Senate Mining and Smelting Company, organized in New York City in 1883. Like Vienna and Sawtooth, towns and mines alike were often isolated by deep snow and frequent avalanches that hampered mail delivery by dog sleds and restricted the seasons during which ore could be hauled over the primitive road to Ketchum by sixteen-horse freight wagons. Early on, the Senate Company brought up a small smelter, but weather, failure to provide the necessary fuel, and generally poor planning delayed blowing it in for several years. Even then it was a crude operation with the ore dragged down the hill over narrow trails on stone-boats—crude horse-drawn sleds of limited capacity.[62] Given such difficulties, it is not surprising that Galena was not a major contributor to the wealth of Wood River.

The Smoky District, twenty-five miles west of Ketchum across Dollarhide Summit, was also tributary to the lower Wood smelting center. From the hub of Carrietown (named after one of the chief mines, the Carrie Leonard) miners were at work developing mines up Little Smoky Creek by 1884. They stockpiled ore and built branch roads to connect with the new Camas wagon road to Hailey. By 1885, the Carrie Leonard, King of the West, Tyranus, Stormy Galore, and other producers were all shipping galena ores to the main Wood River sampling works. In 1887, the Carrie Leonard sent 112 tons of ore to Hailey and Bellevue and 503 tons to Ketchum.[63]

Eleven miles southwest of Hailey, the town of Doniphan flourished in the early 1880s. Named after Judge James Doniphan, its postmaster and most prominent citizen, the town served the mines of the Hailey Gold Belt, especially the Big Camas, the Tip Top, the Hidden Treasure and the Black Cinder. Complete with post office, schoolhouse, general store, shoe shop, boardinghouse, saloon, and a number of dwellings, the town endured for nearly two decades, but its existence was based on gold, not silver.[64]

On the opposite side of Hailey, twenty-four miles due east by wagon road, Muldoon sprouted in 1881 to serve a number of mines in the drainage basin of the Little Wood River. It soon attracted a flurry of optimists. The Silver Spar, Eagle Bar, and John A. Logan were among the promising prospects, but the most productive property of the boom era was the Muldoon Mine on the East Fork of Muldoon Creek about halfway up the canyon at the foot of Muldoon Ridge. About fifty locations quickly followed. In 1882 the district was undergoing a definite boom with a dozen saloons and a population of nearly five hundred. The Muldoon was owned by the Little Wood River Mining and Smelting Company, which was closely linked to the Philadelphia smelter in Ketchum. In the summer of 1882, the firm had about forty men at work on a smelter while others were developing the mine, digging charcoal pits, building a sawmill and hauling 400 tons of Fish Creek iron ore to use as flux. In what proved to be a case of classic overkill, two water jacket furnaces, each of forty-ton capacity, were brought from the Pacific Iron Works in San Francisco. To match the smelters' capacity, the company felt compelled to purchase additional mines and install a tramway system to bring the ore down 1,200 feet from the mine to a road leading two miles to the furnaces, which blew late in September. After a month or so, twenty tons of bullion were freighted to the railhead in Blackfoot.[65]

In 1883, the new manager sent out from Pittsburgh contracted for a forty-mule packtrain to bring a daily load of eight tons of iron ore from upper Fish Creek six miles to the wagon road, where it was freighted another six miles to Muldoon. But high quality galena was limited, lead prices were low, and the company ran out of operating funds and had to close down temporarily in October after having produced about $34,500 during the season. About fifteen men doing development work on the property in 1884 blocked out four to five hundred tons of ore which would keep the furnaces going until weather and roads permitted resumption of operations sometime after mid-May. That was enough ore, the company believed, to justify the addition of a fifty-ton concentrator.[66]

But annual production remained modest. Two hundred thousand dollars was taken out of Muldoon in the 1882–84 period, but the region produced little after that. The company moved its tram and mining equipment to its promising North Star lode on the East Fork of the Wood River. Efforts of other groups to inject capital and develop new properties failed. Isolation and an inability to perfect the technology to handle ores profitably doomed the district's mining industry, and the area eventually became sheep and cattle country.[67]

These outlying areas contributed to the Wood River economy, but were not of major significance. The communities were small; most never grew beyond seven or eight hundred inhabitants and were short-lived. The majority were isolated and their labor and transportation costs so high that only the richest ores could be worked gainfully, thus limiting operations to a few short seasons. The bulk of Wood River's lead and silver wealth during the boom period came from the districts around the larger, wealthier, and more enduring centers of Bellevue, Hailey, and Ketchum—small towns themselves.

Already the Wood River mines were being overshadowed by rich new deposits in the northern part of the territory. Following the discovery of gold along the North Fork of the Coeur d'Alene River in the late 1870s, a rush of prospectors ten thousand strong pushed into the region in 1883–85 taking out a quarter to a half million dollars a year. Next came the finding of silver-lead ores on a tributary of the South Fork in 1884. A year later, Bunker Hill and Sullivan claims in Milo Gulch were discovered. They eventually became the largest silver-lead property in the country.

Thus began the exploitation of the Coeur d'Alenes, a new era in Idaho's mining history, far surpassing the Wood River phase.[68]

CHAPTER THREE NOTES

1. "H" to editor (Hailey, March 28, 1882), *Idaho Tri-Weekly Statesman* (Boise), April 4, 1882; "J. B. F." to editor (Gimlet, February 14 and March 3, 1882), *Idaho Tri-Weekly Statesman*, February 25 and March 11, 1882; *Mining and Scientific Press* (San Francisco), XLIV (April 29, 1882): 280.

2. *Wood River Times* (Hailey) (weekly), April 19, 1882.

3. *Wood River Times*, September 9 and 26, 1882.

4. *Wood River Times*, September 11, 1882.

5. *Wood River Times*, October 7 and 26; November 1, 1882.

6. *Wood River Times* (weekly), November 22 and December 20, 1882.

7. *Wood River Times* (weekly), December 20, 1882.

8. J. Miller to editor (Ketchum, March 16, 1882), *Mining and Scientific Press*, XLIV (April 1 and May 27, 1882): 210, 330.

9. Isaac I. Lewis to Samuel T. Hauser (Ketchum, July 19 and October 30, 1882), Hauser Papers, Box 7, Montana Historical Society Archives, Helena; *Wood River Times*, June 15 and 22, 1882; *Mining and Scientific Press*, XLVII (August 4, 1883): 71.

10. *State Preservation Plan, Idaho*, (Boise, Idaho State Historical Society, 1974), I, p. 52.

11. *Engineering and Mining Journal* (New York), XXXIV (July 29, August 12 and 26, 1882): 61, 86, 112.

12. *Wood River Times*, January 22, March 13, and April 20, 1883.

13. *Mining and Scientific Press*, XXXIX (December 13, 1879): 370.

14. George A. McLeod *History of Alturas and Blaine Counties Idaho* (Hailey: *Hailey Times*, 1938), p. 21; "F" to editor (Bellevue, November 4, 1880), *Idaho Tri-Weekly Statesman*, November 9, 1880; *Mining and Scientific Press*, XLIII (August 6, 1881): 89.

15. *Mining and Scientific Press*, XLII (April 16, 1881): 248.

16. *Wood River Times*, June 24, 1882; Lalia Boone, *Idaho Place Names* (Moscow: University of Idaho Press, 1988), p. 168.

17. *Ketchum Keystone*, March 10, 1883; *Wood River Times*, March 10 and April 21, 1883.

18. *Wood River Times*, April 27, 1883.

19. *Wood River Times*, May 19, 1883; Robert G. Athearn, *Union Pacific Country* (Chicago, New York, and San Francisco: Rand McNally & Co., 1971), p. 316; Carrie Adell Strahorn, *Fifteen Thousand Miles by Stage* (New York and London: G. P. Putnam's Sons, 1911, reprint, Lincoln and London: University of Nebraska Press, 1988), p. 422; *Hailey Times*, June 18, 1931.

20. James L. Onderdonk, *Idaho: Facts and Statistics Concerning Its Mining, Farming, Stock-raising, Lumbering, and Other Resources and Industries, Together with Notes on the Climate, Scenery, Game, and Mineral Springs* (San Francisco: A. L. Bancroft & Co., 1885), p. 72.

21. *Mining and Scientific Press*, XLVII (August 4, 1883): 71; *State Preservation Plan, Idaho*, I, pp. 52–53.

22. *State Preservation Plan, Idaho*, I, p. 52.

23. James Court Blackwood to his brother (Bellevue, April 14, 1883), James Court Blackwood Letters, Montana Historical Society Archives, Helena; *Wood River Times*, May 21 and October 24, 1883.

24. *Wood River Times*, March 14, 1883; *Mining and Scientific Press*, XLVI (March 24, 1883): 205. The total adjusted value figure for 1883 as computed by the Director of the Mint and the Geological Survey was $1,447,237. Joseph B. Umpleby, et al., "Geography and Ore Deposits of the Wood River Region, Idaho" ("With a Description of the Minnie Moore and Near-by Mines," by D. F. Hewett), U.S. Geological Survey *Bulletin* NO. 814 (Washington: Government Printing Office, 1930), p. 82.

25. *Wood River Times*, March 14, 1883; *Mining and Scientific Press*, XLVIII (March 8, 1884): 180; XLIX (December 20, 1884): 386; LVIII (February 2, 1889): 80.

26. *Wood River Times*, August 1 and November 5, 1883; August 27, 1884; *Idaho Tri-Weekly Statesman*, June 28, 1883; *Engineering and Mining Journal*, XXXVI (July 7 and 21, November 7, 1883): 8, 39, 315; *Mining and Scientific Press*, XLVI (May 19, 1883): 341; XLVII (August 18, 1883): 101, 102. Base bullion is argentiferous lead, as distinguished from silver or gold bullion.

27. *Mining and Scientific Press*, XLVI (May 19, 1883): 341; XLVII (August 18, 1883): 101, 102; XLIX (December 20, 1884): 386; *Wood River Times*, August 1, 1883; Onderdonk, p. 71; Walter P. Jenny, "The Occurrence and Behavior of Tellurium in Gold Ores, More Particularly With Reference to the Potsdam Ores in the Black Hills, South Dakota," *Transactions of the American Institute of Mining Engineers*, XXVI (February, 1896, to October, 1896): 1105.

28. Walter Renton Ingalls, *Lead and Zinc in the United States* (New York: Hill Publishing Co., 1908), p. 163.

29. *Mining and Scientific Press*, XLIX (December 20, 1884): 286; LI (August 22, 1885): 137; Edward Norris Wentworth, *America's Sheep Trails* (Ames: Iowa State College Press, 1948), pp. 290–91.

30. Umpleby, et al., pp. 198–99; *Engineering and Mining Journal*, XXXVI (July 21, August 4 and 18, September 9, October 6, 1883): 39, 103, 155, 219; Onderdonk, p. 70; *Mining and Scientific Press*, XLIII (September 17, 1881): 189; LI (August 8, 15, 22 and 29, 1885): 105, 121, 137, 153.

31. *Engineering and Mining Journal,* XXXVI (August 25, September 22, November 17, 1883): 120, 187, 315; XXXVII (June 21, 1884): 469.

32. *Engineering and Mining Journal,* XXXVI (September 8 and 15, October 20, December 1, 1883): 155, 171, 251, 345.

33. *Engineering and Mining Journal,* XXXVI (November 3, 1883): 248.

34. *Ibid.,* (December 1, 1883): 345.

35. Lewis to Hauser (Ketchum, January 27, February 15 and 21, March 27, May 6 and 25, July 12 and 22, November 10 and 11, 1883), all in Hauser Papers, Box 8.

36. *Wood River Times,* July 2 and 13, August 3, 1883; McLeod, p. 163; *Engineering and Mining Journal,* XXXVI (September 1, 1883): 135.

37. Elkhorn Mine, Trial Balance, Dec. 4, 1884, and Lewis to Hauser (Ketchum, April 12, 1884), both in Hauser Papers, Box 10; Statement of Expenses & Proceeds of Elkhorn Mine From August 7, 1885 to December 22 1885, Hauser Papers, Box 11; Lewis to Hauser (Ketchum, July 22, November 10 and 11, 1883), all in Hauser Papers, Box 8; Lewis Statement of Dividends (Ketchum, Oct. 15, 1883); Lewis to Holter (Ketchum, February 18, 1888), both in Holter Family Papers, Box 115; Lewis, "Reminiscences," pp. 171, 177; *Engineering and Mining Journal,* XXXVII (March 29, 1884): 242; XLIV (July 2, 1887): 11; *Hauser, et al. v. Austin, et al.,* 2 *Idaho Reports* (March 3, 1886), pp. 204–15.

38. Lewis to Hauser (Ketchum, July 21 and August 4, 1883), Hauser Papers, Box 8.

39. *Wood River Times,* June 19, 1883; *Engineering and Mining Journal,* XXXVI (August 4, September 22 and 29, November 17, December 15, 1883): 71, 187, 203, 315, 373.

40. *Engineering and Mining Journal,* XXXVI (October 20 and November 10, 1883): 251, 300.

41. *Engineering and Mining Journal,* XXXVII (June 14, 1884): 448.

42. Lewis to Hauser (Ketchum, October 19 and December 28, 1881), Hauser Papers, Box 6; Lewis to Hauser (Ketchum, February 20, April 8 and 14, 1884); Lewis to Hauser, Holter & Hale (Ketchum, March 10 and April 10, 1884); J. P. Ostrom to Lewis (Ogden, April 19, 1884), copy, all in Hauser Papers, Box 10.

43. Wood River Times, March 6 and June 2, 1883.

44. The Bullion Mining Company, Ltd., *Memorandum and Articles of Incorporation* (February 28, 1884), pp. 1–3; *Memorandum of Agreement* (January 17, 1884) between James S. Leeds on behalf of Howard Oviatt and Buna Newton and John Walsh for the company, both in the Companies Registration Office of the Board of Trade, Bush House, London; Bullion Mining Company, Ltd., *Prospectus* (undated), Guildhall Library, London.

45. Wood River Times, March 21, 1884; *Truth*, (March 6, 1884): 347.

46. Wood River Times, April 24, 1884; Bullion Mining Company, Ltd., *Summary of Capital and Shares* (July 11, 1884); *Dissolution Notice* (June 22, 1894), both in Companies Registration Office.

47. *Financial & Mining News* (London), May 2, 1884; *Wood River Times*, October 4 and December 26, 1884.

48. Wood River Times, February 21, 1884.

49. *Ketchum Keystone*, February 27, 1884; *Wood River Times*, March 1 and April 9, 1884; *Financial & Mining News*, March 18, 1884; *Report of Director of the Mint upon the Production of Precious Metals in the United States During the Calendar Year, 1883*, p. 449.

50. Umpleby, et al., p. 220.

51. *Engineering and Mining Journal*, XXXVII (April 12 and May 10, 1884): 282, 356.

52. Wood River Times, December 12, 1884.

53. William M. Bunn, "Report of the Governor of Idaho, 1884," in *Report of the Secretary of the Interior, 1884*, p. 548.

54. *Engineering and Mining Journal*, XLI (January 30, 1886): 79; XLII (July 3, October 23, and November 20, 1886): 11, 299, 370; XLIII (January 15, 1887): 48; XLIV (July 2 and October 8, 1887): 2, 263.

55. *Engineering and Mining Journal*, XLI (January 16 and May 15, 1886): 43, 361.

56. *Engineering and Mining Journal*, XLIV (July 2 and December 31, 1887): 11, 491; Merle Wells, *Gold Camps & Silver Cities: Nineteenth Century Mining in Central and Southern Idaho*, 2d ed. (Moscow: Idaho Bureau of Mines & Geology *Bulletin* No. 22, 1983), p. 130.

57. *Engineering and Mining Journal*, XLII (December 11, 1886): 424; XLIII (January 1 and 15, 1887): 11, 48; XLIV (July 2, 1887): 2, 11; Lewis to Hauser, Holter & Hale (Ketchum, July 6; Hailey, July 31, 1885), both in Hauser Papers, Box 11; Lewis to Holter (Ketchum, February 18, 1888), Holter Family Papers, Box 115, Montana State Historical Society Archives.

58. *Engineering and Mining Journal*, XLI (June 26, 1886): 469; XLII (August 28 and October 23, 1886): 155, 299; Robert W. Sloan, *Utah Gazetteer and Directory of Logan, Ogden, Provo and Salt Lake Cities, for 1884* (Salt Lake City: printed for Sloan & Dunbar by Herald, 1884), pp. 318, 539.

59. *Engineering and Mining Journal*, XLI (January 16 and March 13, 1886): 43, 198.

60. *Engineering and Mining Journal*, XLII (October 9, 1886): 263; Wayne C. Sparling, *Southern Idaho Ghost Towns* (Caldwell: Caxton Printers, 1974), p. 79; *Mining and Scientific Press*, XLIX (September 27, 1884): 201.

61. Donald C. Miller, *Ghost Towns of Idaho* (Boulder: Pruett Publishing Co., 1976), p. 5; *Mining and Scientific Press*, XLVIII (April 19, 1884): 277; XLIX (September 6, 1884): 150; Wells, pp. 111–12.

62. *Mining and Scientific Press*, XLVI (February 17, 1883): 109; XLVIII (May 24, 1884): 353; Sparling, p. 80; McLeod, p. 43; *Wood River Times*, August 1, 1885; Pearl Eva Barber, *The Galloping Ghosts of Galena* (Boise: Capital Lithograph & Printing Co., 1962), pp. 21–22.

63. *Mining and Scientific Press*, XLVIII (June 7, 1884): 385; LI (August 1, 15, and 22, 1885): 89, 121, 137; LIII (November 13, 1886): 317; LVI (February 4, 1888): 75.

64. Sparling, p. 78; Vardis Fisher, comp., *The Idaho Encyclopedia* (Caldwell: Caxton Printers, 1938), p. 102.

65. Elmer B. Fitch, "Muldoon District," in Umpleby, *Geology and Ore Deposits*, p. 106; *Ketchum Keystone*, January 26, 1882; *Mining and Scientific Press*, XLVII (December 15, 1883): 381; *Engineering and Mining Journal*, XXXVI (August 4, 1883): 71; Wells, pp. 129–30.

66. Fitch, p. 106; *Mining and Scientific Press*, XLVIII (April 12, 1884): 261; *Engineering and Mining Journal*, XXXVI (June 21, 1884): 469; Wells, p. 131.

67. Wells, p. 131; Fitch, p. 106.

68. Leonard J. Arrington, *History of Idaho* (Moscow and Boise: University of Idaho Press and Idaho State Historical Society, 1994), I, pp. 352–60; Ingalls, *Lead and Zinc in the United States,* pp. 17–18.

CHAPTER FOUR

"STRANGERS OF ALL NATIONALITIES AND CONDITIONS OF LIFE"

WOOD RIVER ATTRACTED men and women from all over, but adjacent areas contributed the largest numbers. Many of the first arrivals were from Atlanta, Rocky Bar, or Boise City (or as some called it, "Bossy Sitty"). "This is a town, you bet!" one exuberant early resident wrote of Hailey. "Almost everyone I meet seems to be from Boise City or vicinity." A traveler heading to New Mexico from Idaho in 1882 found the road from Mountain Home "lined with men on their way to the Wood River mines," most of them drawn from the capital. According to Carrie Strahorn, "Hailey was made up largely of people from Boise," and many of the first promising finds were made by Boiseans. Others like David Falk, W. H. Nye, and Judge A. P. Turner sought to capitalize on mine and smelter development. Portly Stamps Anderson, a Yale graduate with a Southern accent, had been an early leader of the bar in Boise, then probate judge in Rocky Bar before joining the Wood River migration. Still others provided even more important business: in Ketchum, "James

Judge, of Boise county fame, is chief among the saloon boys and doing well."[1]

Idaho's neighbors were also important. When Isaac Lewis came down from Butte in the spring of 1880, he passed or was passed by a number of Montanans headed for the mines, and Montana's capital supported his and other mining activities. But Utah seems to have had a greater impact. The early newspapers clearly document Wood River ties with both Boise and Utah. The Boise Bakery and Confectionery had a branch in Hailey, as did banker T. R. Jones of Salt Lake City, the Gem Saloon and M. J. O'Neill & Co., dealer in "Wines, Liquors and Cigars"—the latter two both of Ogden.[2]

Almost from the beginning, former Utahans—both Mormons and gentiles—were much in evidence on the river. At least a dozen charter members of the prestigious Alta Club of Salt Lake City had interests in the new Idaho diggings. The Mayflower Mine was originally owned by brothers from Ogden, and the Saturn was owned by capitalists from Bingham. One of the most successful owners and promoters, Enos Wall, brought with him in 1880 a number of miners from Silver Reef who had just lost a wage battle.[3] By 1883 the virulent "Wood River fever" had spread to most Utah mining camps, and perhaps the *Salt Lake Tribune* may be forgiven for speaking of "our neighbor to the north— Utah's great suburb."[4] As John Moore, co-owner of the Minnie Moore, reported when he returned to his Salt Lake City home in the summer of 1880, Wood River miners had treated him and other Utahans well. "They give a grand reception to all the Saints who visit them," he noted, adding: "What the boys want above all things else, however, is wives."[5]

During the following year, David Eccles, a staunch Mormon entrepreneur who would eventually become Utah's first multi-millionaire, joined a Swiss immigrant, A. D. Quantrell, to set up a portable sawmill in Gray's Gulch west of Hailey. When timber there was depleted, the two moved the mill to Elk Creek, three miles east of Bullion, then expanded their operation to provide lumber for the construction of the Wood River branch of the Oregon Short Line. After three years and a profit of $50,000, Eccles dissolved his operation and moved on to even greater successes with the Oregon Lumber Company and later the far-flung Amalgamated Sugar Company.[6]

As early as 1882, there was a good deal of opposition to the "Saints" on Wood River. Editor Picotte of the *Times* thought it "would not be surprising if, at the coming election, a square Mormon and anti-Mormon issue should prevail over all others." Indeed, anti-Mormonism would be much in evidence in subsequent local political campaigns.[7]

Much of this anti-Mormon sentiment was based on opposition to the practice of plural marriage and on the belief that the Latter-day Saints repudiated the mining industry, although the Church not so much opposed mining as relegated it to a lower priority than a diversified economic and social development of Zion.[8] Many opponents of the Mormons and of polygamy had migrated from Salt Lake City and from the Utah mines to the earlier Idaho diggings at Atlanta, Rocky Bar, Salmon, Yankee Fork, and other camps. With the new silver strikes, they followed the stampede to Wood River, which became one of the strongholds of the bitter anti-Mormon movement that wracked Idaho in the 1880s. The coming of the railroad to southern Idaho brought in thousands of gentiles to offset Mormon dominance and intensified the struggle over plural marriage, especially since some of the new Wood Riverites had already been vigorously involved in the movement elsewhere.

Enos Wall had been a prominent anti-Mormon radical in Utah, and would play an active role in the Idaho legislature and in lobbying in Washington for a test oath to exclude Mormons from voting. George A. Black, who had once served as Secretary of Utah Territory, also moved to Wood River, where he was an active part of the conspiracy to curb the Latter-day Saints. After he was removed from the Idaho governorship in 1883, John B. Neil was one of the movers and shakers of anti-Mormonism at the territorial level. After his ousting from the executive post, he acquired Wood River mining interests and continued his political agitation.[9] Such leaders kept the anti-Mormon cauldron bubbling through much of Wood River's boom, along with the anti-Chinese agitation that was part of the era.

There were a few Oregonians present and many "yon siders"—Californians and old Comstockers like "Billy" Anderson, whose passion for mining excitements had taken him to Placerville, Washoe, White Pine, Eureka, Yankee Fork and Wood River before he died in poverty in 1883. J. B. Foster, Bellevue correspondent for the *Statesman,* marveled in 1880 at the old forty-niner with canvas patches on his knees and elbows, surrounded by admiring listeners in a tent saloon, where he expressed vulgar contempt for all tenderfeet (i.e., those who came to the Coast after 1855) and described how his partner, "six toed Pete, and himself made and lost fortunes in California."[10] Charles Gill, a long-time butcher in the Nevada silver camps, opened a shop in Bellevue in 1881 and was pleased to meet "many a Eureka man." Mrs. J. M. Graham, at Wood River to open a boardinghouse the same year, noted that "a large number of Tuscarorans" were on their way or about to leave from northern Nevada. In 1884, the Association of Pioneers of the Pacific Coast, limited to those with at least twenty years' residence on the western slope, could boast 411 members in Hailey, although some saw a number of misfits in the ranks.[11]

The first waves of the rush were distinctly masculine, with an occasional woman in evidence, like Mrs. Loving, Mrs. Graham, Commodore Perry Croy's wife, or Mrs. Griffin, who ran a roadhouse on the stage route to Utah.[12] The usual prostitutes quietly found their way to the district also, but as the towns settled down, women became more conspicuous. As the *Times* editor wrote of Hailey in April, 1882, "Wagons, loaded to the guards with men, women, children, chairs, and cooking utensils, are rolling through the streets of the chief city of the great lead-silver mining country." Soon he could call attention to a more unusual resident—Mrs. C. A. Mahar, a "lady prospector and miner," who had located a number of claims on Deer Creek and was supervising their development.[13]

Overall, they were a mixed lot. Illiterates and college graduates rubbed elbows, Yale men swung their picks alongside those from Harvard, and former Confederates and members of the Grand Army of the Republic toiled together. Mining "experts" were a dime a dozen, and some were pretty precious, according to editor Picotte:

Bellevue was the possessor of a "real, live, genuine, Colorado mining sharp" to-day, and it was dressed up in a light corduroy suit, straw hat, expert boots, a galena look out of his eyes, with a high-assay cut to his hair. The wind blew it over the mountain, and we haven't seen it since.[14]

In addition, according to Picotte, a newcomer examined one of the hotel registers, and "innocently asked the way to the barracks, and explained that he really thought the troops were here, as he saw the names of so many army officers in the list. All of our principal citizens are generals, colonels, majors or captains—with once in a while a professor or two."[15]

The editor did not exaggerate when he commented in 1884 that the town was "full of strangers of all nationalities and conditions of life." "Hailey is becoming cosmopolitan as well as metropolitan."[16] The town sported a French lady barber in 1883. There were enough Irish on hand to make St. Patrick's Day a big affair; indeed, one writer estimates that half the miners at Wood River in the 1880s were Sons of the Old Sod. Newspaper references to "Dutchmen" (Germans) and their wives were common. In 1890, Hubert Howe Bancroft noted that fifty homesteads were taken up in 1881 by an agent of a German colonist from Oregon, who intended to "make a garden of the cultivable parts of Alturas county, a scheme which probably fell through."[17]

Other groups, too, were noted, like the dozen Scandinavians—"tenderfeet, with blankets and packs"—who passed through on a spring morning in 1883, heading for the camps above Hailey.[18] While there were never enough Jews in Wood River to organize a formal congregation, S. J. Friedman led the small group in Hailey in observance of the Sabbath and of the Holy Days, advertising that his dry goods store would be closed for Yom Kippur, the Jewish Day of Atonement, in September.[19]

Since much of the boom came after the census count of 1880, there is no accurate analysis of the population mix. The official figures for Alturas County for 1890, after the numbers had leveled somewhat, showed that roughly one of every four residents had been born outside the United States. More than one-third of these had been born in the British Isles, fully 20 percent were Canadian by origin, nearly 16 percent Chinese, Germans represented 14 percent and Scandinavians about 9 percent of the total.[20]

Wood Riverites were about as tolerant of the foreign-born and held about the same attitudes toward minority races as did other westerners of the late nineteenth century. The few African Americans present were accepted to a point, but in their place, and local newspapers—especially the *Ketchum Keystone*—were often bluntly racist in their remarks about them. One African American, Lew Walker, described by the *Wood River Times* in 1882 as a "colored barber-sport," seems to have been something of an entrepreneur and the owner of a desirable lot for which he was offered $1,200. According to Carrie Strahorn, Walker and whiskey made a dangerous combination. One time, when he was liquored up, Lew and his cohorts attempted to take illegal possession of property in downtown Hailey, only to be thwarted by Robert Strahorn and a few friends, then more firmly by local law officers. Perhaps Carrie embroidered the situation a little because two years later, Walker was still in business and had announced new public bathing facilities in the rear of his barber shop at only fifty cents a bath. Apparently, one black barber on the river was enough. When Tom Brown sought work in this profession in 1882, he found there was no place for him, so he went to work clearing land and building fences for local ranchers.[21]

Another African American, known only as Ike, spent the winter of 1883–84 on Wood River, but was killed in a brawl in Le Grande, Oregon, the following summer.[22] It was hardly necessary to go as far as Oregon for a shooting scrape, however. Only a month later, right there in Hailey, in another "pistol pop," as editor Picotte called such affairs, "a dusky dude known as 'Gus,'" the lover of Ada Radcliffe, "one of the colored women of the town," put a bullet into another Hailey black woman, an episode which involved black pimps and prostitutes in their own bailiwick.[23]

There were never many African Americans in the Wood River communities. The U.S. Census of 1890 counted only thirteen "Persons of African descent" in all of Alturas County.[24] Usually, they were not as newsworthy as Gus and Ike. The personal maid of Homer Pound's New York bride, who had been with the family "since the Flood," came to Hailey in 1884, at a time when the town was reputed to have had but "one Nubian citizen." She remained only a few months before returning East.[25] In the spring of 1886, a few months after the Nevada Hotel had hired three black cooks from Portland, the *Times* editor noted that eighteen "colored people" then lived in Hailey and more were coming. "No better people can settle in an active camp than the men of this race," he commented. "Those who know them, know this."[26] The same newspaper at the end of 1894 announced the arrival of a black woman—"a typical Southern 'mammy'" to keep house for Mrs. George V. Bryan.[27]

Unfortunately, the Chinese were another matter. The

California gold rush and the building of the transcontinental railroad line had attracted large numbers of Chinese to the American West. When restrictions were placed on their immigration in 1882, there were about a hundred thousand Chinese men and five thousand Chinese women in the West, three-quarters of them in California. With the extension of the mineral frontier inland and into the Rockies, growing pockets of Chinese appeared in the mining communities of all the new states and territories, ranging from Oregon and Washington to Arizona, Nevada, Montana, and Idaho.

Everywhere their clannishness and different ways set them apart from white society, which despised their "filthy habits" (usually meaning the use of opium and their competition on the labor market) and frequently proceeded to hem them in with special taxes and limitations. The 1880s were years of vicious reaction and sometimes actual violence directed against the detested Chinese in many parts of the West. A small-scale riot in Denver in 1880 left the Chinese quarter gutted. Five years later, a Rock Springs, Wyoming mob killed twenty-eight Chinese coal miners and ran several hundred more out of town. In the same year there were anti-Chinese outbreaks in Tacoma, followed by others even more savage in Seattle. The Wood River Chinese would feel the same lash of white racial prejudice, but without the actual bloodshed.

How many Chinese there were at any given time is difficult to calculate. The census takers in 1880 recorded 128 in all of Alturas County. In December 1882, when the Chinese Masonic Order met in Hailey to consider building a hall, the lodge had seventy-five members. An estimate a few years later set the town's peak population of Chinese at 150.[28]

As was the case elsewhere, members of the Wood River Chinese community found limited economic opportunity. In this predominantly masculine society, the few women present were likely to be prostitutes. In many of the gold camps of the West, the Chinese men engaged in placer mining, but silver, with it's underground veins and complex ores held little attraction for them. Instead, they gravitated to other occupations, which by dint of industry and competition they made profitable, but not prestigious.

Some operated stores where their compatriots might buy such traditional delicacies as mushrooms, bamboo shoots, dry bean curd, and dry duck. Amidst the smell of herbs and smoked fish, these businesses were social centers where patrons sipped tea and caught up on the latest gossip. Other Chinese entrepreneurs, especially in Hailey, ran local restaurants or gambling houses, where a man might relax over a game of fan tan or pai kow, or even a pipe of opium. A few of the Chinese made a living cutting firewood and distributing it to householders in the Wood River towns. A number were remarkably productive gardeners with large rented plots on the west edge of Hailey, close to Broadford, and on the Brown brothers' ranch, south of Bellevue.[29] Despite short growing seasons, with effective manure and irrigation techniques they could wrest four or five crops a summer from a small plot. Chinese cabbage was one of their important harvests, but they peddled fresh vegetables of all kinds on the streets and from door to door each morning. The demand for their garden produce was indicated in 1882 when two Boise Chinese were killed and robbed of four horses, a wagon, and $1,000 while returning from a successful peddling excursion to Wood River. Many worked as cooks, especially for hotels, restaurants, affluent families, and company boardinghouses. One Chinese servant hired by Homer Pound was regarded as "a model of virtue"—until he used the hearth-brush instead of a crumb-brush to clean the crumbs from the table during an important dinner.[30]

But the favorite occupation of Wood River Chinese was laundry, a business that required little start-up capital. A wash house was often a mere shack on the creek or river bed, and it could be established for as little as six or seven dollars for a stove, tubs, kettles, benches, and flat irons. Chinese laundrymen washed for bachelor residents and did linens for hotels and restaurants and provided tough competition, especially for struggling widows who needed the business.

Apparently there was little harassment in the early years, except for an occasional raid on an opium den. Sheriff Furey of Alturas County and his deputy cooperated with Constable Frank Oliver one September night in 1883 and stormed the dens in Hailey's Chinatown, busting eight Chinese and one white, and capturing two hundred and fifty to three hundred and fifty dollars worth of drugs and drug paraphernalia. At Bellevue in April 1885, eleven Chinese culprits were hauled in "for hitting the opium pipe a lick." Three were let off and the others were fined $100 and jailed.[31]

Early in 1884, a new Bellevue ordinance prohibited Chinese laundrymen from being on Main Street. In response, the Chinese went on strike, leaving the town momentarily "an unwashed community" with a shortage of "boiled shirts." A few months later, forty or fifty anti-Chinese stalwarts met at Easley's saloon in Ketchum to denounce the Chinese and pass resolutions against them.[32]

All the while, pressure against the Chinese was growing throughout the West, the Wood River communities included. Near the end of 1885 the *Times* reported that "the cute ones" were slyly buying up stocks of shirts and collars from Chinese laundrymen, "who are expecting—and not without some reason—to be 'bounced.'"[33] As agitation was stepped up in California, more of the victims migrated inland. Early in 1886, a year of anti-Chinese violence in various western locales, Wood Riverites met more often to plan how to rid themselves of these undesirables. A committee in Hailey issued a preliminary statement in mid-January, employing familiar West Coast rhetoric: "The Chinese Must Go!" The committee claimed that their habits were loathsome, their diseases deadly, they undercut white workers on the labor market and they exported many American dollars to China. Wood Riverites were urged to refuse to patronize or to employ them and to publicize this position.[34]

Thus began the organization of the Anti-Chinese League, with editor Picotte as Secretary and General George Roberts, a hero of Gettysburg and the first attorney general of Nebraska, the featured speaker. The League's avowed goal was the removal of the Chinese by nonviolent means, principally their replacement by white workers. A boycott went into effect. One of Robert Strahorn's buildings on Croy Street in Hailey was rented for a family boardinghouse. "No Chinese need apply," said Picotte, "as the help will all be good-looking American girls freshly imported from the East."[35]

Chinese laundry trade reportedly began to fall off. League spokesmen were confident that as the boycott spread, the Chinese would have no alternative but to leave. On February 1, the Hailey Anti-Chinese Committee served formal notice of their boycott and gave the Chinese until May 1 to wind up their business and leave.[36] In response, Hop Chung and Sam Wing of Hailey, Quong Lee of Ketchum and Ye Lee of Bellevue took a month's advertisement in the *Times* to say that the Chinese did not intend to depart. Their countrymen in the three towns had met and resolved to stay and to appeal to the United States government for protection. They insisted that they were law-abiding, paid taxes, and would lose at least $35,000 in property were they to withdraw, to which their adversaries pointed out that their total taxes paid in the past year amounted to only $108.50.[37] There is some irony in editor Picotte's flexible position: He ardently supported the boycott, but he had no qualms about taking Chinese dollars to run their advertisement.

Harassment of the Chinese continued. In Boise, an Idaho Territorial Anti-Chinese Congress with representatives from nearly every mining community (except Coeur d'Alene, which boasted it had no Chinese) met to pass resolutions to protect the fruits of white labor by boycotting Chinese competition. Wood River opium dens were again raided, but the lone smoker had to be released when it was discovered that no law prohibited smoking opium in one's own home.[38] By early February 1886, when it was estimated that 100 of the 150 Chinese were still in Hailey, the campaign against them was in full swing. Residents were urged not to hire Chinese for such traditional jobs as woodcutting or housecleaning, nor to patronize Chinese laundries or truck gardeners. Town businesses were urged to emulate the Nevada Hotel and replace their Chinese cooks with others. White laundries and especially steam laundries were encouraged. If not enough facilities were available, dirty clothes could be sent to Salt Lake City or even Chicago for washing. With a firm, tough-minded boycott, the Chinese could be ousted in a month.[39]

Outside labor was encouraged. Some urged bringing in Mormon girls from Utah as servants. "They are strong, hard-working, and can doubtless be had for $3 or $5 per week." Of course, all were not desirable employees, "but the worthless ones can be discharged as soon as other help can be secured."[40] Others believed that importing Swedish or Bohemian girls would undercut the Chinese sufficiently to prompt them to leave. Dr. J. M. Rice, promoter of Idaho colonization schemes, promised to do something along this line. Rice was confident that he could bring young Scandinavians to work as servants for eight to twelve dollars a month. "These are a hardy class of girls—good cooks, good housekeepers, moral, and reliable in every respect," he insisted. The idea was widely applauded—although not by local Wood River belles. The good doctor spread the word that he would make arrangements for the girls for a fee of five dollars and fare from Omaha (twenty-five dollars), and interest heightened. When crowds flocked to the Hailey depot, accompanied by a band, to greet Rice and "his colony of girls," gaiety turned to dismay. "The 'colony of girls' consisted of one dried up old maid, which the 'doctor' brought along as a sample!"[41]

Ketchum also formed an Anti-Chinese League, and by resolutions signed by 150 persons, vowed not to patronize the detested
Chinese and requested that they "wind up their business and
prepare to remove from amongst us." Letters to the editor railed
against "the Chinese leper," this "menace to our civilization,"
and urged all nonviolent means to rid the community of the
menace.[42] When territorial governor Edward A. Stevenson issued
a proclamation against any unlawful expulsion of the Chinese,
editor Picotte wrote it off as "bombastic furioso" emanating from
"a small-bore demagogue."[43] At the same time, Stevenson, a veteran Democrat politician, advocated total Chinese exclusion
from Idaho and had officially whitewashed the hanging by vigilantes of five Chinese near Pierce City in 1885.[44]

Picotte's *Times* eventually came out on the other side of the
issue. Early in June 1886 it called the "boycott of Mongolians"
"unlawful, unmanly, un-American" and doomed to fail, just as it
had failed in Butte and elsewhere. The newspaper "is and always
has been anti-Chinese," wrote the editor, "but it will not uphold
a conspiracy to injure any man's business."[45]

The campaign peaked in 1886; it had considerable impact,
although numerous Chinese remained. In June, they operated
only three laundries in Hailey, each with one man, whereas two
months earlier at least ten had been in business, "employing
about 60 heathens." For the three remaining, times were dull—
business "belly bad"—but at least some were hanging on at the
end of the year, when Gus Meyers and his partner, Miss Brown,
"a colored lady who has worked for years in some of the leading
laundries of the East," opened the Denver Steam Laundry in the
old May and Kreig store on upper Main Street. Now, crowed the
Times, "if the people of Hailey wish to, they can soon get rid of
the Chinese, as the Denver Laundry can do the laundering for
10,000 people."[46]

But the Chinese persisted. Instead of leaving, some of them
hired a lawyer to advise them of their rights and remained for

years or as long as their businesses warranted it. It was rumored in mid-1888 that the movement against them, which had been dormant for almost two years, was about to be revived, but it never materialized; however, the traditional Chinese New Years were tame indeed by contrast with earlier years when many whites turned out to witness the festivities. At Ketchum in 1891, because there were so few Chinese, there was no celebration apart from a dinner and a few firecrackers. Enough Chinese remained in 1892 to cause a commotion when Hailey boys threw stones at their wash houses, precipitating a gunshot in response. Isaac Lewis still collected $3.50 a month in rental for his half interest in a Ketchum "Wash House (China)," but no substantial Chinese community existed any longer. The census of 1890 showed ninety-five Chinese living within the bounds of the now shrunken Alturas County.[47]

The anti-Chinese discrimination of the 1880s was not a pretty chapter in Wood River history, but it reflected a malaise that afflicted much of the West, especially the mineral West. Fortunately, apart from the blowing up of a Hailey laundry in 1886, with no personal injury, white bigotry did not erupt into violence against the much maligned "Mongolians," as was the case in Denver, Rock Springs, Tacoma, and other areas. In many ways, Wood River's anti-Chinese thrust was remarkably similar to that in Tombstone, Arizona, not only in its timing, but also in its threat of economic boycott and, in the end, its overall lack of success.[48]

CHAPTER FOUR NOTES

1. James Hart to Judge Kelly (Hailey, May 30, 1881), *Idaho Tri-Weekly Statesman* (Boise), June 4, 1881 and June 28, 1883; *Wood River Times* (Hailey), June 12, 1882; Carrie Adell Strahorn, *Fifteen Thousand*

Miles by Stage (New York and London: G. P. Putnam's Sons, 1911, reprint, Lincoln and London: University of Nebraska Press, 1988), p. 460; *Mining and Scientific Press* (San Francisco), XLIV (May 13, 1882): 313; Thomas B. Donaldson, *Idaho of Yesterday* (Caldwell: Caxton Printers, 1941), pp. 135–36.

2. Isaac I. Lewis, "Reminiscences," (Ketchum, March 28, 1892), typescript, pp. 71–73, American Heritage Center, University of Wyoming; *Wood River Times*, May 20, 1882; Robert W. Sloan, *Utah Gazetteer and Directory of Logan, Ogden, Provo and Salt Lake Cities, for 1884*, (Salt Lake City: printed for Sloan and Dunbar by Herald, 1884), pp. 317, 320.

3. The *Salt Lake Daily Tribune*, July 13, 1880; O. N. Malmquist, *The Alta Club 1883–1974* (Salt Lake City: The Alta Club, 1974), pp. 129, 130, 131, 133, 134, 135, 136; G. W. Barrett, "Colonel E. A. Wall: Mines, Miners, and Mormons," *Idaho Yesterdays*, XIV (Summer, 1970): 6.

4. *Wood River Times*, April 19, 1883; Salt Lake Tribune, quoted in *Wood River Times*, January 3, 1893.

5. *Salt Lake Daily Tribune*, August 14, 1880.

6. Leonard J. Arrington, *David Eccles: Pioneer Western Industrialist* (Logan: Utah State University, 1975), pp. 60–61.

7. *Wood River Times* (weekly), March 6, 1882; *Wood River Times*, November 1, 1884.

8. Leonard J. Arrington, *Great Basin Kingdom: An Economic History of the Latter-day Saints 1830–1900* (Lincoln: University of Nebraska Press, Bison edition, 1970), pp. 241–44.

9. Ronald H. Limbaugh, *Rocky Mountain Carpetbaggers: Idaho's Territorial Governors 1863–1890* (Moscow: University of Idaho Press, 1982), pp. 144–45, 147, 152–53, 155, 163; Merle W. Wells, *Anti-Mormonism in Idaho, 1872–92* (Provo: Brigham Young University Press, 1978), pp. 21–22, 38, 42, 45, 46; Barrett, "Col. E. A. Wall," pp. 9–11.

10. *Wood River Times* (weekly), June 22, 1881 and April 14, 1885; *Wood River Times*, July 7, 1883; "F" to editor (Bellevue, May 15, 1880), *Idaho Tri-Weekly Statesman*, May 27, 1880.

11. *Wood River Times*, June 5 and August 3, 1882; June 4, 1884.

12. Mary Brown McGonigal, *Spring of Gladness: Reminiscences of Pioneer Life in the Wood River Valley* (Sun Valley: High Country Lithography, 1976), p. 52.

13. *Wood River Times* (weekly), April 26, 1882; *Wood River Times,* August 17, 1882.

14. *Wood River Times* (weekly), July 19, 1882.

15. *Wood River Times,* September 15, 1882.

16. *Wood River Times,* May 13, 1884.

17. "The Works of Hubert Howe Bancroft," XXXI (*History of Washington, Idaho, and Montana*) (San Francisco: The History Company, 1890), p. 548.

18. Leonard J. Arrington, *History of Idaho,* (Moscow: University of Idaho Press, 1994), II, p. 265; *Wood River Times,* March 10 and 17, 1883; *Wood River Times* (weekly), March 24, 1883. Bancroft notes that many of the early newcomers were Norwegians, who had no fear of winter weather. See "The Works of Hubert Howe Bancroft," XXXI, p. 548.

19. *Wood River Times,* September 9, 1882; Juanita Brooks, *History of the Jews in Utah and Idaho* (Salt Lake City: Western Epics, 1973), p. 127.

20. *Report of the Population of the United States at the Eleventh Census: 1890* (Washington: Government Printing Office, 1895), Pt. I, p. 618.

21. *Wood River Times,* June 22, 1882; C. Strahorn, pp. 426–28, 430; Marilyn Watkinson, *Emmanuel Church, Hailey: The Early Years 1881–1901* (Twin Falls: Professional Print & Copy, 1991), p. 64; McGonigal, p. 74.

22. *Wood River Times,* September 4, 1884.

23. *Wood River Times,* October 25, 1885.

24. *Compendium of the Eleventh Census: 1890* (Washington: U. S. Printing Office, 1892), p. 481.

25. *Wood River Times,* December 6 and 10, 1884; Ezra Pound, *Indiscretions, or, Une Revue de Deux Mondes,* (Paris: Three Mountains Press, 1923), pp. 39, 40; Waller B. Wigginton, "The Pounds at Hailey," *Rendezvous,* IV (Spring, 1969): 37, 45.

26. *Wood River Times,* February 17 and April 2, 1886.

27. *Wood River Times*, December 21, 1894.

28. *Compendium of the Eleventh Census: 1890*, p. 517; *Wood River Times*, December 8 and 11, 1882; February 13, 1886. An excellent over-all statement of the Chinese in Idaho mining communities is Betty Derig, "Chinese in the Diggings," *Idaho Yesterdays*, XVI (Fall, 1972): 2–23.

29. McGonigal, pp. 140, 172.

30. *Idaho Tri-Weekly Statesman*, August 24, 1882; Pound, p. 51.

31. George A. McLeod, *History of Alturas and Blaine Counties Idaho*, (Hailey: *Hailey Times*, 1938), p. 86; *Wood River Times*, April 4, 1885. For a general treatment of the Chinese and the Idaho legal system, see John Wunder, "The Courts and the Chinese in Frontier Idaho," *Idaho Yesterdays*, XXV (Spring, 1981): 23–32.

32. *Wood River Times*, February 12, 1884; *Ketchum Keystone* (weekly), April 5, 1884.

33. *Wood River Times*, November 16, 1885.

34. *Wood River Times*, January 11 and 13, 1886.

35. *Wood River Times*, January 18, 19, and 26, 1886.

36. *Wood River Times*, January 28 and February 1, 1886.

37. *Wood River Times*, February 6, 8, and 9, 1886; *Ketchum Keystone* (daily), February 13, 1886.

38. *Wood River Times*, February 13, 1886. For the Territorial Convention in Boise, see Derig, p. 16.

39. *Wood River Times*, February 8 and 13, 1886.

40. *Wood River Times*, February 8, 1886.

41. *Ketchum Keystone* (daily), February 20 and April 24, 1886; *Wood River Times*, February 16, March 2, and April 24, 1886.

42. *Ketchum Keystone* (daily), February 20 and 27; March 6, 1886.

43. *Wood River Times*, April 29 and 30, 1886.

44. See Kenneth Owens, "Pierce City Incident, 1885–1886," *Idaho Yesterdays*, III (Fall, 1959): 8–13.

45. *Wood River Times*, June 2, 1886.

46. *Wood River Times,* June 7 and December 18, 1886.

47. McLeod, p. 88; *Ketchum Keystone,* July 7, 1888 and February 7, 1891; *Wood River Times,* July 2, 1892; Lewis, "Reminiscences," p. 200; *Compendium of the Eleventh Census: 1890,* p. 517.

48. *Idaho Tri-Weekly Statesman,* May 8, 1886; Eric L. Clements, "Bust and Bust in the Mining West," *Journal of the West,* XXXV (October, 1996): 45–46.

CHAPTER FIVE

"CITIES ARE SPRINGING UP LIKE 'JONAH'S GOURD'"

T HE GENERIC TERM "Wood River" generally referred to a handful of core towns—including Bellevue, Broadford, Hailey, Bullion City, and Ketchum—all within a distance of fifteen or twenty miles of one another. Small satellite settlements around them rose and fell. Muldoon, Sawtooth, Vienna, Galena, Carrietown, and Doniphan all had their day. More obscure camps mushroomed and sometimes as quickly disappeared: Gilman, west of Hailey on Croy Creek near the mouth of Bullion Gulch; Boulder Basin, isolated far to the north between Ketchum and Galena; North Star and East Fork City, up the East fork of the Wood River; the Mascot diggings farther yet up the East Fork; Gimlet, the ore-loading station at Greenhorn Gulch halfway between Ketchum and Hailey; and Stanton, thirteen miles south of Bellevue.[1] Taken as a whole, Wood River lacked the colorful, graphic placenames of the earlier western rushes. Even the most striking, like Ketchum or Muldoon, paled alongside western maps of a previous generation, speckled with names like Bed Bug, Red Dog, Tin Cup, Pinchem-Tight, You Bet, Gouge Eye, Git-up-Git, or Hell-Out-for-Noon City.

Physically and in spirit, though, Wood River towns were like other mining centers. In these "instant cities," a jumble of tents and log or slab shanties, miners, and those who came to exploit them or to provide legitimate services lived crudely until economic and self-improvement brought greater stability and permanency.[2] Their inhabitants portrayed both the general region and the towns themselves as making up an opulent Garden of Eden. "This whole mountain range, 75 miles from north to south, and at least 50 from east to west, is God's treasure-house," wrote a Michigan man who had visited the new diggings.[3] It was a lush habitat for deer, elk, antelope, bear, and many wildfowl. Streams "are filled with mountain trout," he wrote. There were warm springs every few miles and the valleys provided "the finest grazing country in the world," with "bunch grass thick as it can grow."[4] "A Stockman's Paradise—Room for 10,000 Prospectors" promised the first issue of the *Wood River Times*.[5] In a region in which the air was so light it "took two men to tell the truth," nature had worked wonders: "to draw men here to behold the beauties of her work, she has, like an expert angler, baited her hook with that for which the appetite of man will lead him through all dangers and cause him to endure all fatigues."[6]

But most mining camps, even in scenic settings, were not necessarily attractive places to live, homespun poets to the contrary notwithstanding:

> *Bullion is a beautiful place*
> *As pretty as can be.*
> *'Tis situated six miles up*
> *From the town of Hay-lee.*[7]

But Bullion, the bard forgot, was hemmed in. Situated in a narrow gulch, Bullion resembled the proverbial mining town of fiction—"2 miles long and 18 inches wide,"[8] except that it was more a Y than a straight line. Just as at Bellevue, Ketchum, or elsewhere, visitors might detect the presence of the town before it ever came in sight. Concentrating mills and smelters directly assaulted the senses of hearing and smell, and underground blasts, the pulse beats of mining, rumbled the earth. Soon rusting machinery and piles of tailings gave visual testimony to the unpleasant side of the industry.

Nineteenth-century boomtowns, in Idaho or anywhere else, had problems with sanitary disposal. Housewives threw their garbage into the back yard to rot. Butchers dumped offal into the nearest stream. Ketchum sawmills did likewise with their sawdust, killing fish in the process.[9] Outhouses and livery stables were an affront to the olfactory sense, as well as contributors to polluted water. In narrow streets, spring thaws revealed accumulated layers of manure (five tons per horse per year) and clouds of bluebottle flies. At the capital in Boise City, legislators still discussed what to do about "Hogs Found Trespassing" freely in the towns around the territory.[10]

One animal, however, owned the Wood River towns: dogs. In 1882 Ketchum had an estimated "one dog and a half to every inhabitant and two dog fights to every square rod, and the ugliest, dirtiest lot of canines on the Pacific coast." Any buggy, team, or saddle horse driven at a trot down Main Street in Hailey was subject to attack by "a score of mangy curs," a situation that invited a runaway and accident, and left non-pet lovers facetiously advocating "a tax of about $1,000 on each dog, payable immediately," to "stop the rapid increase of vagrant canines." Editor T. E. Picotte counted fifty-one dogs one day "enjoying a grand picnic" on that street. And "one of them," he said, "evidently was not happy, last night, as he howled until day light, and a score of good people lay awake out of pure sympathy." "Dog fight—this afternoon—Main Street—big crowd of men looked on," he reported a few months later.[11]

Not much is specifically written about health in the Wood River towns, but residents' experiences were no doubt similar to those elsewhere in mining regions. Pollution and lack of sanitation led to high rates of premature death, both for adults and children since disease, especially cholera, dysentery, and intestinal disorders, was common. Youngsters were especially hard hit by pneumonia; such maladies as measles, scarlet fever, and whooping cough ended the lives of many. No doubt laryngeal diphtheria was the greatest child killer. It accounted for roughly a quarter of deaths throughout the Rocky Mountain area.[12]

Physical facilities of the towns gradually improved. In 1880, Robert Strahorn had to consult a local "tonsorial artist" in an unroofed log enclosure and was covered with sleet and snow before he was through with his shave. Two years later, he could have had the services of a lady barber, a Frenchwoman at that, in a cozy shop across from the Grand Central Hotel, although he might have had to pay four bits instead of two.[13]

During the boom days, there was never adequate housing in the Wood River towns. The well-organized miners carried tents and bedrolls; the rest scrambled for a spot in whatever hotel, boardinghouse, or big tents that might be available for lodgers, sometimes five to a bed. Still this was not enough. In Hailey, where a single hotel keeper had turned away fifty men a night in 1881, the streets were full of tired migrants looking for a place to lay their heads.[14]

When the Strahorns first arrived in 1880, they found Bellevue—"the entrepôt of the then brand new Wood River mining country," lively, but without a single bank or even decent accommodations. Avoiding the "corral" (the upper half-story of the only available log hotel where a score of beds was assigned by numbers), they managed to find a tiny, smoke-blackened room off the bar. Three years later, they were able to lodge at Isaac Culp's Grand Central Hotel, billed as "The Largest and Most Commodious Hotel in Wood River." To be sure, the Grand Central was less pretentious than its name. Carrie complained each room had but one chair, and that any guests going to the parlor or to more sociable company on the sidewalk took their chair along. She also protested that the walls and ceilings were paper thin and guests in bed suffered from *mal de mer* by watching the ceiling above swaying up and down "like the waves of the sea" when someone walked across overhead.[15]

As the towns matured, more grandiose hotels were built. The new Dewey House in Bellevue, for example, opened in mid-1884 and was described as "splendidly furnished," as was the New Merchants' Hotel in Hailey a few years later. Matthew McFall's International Hotel in Bellevue was considered one of the best in the territory and McFall also maintained "an extensive boardinghouse and hotel at Broadford." In Ketchum, a "genial and competent landlady," Mrs. Himes, gave the Palace an excellent reputation, while the striking Baxter's Hotel caught the eye: it was painted "to remind one of the principal industry of the country": body of golden yellow, trimming of ruby red, and deep green tree boxes "of unusual size."[16]

One of the most elegant of the new hostelries was the Alturas

The International Hotel was Bellevue's best. *Idaho State Historical Society*

Hotel in Hailey, owned by Robert Strahorn and others connected with the Idaho and Oregon Land Improvement Company. Conceived in 1883, its completion was delayed for lack of funds until Judge Thomas W. Mellon, the father of yet-to-be multimillionaire Andrew Mellon, came up with financing in Pittsburgh. It was opened in 1886 with great fanfare and a grand ball. The structure was said to have cost $35,000 and the furniture $8,000, not including the $5,000 bar and the billiard hall fixtures. According to the *Hailey Times*, "It is admitted to be the finest hotel between Denver and the Pacific Ocean." Reportedly, it was a favorite of the Mellon family, who more than once flocked in en masse from various points to vacation, "making quite a Mellon patch for the highlands of Wood River," according to punster Carrie Strahorn.[17]

Robert Strahorn was also involved in another hotel enterprise. In 1888, with a relative from Chicago who claimed to have benefited greatly from the mineral waters, he bought the Lamb ranch, a controlling interest in the Electric Light works, and Hailey Hot Springs. (The Hot Springs went on the market after the previous owner, J. L. G. Smith, was murdered by his wife.) There, two miles west of town, the Strahorn group built the Hailey Hot Springs Hotel. With improvements and bathhouses, it reportedly cost about $100,000. It opened in June 1889, but Strahorn eventually disposed of this interest. It was regarded by visitors as a pleasant accommodation, but in 1899 the hotel burned and was never rebuilt.[18]

Many local residents lived in cheap log or board structures of their own making, where they subsisted on heavy diets of bacon, beans, and flapjacks, perhaps livened up with fresh local trout or venison. Like young James Blackwood in 1883, some did better and were proud of their newly-acquired culinary arts. Blackwood wrote his mother from Ketchum: "I am batching now, four of us together and today cooked one of my dinners such as you used to get me when I came home—corn-beef & cabbage."[19] Others patronized boardinghouses, a highly important institution of nineteenth-century America in towns both small and large. Frequently kept by women, oftimes by widows, the boardinghouse dispensed cheap food and lodging. A Mrs. Gallagher ran one of the most popular of such places at Broadford in 1881, in which Annie, her teenage daughter, was the customers' favorite waitress. Isaac Lewis's daughter supported her family in Ketchum by taking in boarders while her husband, a dentist, spent most of what he made. He was not dishonest, said his father-in-law, "but money burned a hole in his pocket." Local women did a brisk business selling eggs, butter, and other farm produce directly to the boardinghouse proprietors, who provided basic meals and basic living facilities to their renters.[20] Isolated outfits like the Little Wood River Mining and Smelting Company at Muldoon maintained their own employee lodging and boardinghouses—not always with complete success. One August day in 1882, miners revolted, threw their Sunday dinner into the creek, and demanded a new cook.[21]

As the economies stabilized, better family housing became available, although most still left much to be desired. Commonly, they were built of rough pine boards nailed on vertically with thin muslin covered with paper inside. The lack of insulation took its toll on families. Even Homer Pound's home on Second Avenue in Hailey—reputedly the first house in the territory with plastered interior walls—was so cold that Pound's wife took the infant Ezra to live in the Alturas Hotel during the winter of 1885–86.[22]

Among the first business arrivals in Hailey were J. C. Fox and his wife, Florence. J. C. set up a grocery store while Florence ran a boarding tent with a dirt floor that she "swept" with a hoe. Canny like his name, Fox charged his wife full price for groceries, but made her board him free. Perseverance and frugality paid off: ultimately the pair prospered and expanded to a solid brick building and built a house on the corner of Bullion and Third Avenue that was considered the finest in town.[23]

Soon, a visitor could get a "square meal" for fifty cents at the Delta or "fresh eastern oysters, fried, stewed or plain," at the Nevada Chop House (private rooms for ladies). He could board at Isaac Culp's Grand Central Hotel for eight dollars a week, although Carrie Strahorn thought the fare pretty bad. In Ketchum, John Murray's Cornucopia and R. C. West's Enterprise, both on Main Street, were considered good eating places.[24]

Along with housing and eating facilities, the three towns of size—Hailey, Bellevue, and Ketchum—all boasted the standard essential businesses: banks; general merchandise houses; hardware, drug, furniture, and stationary stores; blacksmith and butcher shops; assay offices; brick and lumber yards; a collection of professional people including doctors, dentists, midwives, edi-

Rupert's Drug Store and the Nevada Chop House were obviously popular places in Hailey in 1884. *Idaho State Historical Society*

tors, lawyers, and a wide range of restaurateurs, brewers, saloon keepers, and gambling hall and dance hall operators. "The light ladies who follow the heavy money" (prostitutes) were always subtly in evidence, too, of course, but they never advertised in the newspapers.

With a population of fifteen hundred to two thousand, at one time Ketchum was said to have sustained two banks, seven daily stages, two hotels, seven stores, seven blacksmith shops, three doctors, three lawyers, several restaurants, six livery stables, two assay offices, a weekly newspaper, and uncounted saloons.[25] According to A. Leonard Meyer, as early as June 1881 the infant Hailey already had eleven general merchandise houses; hardware, drug, furniture, and stationery stores; blacksmith and butcher shops; two assay offices; a lumber yard; several lodging houses and restaurants; and four livery stables. As for drinking establishments, Meyer reported there were plenty: "I shall alleviate the pain it will cause the crusaders by mentioning just 12, and no more, of the leading houses."[26]

Businessmen of all kinds came in lock step with the prospectors and miners. As soon as he heard of the silver strike, Glenns Ferry merchant Nathan C. Delano pulled up stakes to open a lumber yard at Bellevue, then sold it and went into general merchandising with H. H. Clay. At Ketchum, the first tent up was a saloon and the second was an assay office. Barnom "Barney" Mallory was in the Wood River country as early as 1879, and opened a combination grocery, livery stable, and lumber yard. When Donald McKay came to Hailey in April 1881, he had to pile his hardware stock in the sagebrush until a tent arrived. Eventually, the general merchandising house of Cliff & McKay sold "everything for house or mine." A native of Germany, Ernest Cramer, came about the same time and established a lodging house, a tailor shop, and the Pioneer News Depot on Hailey's Main Street, and at one time also owned a beer parlor.[27]

In the summer of 1882, S. J. Friedman had announced that

his "Mammoth Brick Store" on Hailey's Main Street stocked all kinds of dry goods at prices 25 percent less than Bellevue competitors and 50 percent lower than Ketchum merchants. He specifically advertised "1,000-mile shoes, warranted."[28] The German-born Friedman was a pioneer among a small coterie of Jewish businessmen on Wood River. With merchandising experience in both Salt Lake City and Ogden, he reacted quickly to the Hailey boom and had opened his first business there in a twenty-by-forty-foot tent. When the establishment thrived, he began construction of a permanent structure, twenty-eight by fifty feet in size, and soon added an extension which was almost as large. Through him, a younger brother, Emil, was attracted to Hailey, and a cousin, Simon M. Friedman, set up a grocery store.[29]

Some of these early entrepreneurs were remarkably versatile. William T. Riley, for example, was a man of multiple talents. He was one of the three responsible for having Hailey surveyed. He was agent for the Utah, Idaho & Oregon Stage Company, manager of the Hailey Town Company, and a real estate agent; eventually, he became a partner in the Riley & Tracy Drug Store.[30]

Equally as talented was H. Z. Burkhart, who, in the spring of 1881, opened an unusual news stand and stationery store in brand new Hailey: it was in a tent made of two bolts of cloth—one from Bellevue and one from Ketchum, stitched together with a Ketchum sewing machine. Burkhart became the town's first express agent, its first justice of the peace, and its first postmaster. In mid-May, 1883, he was turning out bricks in Quigley Gulch and expected to produce 15,000 a day to meet the demand of 350,000 bricks for the new hotel, the Episcopal church, and other buildings about to go up. He was burned out of business twice, and he eventually sat in the territorial legislature, became a lumber merchant, and had close ties with Strahorn, Senator Caldwell, and others involved in developing downtown Hailey business structures.[31]

Apparently there were other brick kilns in town. Robert

Redway & Dix's store and stage station also acted as agent for the Pacific Express Company in Bellevue, c. 1883. *Idaho State Historical Society*

Strahorn's group bought brickyards on the edge of Hailey about the same time a new brick block was going up on the east side of Croy Street, next to the *Wood River Times* office, and three "of its fine stores" had been rented to Denver merchants by the middle of March 1883.[32]

Another entrepreneur who cut a wide swath was Isaac Lewis, who did not limit himself to mine proprietorship, assaying, or laying out townships, but had multiple business interests in Ketchum. In the summer of 1881 he built a small, one-room drugstore and ran it himself during the winter with a fair profit, with the intent of turning it over to his son, who was in Minnesota taking a course in chemistry. Young George, however, preferred to try newspaper work, so his father staked him to an interest in the *Ketchum Keystone* and put George Steward in charge of the drug enterprise, now expanded to include groceries. In 1883 Lewis "bought in" with Joseph Pinkham in the mercantile business, which included mining supplies, a venture he later admitted was a mistake. While Lewis was busy elsewhere, Pinkham ignored the store in order to play cards and allowed customers to run up large debts. Meanwhile, "the clerks stole us blind," as Lewis put it. With deficits mounting, Lewis sold out to Albert Comstock for $6,000. Comstock paid down $1,000 and soon died insolvent, leaving Lewis in the lurch. At the end of 1884, he turned his drug store over to his son, who was then disenchanted with journalism. By 1899, what had been "Pinkham & Lewis: General Merchandise, Mining Supplies," had become "Lewis, Lemon & Co., Dealers in General Merchandise and Drugs," with Isaac and one of his sons associated with William H. Lemon.[33]

Two years earlier Isaac had been busy at Guyer Hot Springs. He built a bathhouse and restaurant-bar with ten or eleven rooms, including a ladies' parlor, along with a twenty-by-forty-foot dance floor. In addition, a town site had been laid out, to be called Saratoga, but it was canceled by the Land Office because of a clerical error. Lewis was manager and held a one-quarter interest in both the Guyer Hot Springs and the Saratoga town site, along with Sam Hauser of Montana, Captain Henry Guyer, and banker-stagecoach operator Orange J. Salisbury. When James Stover took a twenty-acre placer claim adjoining the Hot Springs property and sought to appropriate water from the springs for a competing bathhouse and saloon, Lewis figuratively waved his U.S. patent for the springs in his face, tore up his water conduits and built a high board fence between the two properties. When Stover threatened a lawsuit, Lewis bought him out for $500, but in 1885 sold his one-fourth interest in the Hot Springs enterprise to Guyer's wife, Mary, who, he said, wanted to run the place "on the Temperance Plan," which was a non-profit approach compared to "the Rowdy Plan."[34]

Early in 1884, Lewis gave banking a try. With a rather questionable operator from New Jersey, and with some Eastern and Montana backing, he organized the First National Bank of Ketchum, controlled three-fifths of its $50,000 paid-up stock, and erected a brick bank building next to Baxter's Hotel. But he failed to make the enterprise a success. His New Jersey cohort and his own bookkeeper skimmed off funds and brought the bank to the brink of disaster. In addition, Lewis owned a number of buildings, including a blacksmith shop, a shoe shop, the Odd Fellows Hall, and half interest in a Chinese wash house, all of which brought in rental income. At one time he was treasurer of the Ketchum & Challis Toll Road Company, and in 1891 was President of the Ketchum Spring Water Supply Company. His mining interests were varied and some of them profitable, but his pride was his ranch with its fifteen miles of fence, forty head of stock, and 200 acres under cultivation. Lewis's first love, though, was Ketchum. "I have virtually made the town," he reminisced, "at least I have expended more money and labor for it, than any ten other men of the country all put together. It is *home*."[35]

Most businesses of the boom era in Wood River communities would be familiar in the twentieth century—and so would the remarkable variety of goods and services available. Trotter chewing tobacco was available at George I. Hurley & Co.; fresh eggs, limes, and oranges could be found at Heckethorns, next to White's furniture store; boots were made to order at Bayhouse's on Main Street; and the miner-shopper was invited to purchase a "Prospector's pocketknife," which came equipped "with Very Powerful Magnifying Glass," for only $3.50 at Riley & Tracy's drug store.[36]

In addition to his smelter, David Falk established a grain and flour business in Hailey, although Bellevue had the only flourishing flour mill on Wood River.[37] Along with a variety of mine and ore treatment facilities that provided jobs, the towns had business that provided support services, like the Hailey Iron Works which, at the end of 1884, employed eight to ten men in the manufacture and repair of such equipment as ore cars, shafting, and pulleys.[38]

At least two standard enterprises—the livery stable and ice cutting and distribution—would soon be either eliminated or changed drastically by technology. In the case of the livery stable, horses were made obsolete by the coming of the internal combustion automobile and truck. The ice business prospered for many years, but eventually large commercial ice-making machines, already in use in some areas by the 1880s, and the cheap electric refrigerator meant the end of the delivery of ice by the block.

At the time of the Wood River boom, the livery stable was as mundane as it was basic. As ubiquitous in its day as the gas station is now, it was an important establishment in any town, regardless of size. It functioned as a social center, a diner, a motel for horses, a business that rented horses for riding or for pulling vehicles, and a car rental agency for everything from buggies to wagons and hearses. It added to the town's unpleasant aromas, and the stamping of horses hooves on wooden stall floors all night long contributed to noise pollution, but the livery stable was a necessary business in every town.[39]

In the spring of 1881 Hailey was barely two months old but already boasted several livery stables, which the *Statesman's* reporter, A. Leonard Meyer, referred to as "horse restaurants, where your dumb brutes may be fed or starved to order."[40] Soon Joe Merrill's "Livery, Boarding and Sales Stables" at Bullion and First Avenue in Hailey was advertising "Unsurpassed Accommodations for Thirty Horses, and the Turnouts and Teams are First-Class."[41] Peter Meves' Capital Feed Stable and Corral, at Silver and Main in Hailey, had "Horses to hay, 50 cents per night," sold baled hay and grain over the counter, and ran a daily hack line between Hailey and Ketchum.[42] When fire destroyed Burnham and Ringgold's livery stable in Bellevue in the wee hours of a September morning in 1884, it left the charred remains of fourteen horses and an estimated $7,000 loss.[43]

Stables were especially busy during the last week of December as miners jockeyed for position in the annual run to relocate presumably abandoned mining claims. Independence Day was their other busy time. As the *Times* announced late in June 1887, "The livery stables of Hailey will realize a bonanza from the Fourth, as every vehicle in them has been engaged for weeks, and the demand for turnouts is far beyond their ability to supply."[44]

Charles Nelson was one of the livery entrepreneurs of Wood River, with establishments in several towns, including a Bellevue structure large enough to house 70 horses inside and 100 more outside. Moreover, he provided "a splendid lot of fine buggies and carriages, and a hearse unequaled in Idaho."[45] A few years later, Nelson's City Livery Stable in Hailey advertised the trotting stallion, "Idaho Boy" at stud. Eventually, like many of its counterparts elsewhere, the same establishment announced it had available choice furniture, wallpaper, upholstering supplies, home sewing machines, and full undertaking services with "Embalming a Specialty." Such versatility was echoed by McNulty & Sullivan, Undertakers and Embalmers, who also advertised furniture, carpets, jewelry, and pianos and organs.[46]

The many bars and saloons helped sustain the local ice industry, although everybody needed ice in the summer for cold drinks and to prevent food from spoiling. Saloon owners gathered their own and stored it in their own icehouses (as did many private households), but usually they bought from professional ice men who cut thousands of tons in the winter with special saws, stored it in sawdust in their own icehouses, and sold it during the warm months.[47]

The suppliers of ice flourished from the beginning. Only four days into 1882, Sam Jones & Co. at Hailey announced that the inventory had been laid in for the coming summer. About one hundred fifty tons, in blocks weighing 75 to 200 pounds each, were packed away in sawdust, ready to be dispensed in any quantity at two and a half to three cents a pound when the weather warranted.[48] At the same time, two Norwegians in Quigley's Gulch, a mile out of Hailey, were making ice by freezing it in five-gallon coal oil cans left out at night. As of February 1, they had a twenty-by-forty-foot log house full of their product "and are still at it." But by mid-May, they had sold their "ice ranch" to Joseph Morrill, the Hailey livery stable keeper, who was interested in the land, not the ice.[49]

Meanwhile, the Wood River Ice Company opened for business, with W. W. Treat of Hailey and E. A. Martin of Bellevue running affairs. Martin took care of his town, while Treat personally handled orders from Cliff & McKay's hardware store in Hailey; and in both places the company delivered ice at half a cent a pound, with "a liberal discount" for over fifty pounds a day.[50] When fall came, Treat and Martin were preparing to put up 1,000 tons of ice for the winter, half for each town. Their firm had leased all the available ponds and sloughs along the river from below Bellevue to six miles above Hailey. In October they were busy clearing out boulders and underbrush and planning new icehouses for both Hailey and Bellevue. Shortly before Christmas, when the ice near Bellevue was ten inches thick, they had six men at work cutting the "crop," as it was called, for the spring and summer trade. Meanwhile, competitors Lew Dorsey, Isaac Culp, and R. R. Rounds had their large icehouse on River Street nearly filled with 140 tons of "perfectly clear and clean" ice "of the finest quality."[51]

In later years Purdam and Ward advertised "ice by the pound, ton, or car-load," with orders taken at Willman and Walkers in Hailey. George Bronaugh, Charles Harvey, and John Boggs were supervising "a corps of aides" in harvesting ice at Hailey Hot Springs, which was eighteen inches thick and "clear as crystal." Of the approximately three hundred tons to be cut, the Springs Hotel would use about fifty.[52]

In all the towns the medical and dental professions were represented; although in Wood River, like mining camps in general, the legal calling was one of the most popular. Newspapers of 1884 indicated twenty-one attorneys practicing in Hailey, including the dean of the Wood River corps of lawyers, Francis E. Ensign, an Oberlin graduate with thirty years experience in California and Idaho. Among others active at the same time were Frank Canahl, Kingsbury & McGowan, Brierly & Co., and two members of the bar with intriguing names, Texas Angel and Lycurgus Vineyard. In Bellevue, N. M. Ruick offered legal services, G. L. Waters had offices in the Ether Building, and B. M. Bruner and A. J. Bruner had offices next to McCornick's Bank.[53]

As Wood River grew into adulthood, canvas roofs and log structures gave way to more substantial buildings of frame, brick, and stone, especially after part of downtown Hailey was destroyed by fire. Indeed, twice Hailey saw its business district leveled by flames. In the fall of 1883, an entire block of buildings burned on the east side of Main between Bullion and Croy for

an estimated loss of seventy-five thousand dollars. Included
were the Hailey Bakery, the Grand Central Hotel, Hilbert &
Company's saloon, a jewelry business, a shoe shop, and several
lodging houses.[54]

Rebuilding took place quickly, with more permanent material
and a volunteer hose company organized to fight future confla-
grations. Just two days before the Fourth of July in 1889, fire
again ravaged the central section of Hailey, this time destroying
one half to three-quarters of a million dollars worth of property.
Although one editor referred to the affair as "the wildest night
ever experienced in Hailey," it commenced in the wee hours of
the morning at the Nevada Hotel, better known as the Nevada
Chop House, when a drunken miner knocked over a candle. It
took almost all of the business district, except S. J. Friedman's

S. J. Friedman's store was the only business to survive the July, 1889, fire in
central Hailey. *Idaho State Historical Society*

brick store, which had a double roof, one of them of dirt. Even so, Friedman desperately battled the flames for several hours and was eventually dragged out of the building with "hair and whiskers singed, a few slight burns on his face, neck and hand, his clothes soaking wet, his face black as a charcoal burner." Among other casualties, the theater was destroyed. Peter Meves's livery stable went up in flames, a loss of $3,000 with no insurance. The Hailey Hotel burned, as did the three-story Merchant's Hotel, considered one of the finest, with a damage estimate of $55,000. Leopold Wertheimer's men's furnishings store was a total loss. Despite a dull economy that fall, most of the devastated area had been rebuilt before winter set in—even as a forest fire in Narrow Gauge Gulch only a mile and a half away threatened the town.[55]

At the same time, grasshoppers invaded the area. The next summer they hit the area below Bellevue. If that were not enough, Wood Riverites also had to worry about the new Russian flu, which was sweeping westward across the country in 1890. The year 1892 brought a cholera scare, a disease which newspapers said could be prevented by drinking a mixture of tea and hydrochloric acid. The next year was no better. Eighteen ninety-three was a time of both depression and diphtheria, the latter, residents agreed, worse than the low price of silver.[56]

Weather was another challenge. In 1879, early prospectors saw no indication of heavy snows or snowslides, but Wood River veterans quickly came to understand the harshness of winter in the mountains. They learned the folly of travel by coach or horseback before mid-May or early June. If they considered two and a half feet of snow a good winter, they knew that even under such positive circumstances this was no area for winter prospecting.[57] Once mines passed the development stage, underground work went on year-round, except in the upper reaches around Galena and Sawtooth City. But the long cold months could be trying, especially if snow accumulated in ten- or fifteen-foot drifts, as it sometimes did. Pessimism and "the blues" often dominated, but once the snow began to melt and "the merry feathered songsters" returned, the outlook improved.[58]

In any given winter, snowfall was unpredictable and could have an unexpected effect upon the economy. In early October 1882, for example, Wood River had a snowfall of a foot and a half, which caught everyone unprepared (see chart opposite). At the Elkhorn mine, Isaac Lewis had intended to "*Rattle out* considerable ore & so increased the force for that purpose, but *Kind Providence* just now giving us fits in the way of snow storms and winter weather." Those engaged in hauling ore, lime, and wood to the smelters moved their teams to more salubrious areas lest they be caught without forage for the animals. But warm weather soon returned and continued for several months. With the animals away, transportation was so crippled that the smelters were forced to close down and the district lost an estimated $1 million.[60]

The rigors of winter prompted many to flee Wood River in the cold months and isolated those who remained. According to the United States Weather Bureau, the mean average snowfall at Hailey was slightly more than eight feet.[61] While the temperature was cold, it was no worse than other areas of the same altitude and longitude—parts of Vermont, for example. Death or severe injury by freezing was not uncommon, especially among those caught up in the relentless search for precious metal. "They have not been accustomed to the luxury of orange groves when seeking fortune in the rocks or placers," the *Times* editor noted. One miner, James H. Allen, froze to death near Bullion early in 1882: "Found Stiff as an Icicle Near the Bullion Slaughterhouse," was the way Picotte put it.[62] During the same winter, prospector T. T. Cox froze both feet, had to have them amputated, and buried them in Hailey. Friends took up a purse to send him to Colorado, but in the summer of 1883 he returned to retrieve his severed members and to inter them properly in the family plot in Iowa.[63]

RECORDS OF TEMPERATURE AND PRECIPITATION AT HAILEY[59]

Month	Average mean temperature	Average mean precipitation	Average mean snowfall
	°F	Inches	Inches
Jan	20	3.72	40.4
Feb	24	1.79	14.1
Mar	31	1.57	6.1
Apr	44	1.01	1.9
May	52	1.47	1.1
June	59	.97	.3
July	67	.62	0
Aug	67	.33	0
Sept	56	.81	Trace
Oct	46	1.17	1
Nov	34	1.30	10.8
Dec	20	1.72	22.2
Annual	43	16.48	97.9

Even in a normal winter, Wood Riverites were in danger from snowslides like the one of 1881 that leveled the buildings at the Kelley mine near Elk Creek, some fifteen miles from Bellevue. When volunteers on skis reached the scene a few days later, they found four men dead: James Bone, a Scot; Irishman James Casey; and the two Kelley brothers, Edward and Meredith, both Mexican War veterans with thirty years experience on the Pacific Coast.[64]

Especially heavy snows in the winter of 1883–84 paralyzed the Wood River area. With five feet on the ground, "the beautiful white," as the poets liked to call it, continued to fall. Mine owners could not reach their property, except on skis. Snow-slides hit both the Queen of the Mountains mine and Narrow Gauge concentrating works on Deer Creek, fortunately both idle for the winter. Muldoon, where the Little Wood River Mining and Smelting Company had fifteen miners doing development work, was reported "pretty badly snowed in," with provisions in short supply.[65] A mail carrier on skis delivering letters between Hailey and Bullion became completely lost in a raging blizzard and when he believed wolves were on his trail, abandoned his mail bag and took refuge in an abandoned cabin. The stages were put on runners, but even they were stymied. It took a sleigh with three teams and seven men with shovels five hours to travel the five miles between Bellevue and Hailey. Train service was canceled and even social affairs, including holiday balls, had to be rescheduled. The weight of snow caved in the roof of the Hailey Theater. Fitzsimmon's Metropolitan Hall, the largest structure in Ketchum, also collapsed. Fitz quickly slapped on a makeshift roof and continued business with a one-story building. Snow shovelers were so much in demand that they commanded the unheard-of pay of a dollar per hour.[66]

Telegraph lines were down temporarily and there were snow-slides and fatalities, especially at Bullion. Meat was in short sup-ply: beef in Ketchum "is like 'hen's teeth,'" the press reported. Finally, on February 27, the railroad snowplow broke the block-ade: a train arrived with thirteen days of accumulated mail and contact with the outside resumed.[67]

In 1890, Wood River was again snowbound, despite the intro-duction of an expensive new rotary snowplow by the railroad three years earlier.[68] There was a fatal avalanche on Lookout Mountain near Bellevue and two people were lost in Quigley Gulch. Mills collapsed at the Mayflower and Jay Gould mines. Snowslides closed a number of operations, while others were forced to shut down from lack of coal and coke, a reminder of two years earlier when coal had been in short supply due to a fire at Union Pacific's Olney mines. With local streets and roads clogged with snow, travel came to a standstill. Carrie Strahorn was marooned in the Hailey Hot Springs Hotel for two weeks, visited occasionally by "a few venturesome miners" who came down from the hills on skis, clad in furs and gunny sacks. "It seemed as if we had been transported to Lapland," she said.[69] Nellie Bly's trip around the world "was not one-twentieth as daring as is a trip from Hailey to Sawtooth, on snowshoes," Picotte reported. But on March 4, with the rotary plow leading the way, the first train since February 22 pulled into Hailey with ten days of mail and 300 tons of delayed freight aboard. Even so, it was another month or so before the coal supply began to improve substantially.[70]

Winter-enforced isolation made it clear how dependent Wood River citizens were on mail and stage and rail links outside. When editors detailed precisely how many passengers departed or arrived, how many freight cars there were, loaded and empty, and whether coaches or trains were ten minutes late or on time, they were passing along information of real interest to the locals. Half the town of Hailey turned out to view the railroad's new rotary snowplow, a pioneer in the United States, on its initial run in 1887. More than two hundred people flocked to the depot in 1893 when the rotary opened up the line. Charlie Sherry got so close he was plowed under, but was dug out unhurt.[71]

In the boom years Wood River weathered the various adversities as it evolved and progressed. One sign of maturity was the presence of banking institutions, beginning with T. R. Jones and Co. in Hailey in 1883. Another was the specialization that came to merchandising. General store keepers narrowed their products as they became purveyors of groceries, liquors or tobacco in the best "citified" tradition.[72]

Another proof of progress lay in Wood River's ongoing publications of many newspapers and in its advancements in public utilities. The towns supported a surprising number of news-papers at various times. A Bellevue weekly, the *Wood River News,* first ran off the presses January 28, 1881. It was followed by Hailey's weekly *Wood River Miner* on May 6 of the same year and by T. E. Picotte's *Wood River Times,* also published weekly begin-ning June 15, 1881. Commencing in May 1882, Picotte issued a daily *Wood River Times.* The *Wood River News* of Bellevue and the *Wood River Miner* of Hailey were consolidated into the weekly *Wood River News-Miner* by Harding and Clay on July 8, 1882, and the *Daily Wood River News-Miner* appeared at Hailey in April 1883. Bellevue had two new papers about the same time: the *Daily Sun* and the *Daily Chronicle,* plus several others at dif-ferent times—the *Weekly Herald,* the *Weekly Logan County Review,* and the *Weekly Silver Blade.* In 1881 George J. Lewis, later Idaho Secretary of State, began the *Ketchum Keystone,* which was purchased in 1886 by Isaac H. Bowman, who contin-ued it for another fifteen years. Meanwhile, C. H. Clay pub-lished the *Daily Inter-Idaho* in Hailey from the summer of 1884 to August 1888. For more than four years, Hailey had three daily newspapers, more than any other town in the territory.[73]

The towns were progressive in another respect—their ad-vances in public utilities. Bellevue, which was chartered by the legislature in 1883, was one of the earliest formal cities in Idaho. Its complex act of incorporation defined boundaries, municipal officers, and various duties and responsibilities at all levels. Two years later, the general assembly granted five individuals a fran-chise for a street railway running from Bellevue to Broadford, and even set the maximum fares to be charged and stipulated during the hours of operation, although apparently the line was never built.[74]

Perhaps because of the feeling of isolation, Hailey had installed a telephone system by October 1, 1883, the first in the Territory of Idaho, although Leadville, Colorado, had its first telephone service in late 1879 with 150 subscribers. The exchange

was in the *Times* building at Croy and Main, and the first operator was twelve-year-old Nathan Kingsbury, who later became
vice-president of American Telephone and Telegraph Company.
The line to Bellevue and Bullion was completed about a week
later and Ketchum was hooked up by the end of November. Two
weeks after the Rocky Mountain Bell Telephone Company ran
its lines in Hailey, about twenty-five residents had phones, for
which they paid eight dollars a month. Non-subscribers could
place calls in Hailey for a dime, but calling Bellevue or Bullion
cost a quarter. Haileyites might have crowed a little that Boise
and Caldwell were still waiting for their hookups; but the lines
between Wood River and Shoshone, Blackfoot, and Boise were
not completed until after the turn of the century.[75]

The Hailey waterworks, dubbed "the first in Idaho," became
operational in mid-December 1883, when water from the Alturas
Water Company reservoir began flowing through the mains, providing water for everyone, including a public hydrant, for three
dollars a month.[76]

The smelters at Ketchum and Muldoon had installed their
own electric lights as early as the summer of 1882, but it was not
until May 1887 when the Hailey electric light works turned on
the current to test the sixty-two lights just installed in the town.
A few days later, a larger trial included 215 lamps, most of them
in stores. When a number burned out, there was a momentary
setback, but while the system was shut down the bugs were rec-
tified. A defective generator had to be rebuilt on the site, and the
engineers worked day and night to have the plant operational by
the contract deadline—Christmas Eve. The contract was met,
but only by a few hours, and Hailey "literally tore itself apart" in
celebrating the event, according to one of the experts in charge.

More than two thousand miners and their companions filled
the night spots and crowded into Art Smith's half finished Tavern
to the cellar, for which expected event Art had imported an extra

carload of wet victuals and set up additional bars all over the place. . . . Drinks were all on the house until ten o'clock that night.[77]

The power plant was located east of the P. K. Saloon, later the site of the Hailey National Bank. Here again, the locals boasted that Hailey was the first Idaho town with an electric light plant.[78]

The first schools were no doubt private, like Professor Gilbert Butler's Hailey Prep School, but public education was not far behind. From the beginning, Wood River had the aid of the office of the Territorial Superintendent of Instruction (created in 1864) to help new communities organize schools, hire teachers, and acquire the necessary textbooks—among them Webster's blue-backed speller and the famous *McGuffey Eclectic Readers*—commonly used to inculcate precepts of high morality and work ethic, and to provide a common body of allusion and a common frame of reference to young nineteenth-century Americans.

Hailey was typical in the way private contributions and the receipts of benefits filled the gap until an adequate tax base could be organized. The town opened its first two-room school early in 1882, but interior trim remained unfinished for another year. From one teacher and an initial enrollment of fifteen girls and twenty-one boys, the student body had grown to a total of ninety, supervised by two teachers, by the fall of 1883. With public funds limited, the women of Hailey staged numerous fundraisers to provide amenities for the classrooms—desks, maps, a chandelier, a piano, and an Estey organ from Vermont.[79]

As the building was outgrown, the town was authorized to issue bonds to erect a larger schoolhouse, which was completed by the spring of 1887. Three of the four teachers hired the next fall had some college training, and the curriculum was expanded to include a kindergarten and a college prep course in high school. The new brick structure came complete with a bell tower, a substantial library, and well over a hundred aromatic balm-of-Gilead trees around the four sides of the school block.[80]

About the same time, Bellevue also constructed a new school. Early in 1885, a territorial law authorized that city to issue up to $8,000 in 10 percent bonds to construct a new building in the town's public square.[81] Soon, the Bellevue public school rivaled that of its neighbor to the north. Almost all children were educated locally, although Mrs. Gallagher's Annie left the Broadford boardinghouse to attend Catholic Sisters School in Salt Lake City.[82]

Perhaps a more conservative outlook, as opposed to the early boom-or-bust mentality, was another sign of community maturity. Society was less egalitarian; more divided into in- and out-groups. A growing split between capital and labor was typical.

Along with such trends came better, more sophisticated court, educational, cultural, and religious facilities. By 1884, Hailey had a miners' hospital that operated on a seasonal basis, closing in the winter when the work force was low. Yet another indication of maturity was that reputable women were becoming more numerous, and the town streets more family oriented, as was the case with Hailey in 1884.

Gay dresses and fashionable bonnets contrast with the togs of the honest miner, and the baby carriage struggles through the piles of wheelbarrows and go-carts on the sidewalks of the stores.[83]

By the end of 1885, one of those baby carriages would belong to Land Register Homer Pound, father of the bouncing boy born in October and named Ezra by his proud parents.[84] Ezra would eventually be the town's most famous citizen.

Physically, the Wood River towns were no longer "babies in swaddling clothes" by 1886. "Their day of pine boards and slab shanties has passed. Their substantial growth demands and warrants substantial structures, and nature whispers 'build of stone and brick.'"[85] Indeed, by this time Ketchum even had a planned subdivision. The Alturas Land Improvement and Manufacturing Company, a group which held title to property in the valley north of town, laid out the Rhodes Addition, named after its president, James M. Rhodes, who also headed the Philadelphia Mining and Smelting Company. According to Major William Hyndman, chief sales agent, the Rhodes Addition included 1,000 acres and by the mid-1880s plats showed it with six wide avenues named Idaho, Arizona, Wyoming, Washington, Oregon, and Montana, intersected by twenty-six streets.[86]

But one trait the Wood Riverites never outgrew was their inter-town rivalry. At least one contemporary believed that there were simply too many competing communities: two towns would have been plenty and would likely have obviated the petty jealousies and spite that so frequently surfaced. Even as early as the summer of 1881, another observer believed that the rivalry between the town sites had "been carried to a pitch bordering insanity."[87] Ketchum, the self-styled "Keystone City," claimed priority of settlement and saw its name as significant: "For we Ketchum (catch 'em); having already allured the prospector, the capitalist, the businessman and caught the trade from every direction."[88] Well located for access to mines, timber, and water power at 6,000 feet in the upper valley at the junction of Trail and Warm Spring creeks, Ketchum's denizens scoffed at "Poor Sick Yop," Hailey; Bellevue citizens referred disdainfully to Hailey as the "Muchroom City," lacking both business and ethics; Haileyites, in turn, spoke of "that place at the mouth of Slaughter House gulch, commonly known as Bunghole, but designated by the Postoffice Department as Bellevue." When the Episcopal priest of Hailey visited the office of the *Ketchum Keystone*, editor Picotte of the *Times* commented: "The afflicted and distressed always require special ministration." One wag, no doubt a victim of Ketchum fever, suggested that the name of

Ketchum was unpretentious in the early 1880s. *American Heritage Center, University of Wyoming*

Hailey be changed to Hogum and that of Bellevue to Skinum: thus Ketchum, Hogum, and Skinum![89]

The transfer of the county seat from Rocky Bar to Hailey in a bitterly contested election of 1881 added fuel to the fire. When the territorial legislature provided that Alturas County residents vote on the issue, it was almost a foregone conclusion that the most populous town, Bellevue (some called it Biddyville),[90] would win. But before the election was held four months later, Hailey "sprang up like a summer breeze and reached out her hand for the persimmon with a long pole," according to Carrie Strahorn, who was on the scene. Bellevue was accused of adding lists of Salt Lake City hotel registrants to the voting rosters; Hailey supposedly counted fourteen more ballots than there were voters in the entire county; the returns from Indian Creek and Canyon Creek precincts went missing; poor Ketchum, according to one partisan, "received the largest number of *honest* votes." Eventually, after the courts counted the Indian Creek returns, which had shown up in Mountain Home, 120 miles away, "Hailey got away with the County Seat by *fraud*," thanks to the machinations of one William H. Watt, "the *chief* light fingered gent," in the eyes of Isaac Lewis.[91]

Town rivalry continued long after each center assumed a slightly different tone and function. Even little Bullion, hemmed in by mountains, regarded itself as the "backbone" of Wood River and a legitimate contender, even though residents disliked wintering there because of heavy snowslides. "Why is the town of Bullion like a Flathead Indian papoose with his head strapped to a board?" asked a Hailey conundrum. "Because he has no room to spread."[92]

Bellevue came in for sarcastic disparagement from both

Bellevue, 1885. *Idaho State Historical Society*

Ketchum and Hailey. "A Boom to Bellevue," ran a headline in Hailey's *Wood River Times*—"Only a Tie Boom, to be Sure, but Better than no Boom." Hailey eventually had "the railroad and the surplus of 'beats and beggars,'" but little else, the Ketchumites insisted. Before Hailey was ever founded, Ketchum was "a city of magnificent distances," "the one oasis in the desert between Bellevue and the Sawtooth Country," "and the fame of her pizen whisky was echoed from one end of the river to the other." "The quality of Hailey whisky was just a little ranker than her own, and Ketchum was envious."[93] At a time when Ketchum had the only really flourishing smelter on the River, her boosters damned her unnamed rival—Hailey—and "those hurrah tiger sensational articles about 14,000 smelters, half a dozen railroad terminuses, and the only town in the whole country." In turn,

Hailey: aftermath of the fire of July 2, 1889. *Idaho State Historical Society*

Haileyites accused "the villagers" in Bellevue, farther south, of assigning local runners to open the doors of the coaches as they pull up to the post office: "Here you are, gentlemen! This is the end of the route," even though the stages ran through to Hailey six or seven miles up the road.[94] On the other hand, Hailey citizens illustrated Bellevue's shaky economy with a story about the visitor who walked into a Bellevue hotel, in which about fifteen residents were sitting, and asked to change his $50 bill. "Not a man made a move to change it, but each one leaned forward and gaped at the money." Continuing on to Hailey, the traveler again entered a hotel and asked to change the bill. "A dozen citizens immediately dove for their pockets, and in an instant twenty-dollar gold pieces and rolls of bills came into sight to the sum of at least $700, and that $50 bill was carelessly slipped into a vest pocket by one of those present."[95]

Town rivalry never waned; it was part of the Wood River experience. But by 1886, it was tempered a little. According to a Ketchum minister, because of their mines Broadford and Bellevue were considered "the workshops"; Hailey was termed "the emporium of law and fashion"; and Ketchum "the center of literature and 'culchah.'"[96] Smart politicians, too, knew how to keep their perspective. In his annual report to the Secretary of the Interior in 1887, Governor Edward A. Stevenson commented on the Wood River centers that "were built in a few days." Bellevue, with a population of 3,000, he called "a fine, handsome business town"; Hailey, with 4,000 people was "a large, fine town"; and Ketchum, with 2,000 inhabitants, was, in turn, "another fine town."[97]

The Wood River Rush indeed made for a dramatic population shift from west to east within Alturas County, which Carrie Strahorn claimed was as large as the state of Ohio. With Hailey's ascendancy, Rocky Bar changed, "as if by magic, from the county seat to a common village."[98] In the fall of 1881, when the *Idaho Tri-Weekly Statesman* predicted that Hailey or Bellevue "may have a larger population some day than Boise City," chauvinistic T. E. Picotte shot back: "Hailey will have a larger population than Boise by the next Fourth of July." And as the population shift continued, partisans pointed out that either Hailey or Bellevue was a more proper site for the capital of Idaho than Boise.[99]

When did Wood River cease to be a "camp" and become a town—or rather a series of towns? Was it when the buildings shed their canvas tops and acquired permanent roofing—say, in 1883 or 1884? Was it in 1885, when the strike among miners at Broadford over wage reductions caught national headlines and indicated that mining was indeed a full-fledged industry? Was it in mid-December 1888 when the Women's Christian Temperance Union opened its free reading room in Hailey? Or was it perhaps December 1892, when the doors opened on the Hailey Ensor Institution at the Hot Springs, where one took the cure for habits in tobacco, liquor, morphine, opium, or cocaine?[100] More likely, 1883 or 1884 would be a realistic point of demarcation. Once established, the coming of efficient smelters and the iron horse put the economy on an industrial basis. Town life adapted accordingly.

CHAPTER FIVE NOTES

1. Wayne C. Sparling, *Southern Idaho Ghost Towns* (Caldwell: Caxton Printers, 1974), pp. 76, 79, 80, 83–84; Lalia Boone, *Idaho Place Names*, (Moscow: University of Idaho Press, 1988), p. 149.

2. For an excellent general detailed treatment, see Duane A. Smith, *Rocky Mountain Mining Camps: The Urban Frontier* (Bloomington: Indiana University Press, 1967).

3. From the *Coldwater Republican* (Michigan), *Wood River Times*, (Hailey), June 10, 1882.

4. Quoted in *Mining and Scientific Press* (San Francisco), XLII (March 26, 1881): 201.

5. *Wood River Times* (weekly), June 15, 1881.

6. *Wood River Times*, October 12, 1882; "F" to editor (Bellevue, April 15, 1881), *Idaho Tri-Weekly Statesman* (Boise), April 23, 1881.

7. *Wood River Times*, March 12, 1888.

8. *Engineering and Mining Journal* (New York), CI (May 13, 1916): 871.

9. *Wood River Times*, January 21, 1884.

10. See, for example, law of January 17, 1883, *General Laws of the Territory of Idaho*, Twelfth Session (1882–83), p. 70; entry of February 5, 1885, *Journal of the Council*, Thirteenth Session (1884–85), p. 251.

11. *Ketchum Keystone*, May 18, 1882; *Wood River Times*, August 21 and September 28, 1882, January 5, 1883.

12. For an analysis of children and disease in western mining communities see Elliott West's admirable *Growing Up with the Country:*

Childhood on the Far Western Frontier (Albuquerque: University of New Mexico Press, 1989), pp. 129–33.

13. Carrie Adell Strahorn, *Fifteen Thousand Miles by Stage* (New York and London: G. P. Putnam's Sons, 1911, reprint, Lincoln and London: University of Nebraska, 1988), p. 294; *Wood River Times*, March 24 and April 17, 1883.

14. *Wood River Times*, October 12, 1881.

15. C. Strahorn, pp. 292–93, 418; advertisement in *Wood River Times*, March 6, 1883.

16. "R" to editor (Bellevue, July 22, 1884), *Idaho Tri-Weekly Statesman*, July 31, 1884; *Mining and Scientific Press*, XLIX (December 13 and 20, 1884): 370, 386; *Wood River Times*, November 11, 1887 and August 18, 1888.

17. *Wood River Times*, May 20, 1886; George A. McLeod, *Histories of Alturas and Blaine Counties Idaho* (Hailey: Hailey Times, 1938), pp. 58, 164; C. Strahorn, p. 586.

18. *Engineering and Mining Journal*, L (November 29, 1890), p. 631; Strahorn, pp. 583, 585, 589, 593; entries for August 7 and 9, 1895, Henry W. Aplington diary transcript, in Pass Mining Company archives, Boise State University, Special Collections Department; McLeod, p. 68.

19. James Court Blackwood to his mother (Ketchum, October 16, 1883), James Court Blackwood Letters, Montana Historical Society Archives, Helena.

20. Mary Brown McGonigal, *Spring of Gladness: Reminiscences of Pioneer Life in the Wood River Valley* (Sun Valley: High Country Lithography, 1976), pp. 34, 36, 121–22; Isaac I. Lewis, "Reminiscences," (Ketchum, March 28, 1892), typescript, p. 181, American Heritage Center, University of Wyoming; Lucille Hathaway Hall, *Memories of Old Alturas County, Idaho* (Denver: Big Mountain Press, 1956), p. 36.

21. Merle W. Wells, *Gold Camps & Silver Cities: Nineteenth Century Mining in Central and Southern Idaho*, 2d ed., (Moscow: Idaho Bureau of Mines and Geology *Bulletin* No. 22, 1983), p. 129.

22. *Wood River Times*, January 23, 1884; Marilyn Watkinson, *Emmanuel Church, Hailey: The Early Years 1881–1901* (Twin Falls:

Professional Print & Copy, 1991), p. 41; Waller B. Wigginton, "The Pounds at Hailey," *Rendezvous*, IV (Spring, 1969): 37.

23. C. Strahorn, p. 417; Watkinson, p. 37.

24. *Wood River Times*, March 27, 1883; C. Strahorn, p. 418; *Mining and Scientific Press*, XLIX (December 20, 1884): 386.

25. McLeod, p. 49.

26. "A. L. M." to editor (June 7, 1881), *Idaho Tri-Weekly Statesman*, June 14, 1881.

27. James H. Hawley, ed., *History of Idaho: The Gem of the Mountains* (Chicago: S. J. Clarke Publishing Co., 1920) I, pp. 716–17; Watkinson, pp. 36, 40, 41.

28. *Wood River Times*, July 11, 1882.

29. Juanita Brooks, *History of the Jews in Utah and Idaho* (Salt Lake City: Western Epics, 1973), pp. 125–26.

30. Watkinson, p. 36.

31. Strahorn, p. 416; McLeod, p. 57; Watkinson, p. 36.

32. *Wood River Times*, March 14, 1883.

33. Lewis, "Reminiscences," pp. 179–80. See also letterheads in Hauser Papers.

34. James L. Onderdonk, *Idaho: Facts and Statistics Concerning its Mining, Farming, Stock-raising, Lumbering, and other Resources and Industries, Together with Notes on the Climate, Scenery, Game, and Mineral Springs* (San Francisco: A. L. Bancroft & Co., 1885), p. 70; Lewis, "Reminiscences," pp. 172, 180; Lewis to Hauser (Ketchum, November 3 and December 23, 1885), Hauser Papers, Box 11; Lewis to Hauser (Ketchum, March 16, 1891), Hauser Papers, Box 21.

35. Lewis to Hauser (Ketchum, February 19, 1884), Hauser Papers, Box 10; Lewis, "Reminiscences," pp. 180, 183–89, 200.

36. See advertisements in *Wood River Times*, May 27, 1882.

37. "A. L. M." to editor (Hailey, June 7, 1881), *Idaho Tri-Weekly Statesman*, June 16, 1881; McLeod, p. 54; *Mining and Scientific Press*, XLIX (December 20, 1884): 386.

38. *Mining and Scientific Press*, XLIX (December 20, 1884): 386.

39. For a general survey of the topic, see Clark C. Spence, "The Livery Stable in the American West," *Montana: The Magazine of Western History*, XXXVI (Spring, 1986): 36–49.

40. "A. L. M." to editor (Hailey, June 7, 1881), *Idaho Tri-Weekly Statesman*, June 16, 1881.

41. *Wood River Times* (weekly), May 10, 1882.

42. *Wood River Times*, November 7, 1884.

43. *Wood River Times*, September 22, 1884.

44. *Wood River Times*, June 30, 1887.

45. *Wood River Times*, May 22, 1886.

46. *Wood River Times*, September 5, 1892 and August 11, 1894; Watkinson, p. 57.

47. *Wood River Times*, January 4, 1882. For a brief, general treatment of the commercial ice industry in early Idaho, see Herman Ronnenberg, "Idaho on the Rocks: The Ice Business in the Gem State," *Idaho Yesterdays*, XXXIII (Winter, 1990): 2–8.

48. *Wood River Times* (weekly), January 4, 1882.

49. *Wood River Times* (weekly), February 1, 1882; *Wood River Times*, May 20, 1882.

50. *Wood River Times*, May 23 and June 5, 1882.

51. *Wood River Times*, October 4 and December 21, 1882; February 26, April 30, and July 4, 1883.

52. *Wood River Times*, July 16, 1887 and January 8, 1894; *Wood River Times* (weekly), January 16, 1889.

53. Leonard J. Arrington, *History of Idaho* (Moscow: University of Idaho Press, 1994), I, pp. 294–95; *Daily News-Miner*, February 22, 1884; Watkinson, pp. 13, 15, 36, 37, 40.

54. *Wood River Times*, September 24, 1883.

55. *Wood River Times*, January 24, 1884 and May 5, 1886; *Wood River Times* (weekly), July 10 and August 7, 1889; Brooks, pp. 125-26, 127; McLeod, pp. 61-62; Watkinson, pp. 52–53; *Report of the Governor of Idaho, 1889*, p. 345.

56. *Wood River Times* (weekly), August 7, 1889; January 22 and June 18, 1890; *Wood River Times*, September 15, 1892 and July 21, 1893.

57. *Mining and Scientific Press*, XXXIX (December 13, 1879): 370; XLII (April 16, 1881): 245, 252; LII (March 20, 1886): 197.

58. *Wood River Miner*, April 5, 1882, quoted in *Mining and Scientific Press*, XLIV (April 15, 1882): 245.

59. These are United States Weather Bureau figures, those for temperature and precipitation based on thirteen years and those for snowfall the mean for eight years. See Joseph B. Umpleby, et al. "Geology and Ore Deposits of the Wood River Region, Idaho" ("With a Description of the Minnie Moore and Near-by Mines," by D. F. Hewett), U.S. Geological Survey *Bulletin* No. 814 (Washington: Government Printing Office, 1930), p. 8.

60. Lewis to Hauser (Ketchum, October 6, 1882), Hauser Papers, Box 7; *Mining and Scientific Press*, XLVI (January 13, 1883): 21.

61. Umpleby, et al., p. 8.

62. *Wood River Times* (weekly), January 18 and April 9, 1882.

63. *Wood River Times*, June 12, 1883.

64. "The Snowslide's Work," letter reprinted from the *Blackfoot Register*, March 5, 1881, in *Idaho Yesterdays*, XXX (Winter, 1992): 19–22.

65. Lewis to Hauser (Ketchum, February 20, 1884), Hauser Papers, Box 10; *Wood River Times*, April 2, 1884; *Mining and Scientific Press*, XLVIII (February 16, April 12, and June 7, 1884): 126, 261, 389.

66. Ron Watters, "The Long Snowshoe: Early Skiing in Idaho," *Idaho Yesterdays*, XXIII (Fall, 1979), p. 23; *Ketchum Keystone* (weekly), January 26, 1884; *Wood River Times*, February 5, 19, and 21, 1884.

67. *Wood River Times*, February 21 and 28, 1884.

68. This mammoth machine was brought out from New Jersey, tested at Shoshone, then put into regular use out of Ketchum. See *Wood River Times*, February 15 and 17, 1887.

69. *Engineering and Mining Journal*, XLVI (December 8, 1888): 486; C. Strahorn, pp. 589–90.

70. *Wood River Times* (weekly), January 29; February 12, 15, and 22; March 5 and April 2, 1890.

71. *Wood River Times,* February 28, 1887 and March 14, 1893.

72. Hawley, p. 398; *Wood River Times,* September 24, 1883 and December 16, 1886.

73. McLeod, p. 25.

74. Entry for February 9, 1883, *Journal of the Council,* Twelfth Session (1882–83), p. 201; law of February 8, 1883, *General Laws of the Territory of Idaho,* Twelfth Session (1882–83), pp. 85–119; laws of January 30 and February 5, 1885, *General Laws of the Territory of Idaho,* Thirteenth Session (1884–85), pp. 28–30, 34–38.

75. *Wood River Times,* October 1, 13, and 19, 1883; November 1, 5, and 14, 1883; Don L. Griswold and Jean Harvey Griswold, *The Carbonate Camp Called Leadville* (Denver: University of Denver Press, 1951), pp. 121–22; Arrington, *History of Idaho,* II, p. 214; McLeod, pp. 23, 53.

76. *Wood River Times,* December 14, 15, and 24, 1883.

77. Quoted in Sidney Alexander Mitchell, *S. Z. Mitchell and the Electrical Industry* (New York: Farrar, Straus & Cudahy, 1960), p. 48.

78. *Wood River Times,* August 15, 1882; May 20 and June 6, 1887; McLeod, pp. 23–24.

79. *Wood River Times,* November 16 and 30, December 6, 1881; January 11, April 5, June 26 and 30, September 6, 1882; September 7, 1883; November 4, 1884; April 6, 1885.

80. *Wood River Times,* January 4, 5, and 19, 1886; January 4, May 23, July 14, and October 28, 1887.

81. Act of February 3, 1885, *General Laws of the Territory of Idaho,* Thirteenth Session (1884–85), pp. 38–40.

82. McGonigal, pp. 123, 125, 126.

83. *Wood River Times* (weekly), December 12, 1884; *Wood River Times,* May 13, 1884.

84. *Wood River Times,* October 30, 1885.

85. *Wood River Times,* March 10, 1886.

86. Onderdonk, p. 72.

87. *Salt Lake Daily Tribune,* July 12, 1884; *Mining and Scientific Press,* XLII (April 16, 1881): 248.

88. *Ketchum Keystone* (weekly), February 2, 1882.

89. *Ketchum Keystone*, February 2 and May 18, 1882; "A. L. M." quoted in *Mining and Scientific Press*, XLII (June 18, 1881): 406; *Salt Lake Daily Tribune*, July 12, 1884; *Wood River Times*, March 24 and August 15, 1883; "A. L. M." to editor (Galena, June 21, 1881), *Idaho Tri-Weekly Statesman*, June 28, 1881.

90. As early as 1882, editor Picotte applied the term "Biddyville" to Bellevue, no doubt facetiously, giving rise to the myth—"one of the great bamboozles in the recorded history of Alturas and later Blaine counties" that the "Gate City" was originally named after early pioneer, Moses J. Biddy. For the demolition of that fiction, see John Price, "Footnote to History: Was There Ever a Biddyville?" *Idaho Yesterdays*, XXXV (Winter, 1992): 16–18.

91. C. Strahorn, p. 414; *Wood River Times* (weekly), November 11, 1881; Lewis, "Reminiscences," p. 182; McLeod, pp. 64–66; *Rupert v. Board of Commissioners of Alturas County*, 2 *Idaho Reports* (September 11, 1882), pp. 19–22.

92. *Mining and Scientific Press*, LXIX (December 20, 1884): 386; *Wood River Times*, January 4 and August 23, 1883.

93. *Ketchum Keystone*, May 18, 1883; "Pilgrim to editor" (Ketchum, January 5, 1881), *Wood River Times* (weekly), January 11, 1881; *Wood River Times*, August 19, 1882.

94. *Mining and Scientific Press*, XLIV (June 24, 1882): 412; *Wood River Times*, March 21, 1883.

95. *Wood River Times*, March 24, 1883.

96. *Wood River Times*, December 18, 1886.

97. Edward A. Stevenson, "Report of the Governor of Idaho," in *Report of the Secretary of Interior, 1887*, pp., 816, 817.

98. Ibid., p. 817.

99. *Wood River Times* (weekly), November 16, 1881; *Wood River Times*, June 15, 1882 and June 12, 1883.

100. *Wood River Times*, December 17 and 27, 1888; December 27, 1892.

CHAPTER SIX

THE UNDERSIDE OF WOOD RIVER

IT HAS BEEN fashionable in popular literature to depict mining towns as godless, lawless, untutored, and uncultured and to focus on violence, saloons, gaming houses, and prostitutes. Lively descriptions of early Wood River tend to do this, in the process giving readers in more "civilized" regions what they expected to hear. Take an account of Hailey, written for the St. Louis press late in 1881:

> Church services are not frequent, and schools do not flourish in the new town. Saloons, dance-houses and faro banks take their places and the accompanying gamblers and female beer-jerkers contribute their share to keep the place lively. The newspapers make no note of fist fights, and officers are instructed to make no arrests unless weapons are called into requisition. Only shooting and cutting scrapes attract more than passing attention. A fist fight is of about as much importance as a street dog fight. There is no Sunday: no Saturday night. Saloons and kindred places of amusement are open night and day, and business is fully as good at 4 A.M. as at 4 P.M.[1]

One wonders. To be sure, among Wood River's first residents were plenty of sharps, long on tricks and short on scruples. Isaac Lewis, who was elected justice of the peace in August 1880, recalled that "some desperate, murderous villains were tried before me," and that "there was a very bad element on Wood River for three or four years, thieves, gamblers and murderers and counterfeiters."[2]

Without accepting Lewis literally—such serious crimes as murder might not be heard before a justice of the peace, even in remote Idaho—there was a plethora of parasites and trouble-makers in the early waves. Many were loafers, so-called "chair-boarders" and "stove-herders" with no visible means of support who inhabited the saloons and the gambling halls. A Bellevue miner wrote a letter published in a Reno newspaper in which he referred to "More dead broke men here than I ever saw anywhere else in my life." "Gamblers look as shabby as Sacramento vagrants."[3] Hailey, too, had its winter hangers-on, "Bums, Beats, Beggars"—so many, reported editor Picotte, the master of farce, that there was talk of halting the practice of beating the gong at meal times at the Grand Central Hotel. "So many impecunious hungry ones are about that this frequent reminder of a spread is looked upon as a species of cruelty to animals."[4]

Even in the more mature towns, there would always be some of the spongers, some of them merely unfortunate, some of them congenitally lazy, like the "Ketchum Bruiser" a local wrote about in 1885 while whiling away his days in jail for arson:

> He said he was a bruiser bold,
> And from Ketchum he had come;
> That he never soiled his hands with work—
> His business was to bum.[5]

In addition, Wood River had its share of bullies cut from cloth common to mining camps.

He dresses in buckskin, goes armed to the teeth, wears long hair, and covers his head with a slouched hat of buckskin, and calls himself a "bad man to handle." When he gets especially jolly he walks through the town, harmlessly firing his pistol and yelling for blood.

One such blusterer late in 1881 was spoiling for a fight and demanded the "big injuns." He could lick any seven men in Hailey, he announced. Instead of seven, he was accommodated by a wiry little gambler who closed up both his eyes and "drew the claret from his proboscis," said the *Times.* Another of the same stripe, "Grizzley Bill," rode up and down the streets, shooting and demanding action, until Deputy Sheriff Steel faced him with his gun, whereupon "Grizzley Bill . . . smelled the unburnt powder in a big navy revolver" and spurred his horse in an unsuccessful attempt to escape.[6]

Law-abiding citizens pointed out that such episodes were endemic to primitive communities, but not typical of the rank and file. Yet they could not deny the presence of violence and crime, the stuff of which pulp and celluloid westerns would be made and which have always been much overdone. The days of murder and mayhem were brief, and mining towns had no monopoly on vice that cities elsewhere could not match. In an era of bare-knuckle journalism, Wood River newspapers gave crime graphic attention and matter-of-fact headlines. "John Palmer Plugged by Horace Lewis" was typical of the kind of shooting episode T. E. Picotte invariably referred to as "a pistol pop."[7]

Perhaps one of the best known "pistol pops" was at Vienna in the summer of 1882. Worthless George Pierson shot and killed good-for-nothing John Hall, better known as "Johnny-Behind-the Rocks," a name that resulted from another scrape in Nevada where Hall killed a man from behind a boulder. The Vienna dispute was over the favors of one Banjo Nell, a local trollop. When Pierson was tried in Hailey and sentenced to hang, Nell became

an involuntary ward of the town of Bellevue, and the case precipitated much interest in the Wood River population centers.
Pierson broke jail in 1883, was recaptured, and finally paid the
penalty for his crime, one of a very few persons actually executed
in the region in the 1880s.[8]

In 1884, a Chinese man, Kuok Wah Chol (also known as Ah
Sam) was indicted for first-degree murder, found guilty, and
hanged on September 18 of the following year. Samuel Ridgeway
had been sentenced to hanging for a murder committed in 1882,
but eventually Governor John B. Neil commuted his sentence to
life imprisonment. J. L. C. Smith, owner of Hailey Hot Springs,
was killed with a shotgun blast by his wife, Margaret, a much
abused woman, who, in the minds of citizens and courts was justified; a change of venue moved the case to Shoshone, and she
was acquitted.[9] Hardly had Margaret Smith been sent on her
blissful way when Wood River residents went through another
tear-jerker. In July 1890, Samuel G. Felsenthal shot and killed
John M. Kinnear, the superintendent of the Minnie Moore, then
took his own life. Felsenthal had been an assayer at the mine,
but lost his job when the operation shut down temporarily. His
wife acknowledged that she had had sexual relations with
Kinnear, but maintained that she had been raped.[10]

There were many other crimes, of course, ranging from theft
to stagecoach robbery and violent assault. Aaron, one of the
Morris brothers who owned a bank in Hailey and a business in
Ketchum, was killed and robbed of a substantial sum of money
while he rode between the two towns one night.

Men resorted to their guns to protect property or their own
person. During the annual New Year's Day round-up of abandoned claims, Captain Edie in Scorpion Gulch "had full need of
his double-barreled shotgun to convince would-be jumpers that
his extension of the Croesus was not re-locatable."[11]

Western society often put a higher value on personal honor
than on legal restraints, and preservation of honor, or what one

perceived as honor, sometimes brought on a "pistol pop." In the summer of 1886, when Robert Strahorn dismissed Charles H. Moore as manager of the Alturas Hotel because of unpaid bills, the stage was set for an explosion. In one day, Moore had been involved in a fistfight with his cook, his wife had engaged in a screaming match with the waiters, and a lien had been served on the dining room after the hotel guests had been seated at the table. Just at that point, the evening edition of the *Times* rolled off the press, with a few choice comments by Picotte's new man in charge, Colonel C. C. Russell, a Southerner who considered himself a "fighting editor," and who always went armed with a gun, as well as a vitriolic pen. This time, Russell outreached himself with a brief item: "The reason C. H. Moore was kicked out of the Alturas was that he did not pay his debts." Later in the day, the popular Moore, goaded to a fury, fired several shots at Russell, wounding him in the neck and groin (his poor marksmanship was attributable to the fact that he was missing several fingers on his shooting hand). Moore was charged with assault with a deadly weapon and fined $100, which friends collected for him. After four months, the Colonel had mended enough to travel and left town, "a sadder and a wiser man."[12]

Many of these shootings—crimes of passion, revenge, or alleged honor—were not indigenous to mining communities in the West: they might have happened in any town between the Pacific Coast and the Atlantic. Wood River was not lawless: Property and life were as safe there as anywhere. Indeed, genteel Carrie Strahorn thought Hailey was "the most orderly mining town imaginable, and its citizens were largely a class superior to those of frontier settlements."[13] Hailey was almost a year old before it felt "the need for a lockup" and fitted out a log house on River Street near Chinatown for the rowdy element. Two years later, when the new brick county courthouse authorized by the legislature was completed at a cost of about forty thousand dollars, its rock basement was fitted with five saw- and file-proof cells. The building itself had been designed and its construction begun by Horace Greeley Knapp, a "young architect and builder" from New York, who left Hailey "rather suddenly" before finishing the job, amid cries of deception and chicanery, leaving the county to complete the most expensive courthouse in Idaho.[14]

Law officers—local, county, and federal—were on the scene early. Town marshals and the Alturas County sheriff handled many of the infractions, often in a casual manner. Early in 1883, the territorial legislature in Boise codified the payment schedule for the sheriff to include a board allowance of $1 a day for each prisoner in the county jail; $.25 for each subpoena served; $2 for each arrest in a criminal proceeding; $8 for empaneling each grand jury; and $75 for executing a death sentence. Two years later it voted to allow Alturas County to pay $3,000 for the relief of former sheriff D. H. Gray, who had served in 1881 and 1882 before the Assembly sanctioned the county's largess to its chief law officer.[15]

In contrast with California and Montana, no vigilantes rode in Wood River, although once a few citizens expressed the opinion that a little "committee work" might reduce the rash of robberies. At Bullion in 1883, thirty-four "good, strong men" with .50-caliber rifles organized as the Mulligan Guards, more to drill and parade than to confront disorder, although some thought the group might also be useful in combating any disturbance or to prevent mine-jumping.[16] The only quasi-vigilante action occurred in 1885, when some fifty volunteers organized as the Bellevue Stranglers to protect the Minnie Moore Mine during a strike situation. This apparently was more a matter of miners wishing to preserve their jobs in the face of disruption by union men, not an issue of suppressing crime.[17]

Many people closely associated violence and crime with alcohol and institutions connected to it: saloons, gambling dens, and dance halls—all Satan's inventions. A few years before the

Wood River rush, a widely traveled man of the cloth remarked that western towns were cities of churches and saloons.

> *Whenever God erects a house of prayer,*
> *The devil always builds a chapel there;*
> *And 'twill be found upon examination,*
> *The latter has the largest congregation.*[18]

This characterization fitted the new Idaho diggings. Mining was hot, thirsty work, and whiskey flowed like the waters of the Big Wood itself. Along with Methodist teetotalers and devotees of the Cold Water Army, the towns included their share of inveterate topers—men like the Rocky Mountain cowboy who swore he "could drink whiskey in ten different languages."[19] When Isaac Lewis came down from Montana in the spring of 1880, near Galena Gulch he found a camp of prospectors, including Jim Hart from Boise, with a barrel of Valley Tan and a sign reading "Only 25¢ a drink, draw and drink all you want." Lewis took "a smile" as he called it, from the barrel and went on to the site of Ketchum to set up the first assay shop in the area. James Hart moved his whiskey barrel down and helped locate the town of Bellevue, but subsequently became a great booster of Hailey.[20]

From that humble beginning came a deluge. As the correspondent of the *Idaho Tri-Weekly Statesman* noted, by mid-1881 there were "too many gin mills on the river, Bellevue having eleven, Hailey eighteen and two breweries, Bullion nine and Ketchum about a dozen."[21] The suds factories were those of George Kohlepp and H. Vorbarg. "If you want to while [sic] away an hour comfortably while drinking a glass of good beer, go to George Kohlepp's Hailey Brewery," the newspaper promotions urged.[22] (Or without the advertising, one might be invited to wile away an hour even more rapidly at Molly's House, or some such place, where the alcohol was not the main article of trade.)

It has been estimated that Leadville had one saloon for roughly a hundred people in the 1880s. Bullion ran close to that in its heyday, but most Wood River towns probably had fewer proportionately. In the early 1880s, Ketchum had a ratio of one to about a hundred and twenty-five; Hailey, one to one hundred thirty-eight; Sawtooth was one for one hundred fifty; and Vienna one for two hundred.[23]

Although they were housed in tents, at least five of Hailey's watering holes were "first-class saloons." John Allen, formerly of Boise, had "the boss place so far," doing business at the corner of Bullion and Main in a tent over a hundred twenty feet in circumference under the sign "Coal Oil Johnny's Saloon, Open Day and Night." There the sound of glasses, the click of poker chips, the tinkling of the piano, and loud laughter were trademarks of a good time.[24]

As canvas gradually gave way to wood and then to brick or stone, places like "Coal Oil Johnny's" were supplanted by more sophisticated houses like Jim Rainey's saloon on Main Street in Hailey, said to have had a polished hardwood bar so slick it took a fly all day to walk across it.[25] When the big two-story Fitzimmons frame building went up in Ketchum late in 1883, the first floor housed Fritz's wholesale and retail liquor business, along with a swank club equipped with fine chandeliers and plate glass doors. Upstairs was a public hall with seventeen-foot ceilings, where the community's blue bloods danced. The structure "would be a credit even in New York City," Picotte of the *Times* remarked.[26]

To show that it had arrived, a substantial mining center had to have a drinking place of size and elegance that set it apart from the run-of-the-mill establishments, of which there were always plenty. With a long, hand-sculpted bar of oak or walnut, preferably by Brunswick-Balke-Callender of Chicago, a polished brass rail at its base, and backed by a large mirror flanked with bottles, the first-class saloon usually boasted multiple tables, a piano, and an array of spittoons, ideally one for every four or five patrons. On the walls hung artwork to be appreciated by a masculine clientele—sometimes nude or barely draped female figures like "Aphrodite Emerging from the Bath" or more often photographs of red-blooded favorites like heavyweight champion John L. Sullivan, the Boston Strong Boy, or the great racehorse, Maud S. Perhaps it is a delusion that miners were a macho lot who liked to stand ankle-deep in sawdust at the bar and toss down straight rotgut whiskey at twenty-five cents a throw. Some no doubt did, and the dingy dives purveying cheap, powerful "forty-rod," "old pop-skull," or "tanglefoot" did a good business. While they resented any effort to "baptize" their booze (i.e., water it down) many customers went for more sophisticated drinks created by a specialist in such things—a "mixologist" or a "spiritualist" he or she might be called casually.[27]

Even as early as 1881, newspaper advertisements gave great promise:

A BIT SALOON!

FRENCH & PURVIANCE

HAVE JUST OPENED ON

MAIN STREET, ONE DOOR NORTH OF WELLS, FARGO

& CO.'S EXPRESS OFFICE

HAILEY.

A SALOON, WHERE FIRST CLASS WINES, LIQUORS, AND

CIGARS ARE SERVED AT

ONE BIT! ONE BIT! ONE BIT!

GO AND SEE THEM.[28]

Nineteenth-century Americans in general and Wood Riverites in particular were likely to bend the elbow on most any occasion. The blowing in of Falk's new furnace, the opening of a place of business, or an anti-Chinese rally called for a nip. If a man struck it rich or sold his claim, that too might mean a drinking spree, not only for him but for all of his friends. Marriages and births brought festive uncorking of the bottle; death often brought men together in alcoholic mourning, especially if the Irish were involved.[29]

Christmas filled saloons with drinkers of such cold weather specialties as negus, hot toddies, or Tom and Jerrys. It was an old American folk adage that "Nobody goes dry/on the Fourth of July." A proper Independence Day celebration always meant cold beer and iced mixed drinks, often with an acute hangover as a chaser.

> *Lovers of Liberty and beer,*
> *We welcome you from far and near,*
> *We welcome you around this rag,*
> *To shout for freedom while we brag.*
>
> *All honor to our brave Squedunks,*
> *All honor to our brave dead-drunks!*
> *Some are groveling in the gutter,*
> *While some have gone home on a shutter.*[30]

Speaking of the Independence Day celebration of 1882, the Ketchum editor noted: "A large percentage of the young men living on Wood River had to hold their heads out of doors until they shrunk enough to permit getting their hats on." Some of the revelers that time no doubt had been at the opening of Isaac Lewis's new Guyer Hot Springs bar, restaurant, and bath, where Judge Henry Prickett, former territorial associate justice, was the orator before the picnic dinner in a shady grove and where the bar receipts ran $253 for the day.[31]

Heavy drinking often brought more than morning-after problems. For some, like Charley Swan, an old miner who came down from Butte with Isaac Lewis, it meant complete disaster. Swan made a pretense of enterprise, but spent most of his time in the saloons drinking and gambling. Ultimately, he headed back to Montana, mixed himself a laudanum cocktail, "and lay down to sleep forever" in a Butte livery stable.[32]

One of the primary functions of the early jails was to serve as a sobering-up place for local drunks like Hogan, "the schtiff," who was a regular visitor in the Ketchum cooler—and the Ada County slammer in Boise as well.[33] Drink was often the underlying cause of brawls and violence, some of which left combatants with cracked skulls or mutilated noses, ears, or even fingers bitten off. Many of the "pistol pops" stemmed directly from barroom quarrels like the one between a belligerent fellow named Biles and a shoemaker named Uhl, which began with Biles repeatedly calling Uhl "hard names" and ended with his shooting Uhl in the face with a revolver.[34]

Another danger, perhaps less common, but still very real, stemmed from the erroneous idea that alcohol warmed the body. In reality, liquor reduces body temperature and acts as a depressant. In substantial amounts, it can cause deep sleep, a danger in cold winter climes like Wood River. Frozen corpses were not unusual and their occurrence provided another occasion for bluenose newsmen to preach against over-indulgence.[35]

As they were elsewhere in America, saloon owners were regarded as upstanding citizens in the community, and their establishments assumed an importance beyond the dispensation of beverages. The saloon was a business enterprise that normally required substantial capital for equipment: the bar itself, tables, chairs, stove, glassware, and a basic stock of liquor and ice. The cost of setting up a good saloon in a prosperous town ranged from $7,000 to $10,000, but some went as high as $20,000. The more elaborate almost always offered gambling and dancing along with drinking. They were usually located on a prominent corner in the business district and were active centers of a town's trade.[36]

In 1884, Sheriff Charles H. Furey, as was his duty, issued licenses to eighteen saloon keepers in Hailey and seven in Bullion. The numbers in Bellevue and Ketchum were less definite; he probably issued fifteen for Ketchum. At that time, Hailey had twelve gambling licenses and Ketchum eight. It is clear that both drinking and gambling houses were excellent sources of public revenue. Saloon taxes ran $9,800 in one year alone. City fathers and pious residents alike saw the advantage of the alchemy involved—levies that converted dirt to gold.[37]

Successful bar owners, and even gambling hall proprietors, often played an active role in public celebrations such as holiday festivals, balls, or other occasions like the Sunday school picnic in the summer of 1881, where the proprietor of Hailey's Parlor Saloon appeared in starched, white apron to distribute candy and lemonade.[38] Such men were upright civic leaders; they were open, gregarious, generous, and honest, according to tradition.

The saloon itself was more than a mere watering place. It has been called the club of the working man; it was a social and recreational center and more. In mining camps, it often had a cabinet displaying ore samples from local mines, an exhibit that was a matter of pride and of use to the miners, not to mention fostering a kind of boosterism that helped business. "It is hard to trace the connection between the sale of whiskey and a taste for mineralogy, but there it is!" a California editor once noted.[39] Saloon business was often large enough to warrant keeping a safe, frequently the first in town. The barkeeper was usually willing to deposit the customers' cash or valuables for safekeeping, generally as a free service.[40]

The local drinking houses were often meeting places. Volunteers planning a rescue mission to the Kelley mine after the avalanche of 1881 assembled at William Parsons' Bellevue Watering Hole. Merchants of Hailey met at Faylor's Saloon early in March 1882 to discuss hiring a night watchman until either the town or the county provided protection. When a group of indignant Ketchumites met two years later to denounce and pass resolutions against the Chinese, they convened in Easley's Saloon.[41]

If one chose to do his drinking in private, he could purchase a wide variety from retailers around Wood River. May, Kreig and Company, general merchandiser in Hailey in the summer of 1882, advertised a California white wine, "a splendid drink in such hot weather as this" at only $1.50 a gallon from its Main Street store. The Wine House, next to the post office in Bellevue, offered a broad selection. Big retail dealers, like Fitz's in Hailey, had imported bourbon, Scotch, brandy, gin, California wines, Irish whiskey, and cases of champagne, ale, and porter.[42]

Those who wouldn't be caught dead in a saloon or liquor store could buy water at fifty cents a barrel delivered in Hailey by Sam Jones. At Riley and Tracy's Drugstore, people could purchase "Dr. Hohly's Celebrated Miners' Bitters, a superior tonic and appetizer," no doubt with as high an alcoholic content as the California wines or perhaps even Lydia E. Pinkham's Vegetable Compound for women, which at nearly 20 percent alcohol was even more potent.[43] The world of patent medicine was full of products like Ballard's Horehound Syrup, Dr. B. J. Dendall's Blackberry Balsam, or "Indian Sachem's Electric Health Restorer," all with an alcoholic content of over 60 percent.[44]

Many saloons also included dance floors and gambling facilities. After all, wasn't mining itself a form of gambling—an underground lottery? Wasn't it rough, dirty, throat-parching work that justified occasionally kicking up the heels or "bucking the tiger" (so-called because early establishments featuring faro games displayed a picture of the striped beast).

Gambling followed the saloons closely and tapered off as the boom period passed. Odds invariably favored the house, even when the games were honest, which was often not the case. Tinhorn gamblers and dedicated professionals alike tended to be drifters, following in their own way the siren call of precious metal. A few were women, although the calling was predominantly a masculine one.

At the same time, as one faro bank operator noted, the lot of the gambler was not an easy one. "It is a dog's life. It keeps a man on the strain day and night, and I don't wonder that so many gamblers lose their minds. Then it throws a man into the meanest and most unprincipled crowd of rascals that walk the earth."[45]

If novelists and eastern visitors created a romantic image of the gambler, even western critics of the evils of such businesses could recognize positive traits in their proprietors. Some lauded them for their grubstaking of prospectors and their liberal contributions to charity. Ethelbert Talbot, Episcopal bishop of Idaho and Wyoming, knew well Joe Oldham, the popular operator of a Hailey gambling hall, and thought highly of this tall, dignified man who wore "a faultless suit of broadcloth" and acted in a "most gracious and dignified manner," especially when he invariably slipped a twenty-dollar gold piece into the Bishop's hand. Despite his profession, Oldham was "a generous soul, warm hearted and loyal to his friends. His kindness to the widow and the orphan, to the man hurt in the mines, and to all in trouble, made him greatly beloved."[46]

In any isolated boom camp where men outnumbered women by five to one or even ten to one, the feminine touch in the barroom, at the gambling table, and on the dance floor could only enhance business. The so-called "pretty waiter girls" in the saloons attracted customers; and the Hurdy-gurdy dance hall girls made good profits for the proprietors as they danced with all comers for a set charge per round and encouraged their partners to ante up for the house drinks, overpriced as they were.

Normally, the "pretty waiter girls" and the Hurdy-gurdy girls were not prostitutes, although some did augment their regular income after hours. But the world's oldest profession was an integral part of western life, especially in the male-dominated camps, where flocks of prostitutes appeared as if by magic to help separate the lucky miner from his new-found wealth: First came the miners to work in the mine, / Then came the ladies who lived on the line.[47]

Every town had its thriving "sporting district," conveniently located on a live-and-let-live basis, like that of Hailey on River Street.[48] The "girls" were beyond the pale of respectability and legally or implicitly limited to specific areas. Some worked in fancy houses, some out of rooms in the dance halls, and some in squalid cribs just off the sidewalks. These "single men's wives" had their own caste system, with Chinese, Hispanics, and African American women at the lower end, and with drugs, alcohol, and suicide often part of their sordid world. Because local census takers were loathe to ruin a town's image, few sporting women appear in the returns. The profession remained generally invisible, carried officially as "servants," female "hotel keepers," or "boarders." Few census takers were as frank as one in western Kansas who wrote of one: she "does 'horizontal' work."[49]

Although all but invisible to newspaper editors, the highly mobile girls of the line and of the better-class brothels were more obvious to those who knew where to look in the Wood River towns, but polite society elsewhere on the scene chose to ignore them. Eastern writers and their reaction to the red light district had much to do with creating an image of mining camps among Americans in general.

Something of a bluenose, a bit naïve, and, in her gentle way, a snob, Carrie Strahorn was impressed and thought Hailey an unforgettable, exciting place, yet comfortable and secure. "Everything was happening that always happens in new camps; saloons, dance halls, and gambling dens far outnumbered any other money-making or money-losing enterprises. . . . Yet with all the wild dissipation one never heard of a woman being insulted or assaulted and those very debauchers would shoot to kill any one who would molest the fair sex."[50]

CHAPTER SIX NOTES

1. Correspondent to *St. Louis Globe Democrat* (Omaha, November 20, 1881), quoted in *Wood River Times* (Hailey) (weekly), December 7, 1881.

2. Isaac I. Lewis, "Reminiscences," (Ketchum, March 28, 1892), typescript, p. 175, American Heritage Center, University of Wyoming.

3. *Wood River Times,* March 28, 1884; *Wood River Times* (weekly), May 3, 1882.

4. *Wood River Times,* January 22, March 13, and April 20, 1883.

5. William B. Campbell, "The Ketchum Bruiser," quoted in *Wood River Times,* October 23, 1885.

6. *Wood River Times* (weekly), December 7, 1881.

7. *Wood River Times,* October 17, 1883 and October 25, 1884.

8. *Wood River Times* (weekly), August 30 and December 6, 1882; *Wood River Times,* March 12, August 17, and September 8, 1883; George A. McLeod, *Histories of Alturas and Blaine Counties Idaho* (Hailey: Hailey Times, 1938), p. 140; *People v. Pierson,* 2 *Idaho Reports* (February 20, 1884), p. 79.

9. *People v. Kuok Wah Chol,* 2 *Idaho Reports* (February 17, 1885), pp. 90-95; Carrie Adell Strahorn, *Fifteen Thousand Miles by Stage* (New York and London: G. P. Putnam's Sons, 1911, reprint, Lincoln and London: University of Nebraska Press, 1988), pp. 583, 585; McLeod, pp. 139, 141, 143.

10. *Wood River Times* (weekly), July 23, 1890; *Weekly Wood River News-Miner* (Hailey), July 25, 1890.

11. Juanita Brooks, *History of the Jews in Utah and Idaho* (Salt Lake City: Western Epics, 1973), pp. 126–27; *Wood River Times,* January 3, 1887.

12. *Wood River Times,* July 21, 1886; McLeod, pp. 171–73; C. Strahorn, pp. 531–32. In mid-March, 1886, Picotte had announced that he would retain ownership of the *Times,* but that "editorial charge and direction" would be in the hands of the "wide-viewed" Russell. See *Wood River Times,* March 15, 1886.

13. C. Strahorn, p. 421.

14. *Wood River Times* (weekly), March 22, 1882; *Journal of the Council of the Twelfth Legislative Assembly of the Territory of Idaho Convened on the Eleventh Day of December, A.D. 1882, and Adjourned on the Eighth Day of February, A.D. 1883* (Boise: Milton Kelly, Territorial Printer, 1883), pp. 102, 204; McLeod, pp. 57–58. Early in 1883, the Twelfth Assembly had sanctioned the issue of $40,000 in 6 percent bonds by Alturas County, and went so far as to specify a foundation "of durable stone, the walls of good brick." See Act of February 8, 1883, *General Laws of the Territory of Idaho Passed at the Twelfth Session of the Territorial Legislature Convened on the Eleventh Day of December, A.D. 1882, and Adjourned on the Eighth Day of February, A.D. 1883, at Boise City* (Boise: Milton Kelly, Territorial Printer, 1883), pp. 119–22; *Wood River Times*, June 5 and 6 and October 3, 1883; January 12, 1884; Waller B. Wigginton, "The Pounds in Hailey," *Rendezvous*, IV (Spring, 1969): 35.

15. Act of February 6, 1883, *General Laws of the Territory of Idaho,* Twelfth Session (1882–83), pp. 83–84; *General Laws of the Territory of Idaho Passed at the Thirteenth Session of the Territorial Legislature Convened on the Eighth Day of December, A D. 1884, and Adjourned on the Fifth Day of February, A.D. 1885, at Boise City* (Boise: James A. Pinney, Territorial Printer, 1885), pp. 27–28.

16. *Wood River Times*, March 29, 1883 and August 20, 1884.

17. Frank Thomason, "The Bellevue Stranglers," *Idaho Yesterdays*, XIII (Fall, 1949): 31–32.

18. W. W. Ross, *10,000 Miles by Land and Sea* (Toronto: James Campbell & Son, 1876), p. 17.

19. Lispenard Rutgers, *On and Off the Saddle* (New York: G. P. Putnam's Sons, 1894), p. 75.

20. Lewis, "Reminiscences," pp. 168-69; *Idaho Tri-Weekly Statesman* (Boise), June 4, 1881.

21. "H" to editor (Hailey, July 18, 1881), *Idaho Tri-Weekly Statesman*, July 21, 1881.

22. "A. L. M." to editor (June 7, 1881), *Idaho Tri-Weekly Statesman*, June 14, 1881; *Wood River Times* (weekly), June 22, 1882.

23. Elliott West, *The Saloon on the Rocky Mountain Frontier*

(Lincoln and London: University of Nebraska Press, 1979), p. 122. Wood River figures are based on rough estimates of both population and the number of saloons in the early 1880s, statistics that are general, to say the least.

24. "H" to editor (Hailey, April 29, 1881), *Idaho Tri-Weekly Statesman*, May 7, 1881.

25. *Wood River Times*, March 27 and April 14, 1883.

26. *Wood River Times*, May 10, 1884.

27. *Wood River Times*, January 25, 1882.

28. *Wood River Times*, June 22, 1881.

29. *Wood River Times*, September 28, 1881.

30. *Wood River Times*, July 6, 1881.

31. *Ketchum Keystone*, July 6, 1882; Lewis, "Reminiscences," p. 180.

32. *Helena Daily Herald*, September 12, 1881; Lewis, "Reminiscences," p. 175.

33. *Wood River Times*, May 13, 1887. One well-known photograph of 1901 shows "Hogan the Stiff," described as "Boise's town drunk," posing with the Ada County Sheriff and others. See Merle Wells, *Boise: An Illustrated History* (Woodland Hills, California: Windsor Publications, Inc., 1982), p. 71.

34. *People v. Biles*, 2 Idaho Reports (February 25, 1885), pp. 114–19.

35. *Wood River Times*, January 4 and November 29, 1882.

36. The standard work on western drinking oases and their proprietors is West's *Saloon on the Rocky Mountain Mining Frontier*.

37. West, *Saloon*, p. 102; McLeod, p. 60.

38. *Wood River Times*, August 17, 1881.

39. *Wood River Times*, March 29, 1882; *The Engineer* (San Francisco), I (October, 1876): 2.

40. *Wood River Times*, November 1, 1882.

41. "The Snowslide's Work," letter from the Blackfoot Register, March 5, 1881, in *Idaho Yesterdays*, XXX (Winter, 1992): 18; *Wood River Times*, March 1, 1882 and February 12, 1884; *Ketchum Keystone* (weekly), April 5, 1884.

42. *Wood River Times,* July 12 and November 29, 1882; March 27, 1883.

43. *Wood River Times,* May 20 and December 20, 1882.

44. Richard Erdoes, *Saloons of the Old West* (New York: Alfred A. Knopf, 1979), pp. 44, 98–100.

45. Ethelbert Talbot, *My People of the Plains* (New York and London: Harper & Brothers, 1906), pp. 147–48.

46. Talbot, pp. 67, 69.

47. W. P. A. Writer's Program, *Copper Camp* (New York: Hastings House, 1943), p. 175.

48. A sound, thoughtful article, although it has little specifically on Wood River, is Elliott W. West, "Scarlet West: The Oldest Profession in the Trans-Mississippi West," *Montana: The Magazine of Western History,* XXXI (April, 1881): 16–27. See also Anne M. Butler, *Daughters of Joy, Sisters of Mercy: Prostitutes in the American West 1865–90* (Urbana and Chicago: University of Illinois Press, 1985), and Marion S. Goldman, *Gold Diggers & Silver Miners: Prostitution and Social Life on the Comstock Lode* (Ann Arbor: University of Michigan Press, 1981), both excellent works although they do not deal with Idaho.

49. Joseph W. Snell, *Painted Ladies of the Cowtown Frontier* (Kansas City, Mo.: Kansas City Posse of the Westerners, 1965), p. 3.

50. C. Strahorn, p. 473.

"SAMSON SEEMED TO ENJOY THE FUN"

IF INHABITANTS SPENT too much time boozing, bucking the tiger, or patronizing the cribs or brothels of the towns, it is more impressive to look at the opposite side of the coin to see what else they were doing—especially the majority who were God-fearing and law-abiding. Basically they were seeking to establish the same kind of society they had known before; they wanted to retreat to the usual patterns of American life.[1]

At first, egalitarianism seemed to prevail, but after a year or two "of joining hands with everybody in a social way," according to Carrie Strahorn, some of the Hailey elite met secretly to exclude the gambling and saloon elements from social functions. Circulars and even invitations signed "By Order of the Committee" weeded out the riffraff and established a mild caste system, of which Mrs. Strahorn strongly approved:

From that time on parties were as select as anywhere in the United States, and no gentleman appeared at a dinner or other social affair except in the conventional dress suit. . . . Hailey was ever an unusual town for its social culture and conventionalities

and when the line for the four hundred was drawn, it was so clev-
erly brought about that no one was offended.[2]

Yet compromises often had to be made. When the ladies in
Hailey gathered for afternoon tea during Carrie Strahorn's first
year, each brought her own plate, knife, fork, and spoon and
often her own chair. If the elegant and matronly Mrs. Strahorn
had established herself as a kind of social arbiter, her role may
have been limited. Whether her influence extended beyond "the
best people" to the average Wood Riverite is questionable.[3]

Dancing was a popular recreation, and, like drinking, often a
celebration of some unusual occasion—the completion of the
rail-road, the opening of a new hotel, or a major holiday. A gala
affair held in Hailey before the rail lines came in was much in
keeping with Carrie Strahorn's philosophy:

> There were the unusual conditions of a new mining town and
> everybody was at the ball from bartenders and table waiters to
> miners, merchants, professional men, and ministers of the Gospel
> with their wives and sweethearts. . . . Every man wore a full-dress
> suit.[4]

In addition to the larger dance extravaganzas, there were
many smaller ones sponsored by specific clubs. As early as 1881,
members of the F.F.P.C. ("First Families from Pike County")
formed the Ketchum Silk Stocking Club, a social dance group,
which planned to trip the light fantastic every two weeks at the
newly-completed Baxter's Hall. At least one of its affairs was a
decided success, as its members' "lively steps kept time to the
soul-stirring music of the Ketchum String Band."[5] Not to be out-
done, the Hailey Theater Social Club sponsored a number of
exciting affairs, dancing to the beat of Dixie Boone or Professor
Delius and his full quadrille band. One ball early in 1883 had a
goodly number of couples "and wonder of wonders!—THREE
EXTRA LADIES." The club was delighted. As its next regular

dance, they planned a grand masquerade ball at the Grand Central Hotel, admission one dollar and supper one dollar extra. Masquerades were always popular. Friedman's store on Main Street stocked masks for them and local seamstresses announced their availability for sewing costumes.[6]

Some affairs were more formal. The initial "sociable" of the Hailey Saturday Night Quadrille Club early in 1884 was attended by forty-three gentlemen and thirty-six ladies. Wrote editor Picotte: "for the first time in the history of terpsichorean festivities in this city, printed programmes were supplied, and—wonder of wonders!—actually adhered to."[7]

Even in Bullion, "a fine lot of old stiffs" organized dancing classes, while Long's dancing school at the Hall of French and Stinson in Hailey instructed gentlemen on Tuesday evenings and ladies and children at other times, charging a fee of seventy-five cents per lesson.[8]

Ketchum had the first silver coronet band on the River, but Bellevue soon had a twelve-piece brass band, although town rivalries intervened when the quality of the local ensembles were being assessed. Editor Picotte was less than objective when he described the more sprightly numbers of the Ketchum band as like "a regiment of tom-cats with their tails tied together and strung on a clothes-line," while its more sedate selections resembled "the last groan of a dying calf."[9] Most other people enjoyed their music, as they did that of the Hailey Quartet Club and the Hailey Choral Association, both formed in 1882.[10]

In 1882 and 1883, Ketchum had both a debating club and the Alturas Literary Society, but Hailey's young people's efforts to organize a drama group were a disappointment.[11] Bellevue formed a minstrel group, a company of "Ethiopian delineators" they were called. Seventeen of the Knights of the Burnt Cork were well received at the Coliseum in the Gate City and were booked to perform at the Hailey Theater in June 1883. Bellevue also organized the Hawthorne Club, which was both literary and musical. They held benefits and debated important questions like "Resolved, That Bellevue will become the largest and most influential city on Wood River."[12]

About the same time some of the old fuddy-duddies got a self-improvement society going: meeting in the Hailey schoolhouse, they sang gospel hymns and college songs, listened to Professor Gilbert Butler on the organ, and heard a "declamation" and anecdotes from their members, who included two ministers. Less serious were Hailey's Order of the Cranks and Bellevue's Liars Club, The Damphools, both of them full of foolishness. By 1884, Hailey had also founded an Association of Pioneers of the Pacific Coast, comprised of old-timers on the Pacific Slope. Rumor was that the more than four hundred members might control Wood River politics, but it never came to that.[13]

Lectures were frequent in the Wood River towns: serious listeners could hear one of their own, Civil War General George Roberts of Hailey, hold forth on "Joan of Arc," "a rare treat" for only fifty cents admission or a dollar for the course. In 1883 Wiley McDowell spoke on "Woman's Rights," a topic editor Picotte thought important "in Europe and with Squaws," but superfluous in Wood River, where "the ladies rule, and it is the patient, suffering man whose wrongs need to be redressed." A few years later, when Bellevue students debated woman suffrage and decided twenty-four to four that women ought to be able to vote, the *Times* had a much more positive view. "Bellevue Kids on the Right Side," read the headline.[14]

As transportation improved, more outside attractions arrived, many of them making the Salt Lake City-Idaho-Montana swing. Professor G. E. Gailey, "Famous Illusionist and Wizard Violinist," shared a card with Percy Williams, "the Pleasing Character Vocalist and Humorist," with performances in Bullion, Hailey, and Bellevue. "Zamloch, the Wizard," did a clever magician's act in Hailey; Professor McDonald of San

Francisco promised lectures on phrenology as soon as his trunk arrived from Boise; Abigail Scott Duniway, the pioneer Oregon suffrage leader, lectured several times on women's rights; and Madam Ombra Esparaza Luis spoke in the Hailey Theater on the "Negro Race: its Past, Present, and Future" and on the "Habits and Customs of Haitians."[15] Wood River audiences relaxed with Sam Spence, "silver-tongued tenor," and the Savannah Minstrels; they enjoyed Katie Putnam starring in "Lena, the Madcap"; and were convulsed with laughter as actor Jack Langrishe did a five-night run of "Man in a Maze" at the Hailey Theater—admission, $1.00, reserved seats, $1.25. Perhaps they were more subdued when Nellie Boyd's touring company presented seven "emotional and society dramas" in late August and early September, 1882.[16]

In most mining towns, theaters, or opera houses as they were often called, provided facilities for respectable dramatic and musical events, dances, or public dinners and fund raisers, as opposed to the less wholesome entertainment of the saloons or hurdy-gurdy houses. The forty-by-fifty-foot Hailey Theater on Main Street served these purposes well. Connected by a hallway to an adjoining restaurant, it had a seating capacity of 500, and boasted a large stage with footlights, dressing rooms, and a drop-curtain comparable to those in large urban theaters: "a landscape viewed through a grand archway with mountains, streams, and cottages in the background. . . ." A gallery of "family circle boxes" was added, suspended from the ceiling to keep the floor free for dancing.[17]

Such structures hosted both traveling shows and local efforts. In Hailey, many of the cultural events seem to have been dominated by the Ladies Guild of the Episcopal Church, and for a time especially by the stalwart Pound family, all musically or theatrically inclined: Homer, the U. S. Land Office Register; his wife, Isabel; his sister; Florence Foote; and Florence's husband, David H. Foote. Florence had studied in Philadelphia and gave instruction on the harp, organ, and piano in Hailey. Foote came to Wood River as an assayer from Salt Lake City and was employed for a time in Pound's office before he entered into partnership with John J. Tracy in a drugstore at the corner of Bullion and Main, only to withdraw soon to devote himself to music full time. He went into business with "Professor" Delius, leader of the popular dance orchestra, organized the Hailey Glee Club, and eventually became director of the Hailey Silver Band, in which he played E-flat cornet.[18]

Only a few months after his arrival in Wood River, Homer Pound was serving as secretary of the somewhat nebulous Hailey Literary Society, and early in 1884 he helped manage the highly successful opening event of the Saturday Night Quadrille Club. Not long thereafter, just before he went east to take a bride, he played a role in the three-act comedy, "Married Life," to benefit the Episcopal building fund.[19]

His new wife (nee Isabel Weston of New York City) would soon be active in plays and performances, especially functions of the Ladies Guild. At the Guild's sociable at the Theater on July 16, 1885, where Florence Foote accompanied her husband's solo, Isabel, six months pregnant, starred as a matron in a skit, "Peak Family," while a number of other women played "virgins from distant Alaska."[20] In most of Hailey's amateur musical and theatrical events in the mid-1880s, the Pounds and the Footes were active participants.[21] They enjoyed generally favorable reviews until 1886, when Picotte's *Times* began to viciously castigate "the Mossback Mutual Admiration Society." [22]

More than once, traveling medicine shows provided both entertainment and "cures" for a variety of ailments. Typical was Dr. Joseph Durham's Kickapoo Sagua Remedy Company, which did an estimated one thousand dollars' worth of business in its short stay in Hailey. Durham practiced on-the-spot dentistry, medicine, and surgery and was said to charge according to the gullibility of his patients. He was assisted by two gifted black men and two Indians, who alternated song and dance routines with hawking tonic, liniment, salve, electric belts, and Dr. Durham's own book of remedies and cures to the audience. Unfortunately, the good doctor later ran afoul of both the law and a jilted sweetheart, who aimed a bullet at him but put it through his diploma from the American Eclectic Medical College of Cincinnati instead, before he fled town with his bride of two months.[23]

Children of all ages marveled at the circuses that came to Wood River. J. B. Shaw's Silver-Plate Circus & McKee's Museum of Living Wonders had hardly left Hailey in the summer of 1884 when W. W. Cole's Colossal Shows arrived. Its visit became a legend in its own time, although how much of the legend is fact and how much is T. E. Picotte is hard to say. Early in August, while three thousand people jammed Hailey in anticipation, the twenty-one-car Cole circus train steamed in, including Samson, the five-ton elephant. According to Picotte, who issued a special supplement for the occasion, Samson went on his annual toot, smashed three flatcars "into kindling wood," rolled the lion cage over three times, demolished four wagons (one an ore carrier), and killed three horses. All the while, according to Ezra Pound, who got the story second-hand from his father "twenty times over," "you could have seen the cowboys out after it, letting off their six-shooters into its rear." Actually, as Picotte's *Times* pointed out, fifteen or twenty local marksmen—prominent Haileyites—peppered away, without effect, with everything "from the small bird shotgun to the heaviest two-ounce Winchester" until Samson's keepers brought him under control with hot crowbars and hobbles and finally led him away "gentle as a lamb." "Samson seemed to enjoy the fun," said Picotte, and "elephant hunting was just what the sports of Hailey had longed for for a long time."[24]

Cole's subsequent circus posters would feature "mighty Samson . . . the elephant which nearly destroyed the beautiful town of Hailey, Idaho." It was good promotion, local boosters thought:

It proved Cole would visit a one-horse town. As to Samson, eventually he was reported to have perished in a fire in Bridgeport, Connecticut, and his bones mounted at the American Museum of Natural History in New York City.[25]

Other circuses followed, including Robinson's in the following summer, although the elephants were not as large as Cole's, and the procession only half as long. J. B. Cushing's one-ring circus was scheduled to perform the same summer, but in Ketchum it was attached for non-payment of San Francisco debts. It was ten days before the show could be reorganized and play in Hailey.[26] Cole's circus was back again in the fall of 1886, including W. F. Carver, sharpshooter extraordinaire; White Cloud, "the Noted Young Sioux Chief"; "50 cages of the Earth's Rarest Zoology"; but above all "mighty Samson"—"God's Most Wondrous Creation."[27]

Picotte's *Wood River Times* was a kind of circus in itself. The Waspish Canadian-born editor also had a puckish streak. Who else could, out of whole cloth, create the "Camas Wild Man," reported by cowboys late in 1882 as a muscular giant, thick black hair over his body, fingers like claws, tusks protruding from his mouth and able to jump fifteen feet "growling terribly as he went." Newspapers in Butte, Salt Lake City, and San Francisco copied the story, and, according to Picotte, so did the *Illustrated Police News* of London, which included a half-page illustration of the creature. While hunting parties allegedly sought to capture the brute, Picotte strung everybody along for several months. Alas, in early 1883, the editor of the rival *Bellevue Sun* "killed off" Picotte's wild man and the hoax was revealed, thus depriving Wood River "of a great deal of free advertising" in the eastern and foreign press, Picotte complained.[28]

Holidays were always celebrated with enthusiasm and the appropriated alcoholic lubrication. According to the census of 1880, the population of all of the Territory of Idaho was only 32,610.[29] But at the Fourth of July festivities in the following year,

T. A. Picotte's stern visage in his GAR uniform belies his puckish approach as long-time editor of Hailey's *Wood River Times. Idaho State Historical Society*

about three thousand people were supposed to have been present, largely miners and railroad workers from the Utah and Idaho Northern. Hailey's Independence Day celebration two years later had "the biggest crowd ever assembled there," a little more than three thousand. The imposing parade was headed by a brass band and the Miner's Union of Bullion—four hundred strong and dressed in their best. Following came an estimated two hundred floats and vehicles of all types, including a grand "pageant of beauty" hayrack drawn by six horses and carrying "Miss Idaho," plus a representative damsel from each of the then thirty-eight states and most of the territories—all beautiful, but modestly covered from chin to shin. The band played "Columbia, the Gem of the Ocean," the Hailey Choral Union sang the national anthem, and the crowd heard the reading of the Declaration of Independence, followed by a twenty-minute declamation by the Honorable J. H. Harris and lunch at Dorsey's Grove. Next, the citizens returned to town to enjoy the antics of the "procession of horribles"—a group of zany cut-ups who marched as the "Pacific Coast Pie-on-ears" and the "Bellevue Band," a group with huge elongated tin horns and rectangular-shaped trombones. Bands played through the afternoon, horse racing began, and in the evening came the fireworks display. The town's buildings were decorated with flags and evergreen boughs

Hailey Fourth of July parade, 1883. *Idaho State Historical Society*

and all the while its twenty saloons worked overtime. Frequent brawls broke out, especially between the Green and the Orange, who may have confused the date with St. Patrick's Day. For the better social strata, the day ended with a Grand Independence Ball.[30]

Equally impressive, although not without its glitches, was the combined Fourth of July and Statehood celebration of 1890, when Idaho was admitted to the Union. Along with the usual brass bands, hose companies and marching Grand Army of the Republic (G.A.R.) veterans, the parade featured producing mining properties. Large flags bore the names of individual mines and were followed by a number of employees of the mines. Later came "literary exercises" before the courthouse and prayer by Reverend I. T. Osborn, the Episcopal minister, then baseball and a horse race down Main Street, during the course of which one horse plunged into the crowd and injured seven people. Evening fireworks also went awry when a rocket fell into the fireworks box, setting it off in all directions. No matter. The finale was a grand ball at the Alturas Hotel for the benefit of the Hailey Hose Company.[31]

St. Paddy's was also quite a bash. March 17, 1883, brought hundreds of miners and prospectors in from the gulches to celebrate the occasion with the citizens of Hailey. Speeches were given, the Ketchum Brass Band played, Ernest Fisher sang "Kathleen Mavourneen," and the Bellevue Dramatic Association presented "Miss Chester" to a good house. The day ended with a grand march and ball for the benefit of the Catholic Church.[32] No saloon keeper lost money on that day.

The Civil War, the bloodiest conflict in the American experience, was still in the recent past, so Memorial Day, then known as Decoration Day, also brought forth large crowds. With G.A.R. veterans much in evidence, the general public gathered to view a procession and to listen to local musical groups, home-grown orators, and poetry hammered out right there in Hailey. The day usually ended with a cemetery ceremony where children placed wildflowers on the soldiers' graves.[33]

Christmas was celebrated much as it was elsewhere in the country, as a religious holiday built around the family, but the community was involved as well. In 1881, a Christmas Tree Festival was held in Hailey for all children, with songs, recitations, and gifts from Santa, followed by dancing and dinner attended by eighty-two couples. Local businesses ordinarily provided free eggnog or other customary Yuletide drinks, and fancy balls were usually part of the festivities. Carrie Strahorn recalled that once, after a funeral, half a dozen of Hailey's young blades made off with Joe Morrell's hearse, the only vehicle available, to attend a Christmas ball in Bellevue.[34]

Those who weren't out getting primed to relocate abandoned mining claims often saw the new year in with gusto. Indeed, a few dedicated consumers of wet goods continued their Christmas binges without break, but most were more temperate. According to the editor of the *Times*, about two hundred shots were fired in Hailey to greet the arrival of 1884. For the ladies, New Year's Day was a time for calling, when socially responsible women plied their visitors with refreshments and good cheer.[35]

At least one advocate believed there was some interest in the fine arts in Hailey: George R. Davis opened an art gallery next to the Bonanza Lodging House in July 1882, and offered for sale "the finest collection of oil paintings and chromos ever seen on Wood River."[36] Two years later, Gilbert Butler, the principal of the Hailey Prep School, announced plans to open a photographic gallery at First and Bullion Streets, but he died before he could carry out the project, leaving a destitute wife and four children. Known locally as a fine artist, instrumentalist, and lecturer, Butler had studied at Oxford and in the studio of his uncle, Sir John Gilbert, before coming to the United States in 1869.[37]

Such occasions as weddings, birthdays, or anniversaries were celebrated casually or with fanfare, at home or in rented facilities. One of the most elaborate affairs was the fashionable evening wedding of William H. Greenhow and Alta Wheat which opened the 1883 social season in Hailey just a day after the new year began. The ceremony was performed by the newly-arrived Episcopal Rector, Israel Osborn, in the bride's parents' home, which was "crowded with representatives of the beauty, the intelligence, and the wealth of Wood River." Local papers gave a detailed explanation of the decorations in the south parlor where the knot was tied, and a stitch-by-stitch description of the bride's dress and her trousseau. Once the groom had properly kissed his new wife, the party adjourned to the dining room where wine was served and the cake table "fairly groaned beneath its weight" of "nine large cakes, and a variety of small ones." For those not present to view the wedding gifts on display in the sitting room, Picotte published a list. The gifts ranged from his own selection of a "large Bohemian glass berry dish, with silver base," to the pickle stand given by the S. B. Kingsburys and the "large bronze pendulum clock, with figure of Diana one-fourth life size" given by the Friedman brothers. After the wedding itself came a reception at the theater with Professor Delius's band and "a joyful throng going through the evolutions so captivating to the disciples of Terpsichore." Following a break at midnight for supper provided by the steward and assistants of the Grand Central Hotel ("chickens, turkey, etc., were brought in by express"), dancing continued "until near daylight."[38]

Another plush wedding was that of David Howard Foote and Florence Leonia Pound in the fall of 1884. The ceremony was performed at the bride's mother's house by Reverend Father Emanuel M. Nattini, the Catholic priest at Hailey. Among the gifts, the bride's brother, Homer, gave the pair a Sevres porcelain tea set, a cord of wood, and a year's supply of potatoes from his own substantial garden.[39]

If the Greenhow-Wheat and the Foote-Pound marriages were spectacular events for Hailey's elite, countless others were small, modest neighborhood affairs. So, too, were casual home affairs—surprise parties, taffy pulls, or especially parlor games for enthusiasts of Pedro, euchre, whist, five hundred, cribbage, or backgammon.

Especially popular among the younger generation were such "social" games as charades, traveling to Jerusalem, or spin the Platter. In vogue, too, were the "electric" parties of the 1880s—easy and pleasant ways to pass leisure hours during the long cold winter months. Electric parties required a room with a heavy carpet so participants could shuffle their feet to generate static electricity, which they discharged by touching fingers or even lips with another person.[40]

Parlor singing was an agreeable and easy entertainment. Favorites might include songs like "Old Black Joe" or "Old Folks at Home," introduced by traveling minstrels, or traditional Scottish or Irish ballads like "Annie Laurie" or "Comin' Through the Rye," or such favorites as "On the Banks of the Wabash" and "Sweet Genevieve."

Outdoor recreations were low-key and widespread. Outings and picnics were common for school, church, or fraternal groups at a pleasant place like Dorsey's grove. Especially in the summer, public sociables were held to raise funds for worthy causes, often by serving cake and ice cream on the school or courthouse lawn, complete with music and recitations.[41] Croquet, "the courting game," also known by some as Presbyterian billiards, was popular because of its coeducational nature.

Children amused themselves on Wood River much as they did elsewhere. Youngsters moving west brought with them a rich lore of songs, rhymes, jokes, games, and word puzzles—some of them centuries old. Thus from the beginning, there was a common heritage that drew children together. Marbles was a universal diversion for boys when spring warmed the air. Though their names might vary slightly, games like peg a Tory, mumbltey-peg, anti-i-over, or hide-and-seek were as popular in Hailey or Ketchum as they had been for generations in Boston. Little girls played hopscotch, threw jacks, and skipped rope to the same rhyming chants their grandmothers had used. A dozen variations of tag games were common and baseball was already as ubiquitous as houseflies in August. Wood River's small town boys played sand-lot versions that ranged from one old cat and rotation to the more orthodox game. In addition, the scope of youngsters' warm-weather activity ran the gamut from swimming in the Wood River or in the springs, to exploring local caves, hooking rides on ore wagons, fishing for trout, hunting rabbits, or experimenting with tobacco and profanity out behind Morrill's livery stable.[42]

Residents of all ages quickly became aware that the Wood River area promised some of the finest fishing and hunting in the United States. For some in the boom period, taking trout, grouse, or deer was simply harvesting resources for everyday living rather than a sport. But for others, the pursuits of Nimrod and of Isaac Walton were purely recreational. At Hailey, the Alturas Rod and Gun Club sought to protect wildlife from those who blatantly violated hunting and fishing laws by, for example, killing fish by dynamiting the river.[43]

Sports were always popular. At Bellevue as early as the winter of 1880, snowshoeing during the day and dancing at night were the main amusements. At this time, the term snowshoe referred to the so-called long snowshoe or ski, as opposed to webs, the other type. The skier utilized a single balancing pole, which was also used as a downhill brake, and the sport was ever a favorite winter diversion. As early as February 1881, it was reported that women at Bellevue "were the most expert snowshoers and races among them are of daily occurrence." Even a dozen years later, homage was still being paid to the area's comely skiers:

The ladies are few, but the fairest
That ever graced beautiful snow;
On snowshoes they're surely the "dearest"
In the mountains of Idaho.

At times the hills around Hailey were said to "have the appearance of a railroad map, so numerous are the tracks along their sides."[44]

Ice skating also had its enthusiasts, who had their choice of either the frozen streams and ponds or a makeshift rink in the upper end of Hailey that was flooded for that purpose—and where skates were available for rent at a quarter a pair. "Ketchumbergers," as Picotte called them, formed a Driving Club, pledged to admit to "honorary membership" every man or woman who could supply at least one horse for sleighing. "When thoroughly drilled to dodge snowslides and withstand the cold," the *Times* reported, "the club will visit Bullion, Bellevue, Broadford and Hailey and may even take a two-days' trip across the Sawtooth Range into Beaver Gulch." Even without the advantages of a club, what young woman could resist the kind of vehicle acquired by Michael Brown in 1892: a shiny new black bobsled with two high-backed seats, upholstered in red velvet, and complete with warm lap robe and chiming Swiss sleigh bells.[45]

Those with stamina and perhaps a pair of S. J. Friedman's "1,000 mile shoes" might enjoy themselves and even win a prize at the big Pedestrian Contest—"an Eight Hour Go-As-You-Please Walking Match"—held in Ward's Hailey Theater on August 26, 1882.[46] That was nothing alongside of the national craze of roller skating, which crowded the floors of Wood River theaters that same year. In one hour, on the opening night of the season in Hailey, "there was more solid fun in chunks to the square rod in the rink than on all the balance of Wood River for six months." Eventually, the skates so damaged the theater floor that it had to be refinished so that dancing could continue. Ward and Quantrell planned to lease the coliseum in Bellevue and lay down a new floor, and one wag suggested building an asphalt road between the two towns on which skaters might travel with speed and economy. One of the problems, it turned out, was that the impresario in charge kept moving his limited supply of skates from one town to another.[47]

A few years later, bicycles were the rage. A riding school in the Hailey Theater was jammed with learners and amused spectators.[48] By this time, the national League of American Wheelmen had been organized. The old bone crusher, with a postage-stamp saddle atop a sixty-inch wheel, still dominated. The safety bike and the drop frame for women were still a few years away, but energetic young ladies could enjoy the sport on their Quadrant or Coventry Rotary tricycles.[49]

Baseball was already America's favorite outdoor pastime, and the Wood River towns were no exception. Locals were so enthusiastic about the game that in 1883, when the Gate City club beat the combined Hailey-Bullion team (with side bets of $100), Picotte bordered the column in black.[50]

Betting improved any sport. When "Old Mose," a well-known fighting dog, scrapped in Hailey in 1881, it was for $3,000, and two men were said to have been killed in a follow-up bout connected with the main event. Cock fighting took on a partisan town flavor in July 1882, when a Hailey bird whipped a Ketchum bird at Faylor's Saloon.[51] Prize fighting was popular but relatively infrequent—after all, the real thing occurred in the drinking houses and gambling halls with regularity. In a bout between Frank McCormick, a "Colorado Light-weight," and Bill Thomas, "an unknown," for $150 a side and the gate receipts, McCormick, in "natty white knee-britches" and "stripped to the buff" from the waist up, won on a foul in the fourth round. The press did the story up right in coverage that took up almost two columns. Mac "laid a sockdologer" on his opponent's nose and struck "telling blows to the breadbasket." For his part, Thomas administered "square bone-to-bone knuckle-smashers" and "worked like a blacksmith hammering red-hot iron."[52]

In the summer of 1881 the contractor turned over the new mile race track to the Hailey Jockey Club. Although the town prided itself on having the finest buildings and "the most get-up-and-go of any town on the river," some race enthusiasts were embarrassed that their track equipment was far from state-of-the-art: indeed, the starter had to use a big milk pan for a drum. Apparently, Hailey had a second track completed during the following year after Commodore Perry Croy bought Mose Biddy's ranch on the town's west side and converted it.[53] Under the drive of Henry Miller, Bellevue was a strong competitor; in time, they boasted one of the finest mile tracks in Idaho where races sometimes drew entrants from as far away as Europe.[54]

As elsewhere in the West, almost any civic or governmental affair was cause for celebration—including public executions. Carrie Strahorn, whose house was just across from the courthouse, described Hailey's first hanging, that of convicted murderer George Pierson on August 1, 1884. She noted that the mines closed for the day and onlookers "seemed to come from the bowels of the earth and drop down from the sky."

Down from the hills came the trooping miners, and up from the valleys came the ranchers and the cowboys. Yet the crowd of such great magnitude kept a silence that was appalling. . . . And when the man was brought from the jail, the pall of silence and oppression was succeeded by a series of groans and moans that swelled into frantic and unnatural shouts of the multitude until the procession moved on down to the gallows of death, followed by thousands of curious and ghoulish people.[55]

Accompanied to the scaffold by Episcopal Bishop Daniel Tuttle and the Reverend Israel Osborn, Pierson seemed indifferent to his fate. From the gallows, the prisoner gave a long rambling discourse justifying the shooting of his victim; while Osborn offered a prayer, Pierson struck a match to light a final cigar as the mass of "sober, silent and reverent" citizens looked on:[56]

> When the ordeal was over and the crowds came back into town, the over-strained nerves of most of the witnesses headed for substantial spirits at the groggeries, and they held a night carnival almost as repulsive as the day had been, but wondrously free of crime.[57]

In terms of their amusement and recreational patterns, Wood Riverites were, like other Americans, organizers and joiners. Their countless clubs and associations reflect a desire to belong and be part of a larger group. Fraternal lodges played an important role: They furnished a place for men to meet and discuss a variety of matters ranging from individual improvement to local politics. They provided a continuity for members scattered throughout the mining West and they served as benevolent agencies in establishing cemeteries, life insurance programs, and charitable aid to survivors and the unfortunate. Among the numerous lodges in the western mining communities, the most popular were the Masons, the Odd Fellows, the Ancient Order of United Workmen, and the Knights of Pythias.

Bellevue's Odd Fellows lodge, the first on the river, was begun in July 1882. A year later, it had thirty-five members and $1,000 worth of property. Apparently there was another lodge later in Ketchum, because Isaac Lewis received $10 a month in rent for the Odd Fellows Hall in that town. In 1886, Hailey also organized the Daughters of Rebekah, a secret order for women, to supplement the work of the Odd Fellowship. The Masonic Grand Lodge of Idaho went back to 1867. By 1883, it had sixteen lodges under its jurisdiction, including the Hailey Lodge and the St. John Lodge at Bellevue, which had twenty-two members. Hailey also had Royal Arch Masons (Alturas Chapter Number 5) and the Chinese Masonic Lodge.

The Ancient Order of United Workmen had an all-white membership, but it included all classes and kinds of labor. The first brotherhood was organized in Hailey in the fall of 1883, and soon lodges had been added in Ketchum, Bellevue, and Bullion as well. Branches of national non-fraternal groups were also formed, especially the Good Templars—advocates of cold water refreshment—and the Civil War veteran's organization, the Grand Army of the Republic, of which Bellevue's James A. Garfield Post Number 4 was the most prominent on the river. Socially active, Post Number 4 announced that "the best String Band in Idaho" had been engaged for its gala ball of March 3, 1884, and that the town's leading hotels and restaurants had agreed to serve hard-tack, bacon, and beans at midnight.[58]

For the loafers who liked their recreation casual and unstructured, pleasant hours could be spent in a number of common commercial or governmental facilities. If saloons and billiard parlors were centers of social activity and business talk and provided companionship for the price of a beer or two, livery stables were traditionally places where idlers wiled away their hours around the potbellied stove, spinning yarns and passing the time of day. In like fashion, the Hailey premises of the Receiver and Register of the U.S. Land Office, first in the Strahorn block on Croy Street, then on First Avenue, also attracted men to socialize and hear arguments in land disputes, just as cases heard in the courts lured loafers and solid citizens off the streets to listen. While Homer Pound was Register, the office also served as a kind of showcase in which to exhibit farm products grown in the lower valley, including, in 1883, wheat and a turnip weighing "fully thirty pounds."[59]

For many people, the bulk of Wood River social activities were not particularly wild or raucous; rather, most were conventional and reflected the hopes of citizens to recapture as soon as possible the traditional ways of doing things. Even the reaction to public execution was not new or western, it was part of a time-honored ritual. People were recreating the society they had known before, and religion, law and order, and at least a smattering of culture were part of it.

CHAPTER SEVEN NOTES

1. For an assessment of such developments in two mining centers, see Margaret Atherton Bonney, "Recreating Culture and Society in Rocky Mountain Silver Mining Towns: Hailey, Idaho, and Aspen, Colorado, 1881–1887," *Journal of the West,* XXXIII (January, 1994): 24–36.

2. Carrie Adell Strahorn, *Fifteen Thousand Miles by Stage* (New York and London: G. P. Putnam's Sons, 1911, reprint, Lincoln and London: University of Nebraska Press, 1988), pp. 421–22, 473.

3. *Ibid.,* p. 418.

4. *Ibid.,* p. 473.

5. *Wood River Times* (Hailey) (weekly), December 7, 1881 and January 11, 1882; *Ketchum Keystone,* February 2, 1882.

6. *Wood River Times,* August 31, October 5, November 30, December 6, 1881; January 11, February 8 and 15, July 5, and December 8, 1882; January 11 and 23, 1883.

7. *Wood River Times,* January 28, 1884.

8. *Wood River Times,* January 16, 1883 and January 28, 1884.

9. *Wood River Times,* January 11, 1882.

10. *Wood River Times,* October 12 and December 6, 1882.

11. *Ketchum Keystone,* February 2 and November 3, 1882; January 9, 1884; *Wood River Times,* May 31 and June 5, 1883.

12. *Wood River Times,* June 5 and October 15, 1883; *Wood River Times* (weekly), January 25, 1882.

13. *Wood River Times,* June 12 and October 6, 1883; June 4 and 5, 1884.

14. *Wood River Times,* May 14, 1883, March 10, 1884, and February 21, 1887.

15. *Wood River Times,* May 24, 1882, July 21, 1883, August 30, 1884, May 26, 1886, August 15 and 17, September 15, 1887.

16. *Wood River Times,* September 2 and October 26, 1882; October 12 and 16, 1883; November 21, 1883.

17. *Wood River Times,* August 15 and 21, September 25 and 30, 1882; March 29, 1883.

18. *Wood River Times,* February 9 and December 10, 1884; January 17, April 6, July 29, August 15, and September 10, 1885; January 19, 1886.

19. *Wood River Times,* October 10, 1883; January 28, October 23, October 24, December 3, 4, and 6, 1884.

20. *Wood River Times,* July 17, 1885.

21. *Wood River Times,* June 13 and October 10, 1885; February 26 and March 1, 1886.

22. *Wood River Times,* March 10 and 19, April 28, June 19, 1886.

23. George A. McLeod, *History of Alturas and Blaine Counties Idaho* (Hailey: *Hailey Times,* 1938), pp. 170–71, 173–75.

24. Ezra Pound, *Indiscretions; or, Une Revue de Deux Mondes* (Paris: Three Mountains Press, 1923), p. 50; *Wood River Times,* August 4, 1884.

25. *Wood River Times,* July 11, August 4 and 11, 1884; Dick d'Easum, *Sawtooth Tales* (Caldwell: Caxton Printers, 1977), pp. 71–72.

26. *Wood River Times,* July 28, August 12 and 21, 1885.

27. *Wood River Times,* September 19, 1886; *Ketchum Keystone,* September 11, 1886.

28. *Wood River Times,* October 10 and November 15, 1882; February 5, 1883; *Wood River Times* (weekly), October 11 and December 6, 1882; *Helena Herald,* October 17, 1882.

29. *Hailey Times,* June 18, 1931; *Statistics of the Population of the United States at the Tenth Census, I, Population,* p. 56.

30. *Wood River Times,* July 5, 1883; *Hailey Times,* June 18, 1931.

31. Marilyn Watkinson, *Emmanuel Church, Hailey: The Early Years 1881–1901* (Twin Falls: Professional Print & Copy, 1991), pp. 54–55.

32. *Wood River Times,* March 17, 1883.

33. *Wood River Times,* May 29 and 30, 1884.

34. *Wood River Times,* December 21 and 28, 1881; December 24, 1883; December 27, 1886; C. Strahorn, p. 426.

35. *Wood River Times,* January 4, 1882 and January 2, 1884.

36. *Wood River Times,* July 19, 1882. "Chromos" are undoubtedly chromolithographs.

37. *Wood River Times,* March 19 and June 20, 1884.

38. *Wood River Times,* January 3, 1883.

39. *Wood River Times,* October 28, 1884.

40. *Wood River Times,* December 14, 1881, December 6, 1882, October 28, 1884, and September 19, 1885; Watkinson, *Emmanuel Church, Hailey,* p. 8.

41. *Wood River Times,* August 15, 1882; September 3, 1884; April 21, May 8, July 14, 1885; April 27, 1887.

42. On children's play in general, see Elliott West, *Growing Up with the Country: Childhood on the Far Western Frontier* (Albuquerque: University of New Mexico Press, 1989), pp. 107–14.

43. *Wood River Times,* August 7, 1884.

44. "F" to editor (Bellevue, December 14, 1880), *Idaho Tri-Weekly Statesman* (Boise), December 28, 1880; *Wood River Times,* January 22, 1890; Ron Watters, "The Long Snowshoe: Early Skiing in Idaho," *Idaho Yesterdays,* XXIII (Fall, 1979): 21–22, 25. The verse is from "Beautiful Snow in Idaho," written especially for the *Times.* See *Wood River Times,* March 13, 1893.

45. *Wood River Times,* December 6, 1882; February 12 and December 10, 1883; *Wood River Times* (weekly), December 7, 1881; Mary Brown McGonigal, *Spring of Gladness: Reminiscences of Pioneer Life in the Wood River Valley* (Sun Valley: High Country Lithography, 1976), pp. 134–35.

46. *Wood River Times,* August 26, 1882.

47. *Wood River Times,* November 23 and 29, December 6, 1882; July 2, 1884; *Wood River Times* (weekly), October 11 and November 29, 1882.

48. *Wood River Times,* February 25, 1886.

49. See Foster Rhea Dulles, *A History of Recreation: America Learns to Play*, 2nd ed. (New York: Appleton-Century-Crofts, 1965), pp. 194–96.

50. *Wood River Times*, May 16 and May 23, 1883.

51. "R" to editor (Bellevue, July 22, 1884), *Idaho Tri-Weekly Statesman*, July 31, 1884; *Wood River Times*, July 29, 1882.

52. *Wood River Times*, August 7, 1882.

53. "Houston" to editor (Hailey, June 27, 1881), *Idaho Tri-Weekly Statesman*, July 2, 1881; *Wood River Times*, July 22, 1882.

54. "A. L. M." to editor (Hailey, June 7, 1881), *Idaho Tri-Weekly Statesman*, June 16, 1881; McLeod, p. 54; McGonigal, p. 128.

55. C. Strahorn, p. 431.

56. Daniel Sylvester Tuttle, *Reminiscences of a Missionary Bishop* (New York: T. Whittacker, c. 1906), p. 423.

57. C. Strahorn, p. 431.

58. Isaac I. Lewis, "Reminiscences," (Ketchum, March 28, 1892), typescript, p. 200, American Heritage Center, University of Wyoming; McLeod, p. 54; James L. Onderdonk, *Idaho: Facts and Statistics Concerning its Mining, Farming, Stock-raising, Lumbering, and Other Resources and Industries, Together with Notes on the Climate, Scenery, Game, and Mineral Springs* (San Francisco: A. L. Bancroft & Co., 1885), pp. 141–42; *Wood River Times*, August 9 and December 13, 1882; September 10 and 17, 1883; June 29, 1885; January 6, 1886; facsimile of advertisement from *Daily News-Miner*, February 22, 1884, in Watkinson, p. 14.

59. *Wood River Times*, October 2 and 23, 1883; September 12, 1885.

CHAPTER EIGHT

"GIVE 'EM HELL, BISHOP!"

RELIGION WAS NEVER very far from the surface, although more than one clergyman who visited western mining camps expressed dismay at the lack of interest in religion displayed by the average miner. They attributed this to a preoccupation with wresting a fortune from nature and the absence of home and community ties and restraints. Moreover, the Sabbath in the mining town was not especially a day of rest and meditation: It was simply another day when establishments of all kinds—grocery shops, meat markets, liquor stores, saloons, gambling dens, and bawdy houses—proceeded full-throttle in the business of separating the mining man from his money.

The first church service in Wood River was given by the Methodists at Bellevue in the fall of 1880.[1] Although preachers were among the firstcomers, the construction of church buildings took time. A new settlement had to prove itself first before such an investment was justified. In the interim, visiting clergymen made the circuit in the summer and spread the gospel in saloons or dance halls that were also used for political meetings, lectures, theatricals, and other events. In an isolated camp such a visit was an occasion, especially if someone as popular as Daniel S. Tuttle, the strapping six-foot Episcopal Bishop of Montana, was the visitor. Ethelbert Talbot, who became the Bishop of Idaho and Wyoming in 1887, at a time when there were only four Episcopal ministers in each territory, was also popular.[2]

Daniel Tuttle was the Episcopal Bishop of Montana for thirteen years. He laid down the robes of Montana in 1880, but continued to visit Idaho regularly in the summers. He traveled nearly four hundred miles on horseback, sleeping on the ground in blankets and buffalo robes, and preaching in thirteen different towns, sometimes in rooms with dirt floors. By the time Tuttle first saw the Wood River country in the summer of 1881, he had visited dozens of mining camps in Idaho and Montana and knew them for what they were: "eminently excitable, unruly, defiant, without fear of God or man." "These sheep in the wilderness," both there and on the Salmon River, needed help. "No

Episcopal Bishop Daniel S. Tuttle served Montana, as well as Idaho and Utah from 1867 to 1886. *Idaho State Historical Society*

Sacraments, no Lord's Days, no Sunday Schools, did I anywhere find," he reported.[3]

While on the River that summer, "Bishop Dan" bought some "ample and eligible church lots" in Hailey and Ketchum, but it would take time to establish a resident minister in a parish. Meanwhile, Tuttle directed missionary activities in Idaho for another five years; he even worked the Bellevue-Hailey-Ketchum circuit himself for a week or ten days in the summers of 1882, 1884, and 1886. During his 1883 travels, Tuttle covered about a hundred miles on horseback and eleven hundred by stage coach. In many camps, he gave the only service people had heard in more than a year.[4]

Before he could preach, the itinerant minister usually had to publicize the forthcoming services, sometimes by tacking up notices, sometimes by personally spreading the word in the local bars. Bishop Talbot visited seven bars in one town in which he preached.[5]

Itinerant preachers had to be flexible in the rough Idaho camps where there were constant surprises. Talbot may not have been puzzled by the language of a saloon keeper's request ("Bishop, we have three kids for you to brand, and the old woman asked me to come and see if you could not do it some time tomorrow."), but he was astonished by the decorum and demeanor with which the entire baptism was handled.

The tastefully dressed men and women, the modest and reverent behavior of all during the service, the delicious refreshments served in perfect form—for all this I was hardly prepared myself. Then the toasts proposed for the health of the newly baptized little Christians completed a function in every way seemly and appropriate.[6]

On the other hand, Talbot and Tuttle also quickly learned the seamy sides of mining camp life—the rowdy world of saloons, gambling halls, and brothels. Even during their services they sometimes saw the consequences, humorous though they sometimes were, of the mixture of alcohol and religion. In the summer of 1881 Tuttle held the first religious service in the new camp of Bullion in a boardinghouse run by a Roman Catholic woman. A small commotion went on, as Tuttle recounted:

A man, the worse for liquor, near the open door was vigorous and frequent in his efforts to keep a dog from coming in to disturb the assembly. Succeeding in that, and conscious of his excellent service rendered, he now gave heed to me and my words. I ended, what from a literary standpoint was to be considered a fairly telling sentence, and gave the rhetorical pause to ensure the full effect. He was pleased. With eyes and ears he had followed the long sentence all through. He was wound up to a pitch of admiration, and not a half second of that dreadful pause rhetorical had passed before his honest tribute loudly struck on our startled ears—"good boy!"[7]

A few years later, when Bishop Talbot preached on the evils of liquor and gambling at a camp north of Wood River, another tipsy listener, who had previously heard him in Ketchum give what was "a hell of a good talk," now constituted a one-man cheering section: "That's right, Bishop. Go for 'em. Hit 'em again," and "Good, good! Give 'em hell, Bishop. Give 'em hell."[8]

In another instance, Bishop Talbot recalled the case of the Colonel, "a most lovable man" in the Wood River country, whose wife, "a cultured gentlewoman" was deeply interested in the Church, but concerned that her husband had never been confirmed. On his part, the spouse sometimes punctuated his otherwise normal behavior with alcoholic sprees that might continue for days. Ultimately, the Bishop agreed to try to persuade the wayward one to join the Church, and in the course of the conversation found himself being questioned about the chances of the Colonel's wife in the hereafter: "Do you think that St. Peter will let the old lady pass through the pearly gates?" When Talbot assured him that there was no doubt in his mind, that settled the issue. In that case, the Colonel saw no need for confirmation. "If the old lady gets in," he said, "and they lock the door against the old man, she will simply raise hell until she gets me let in. And she's sure to succeed."[9]

The bishops were not alone in their efforts. Father Thomas is reported to have said Catholic Mass in John Cunningham's store in Broadford on May 4, 1881, and he apparently returned every few months during good weather. Other roving soul savers were on hand from time to time. Dr. H. D. Fisher, the District Superintendent of the American Bible Society for Montana, Idaho, and Utah, was in Hailey in June 1882 preaching "to a large audience" from the sidewalk in front of the Merchant's Hotel and selling Bibles and other religious literature.[10]

As the rush subsided and gave way to a small industrial economy, and as camps became towns, more permanent religious establishments developed. St. Charles Catholic Church in Hailey was the first church built in the Wood River Valley. It was the work of Father Emanuel M. Nattini, a native of Genoa and a member of the Society of Jesus, who served in California after his ordination, taught at Santa Clara College, and was Prefect of St. Ignatius Church of San Francisco before coming to the Wood River country in the autumn of 1881, at first on a temporary and somewhat roving basis. By June of 1883 he was serving as resident pastor in Hailey and as missions pastor at Shoshone, Bellevue, Broadford, Bullion, and Ketchum. St. Charles was dedicated on June 17, 1883. Subsequently, Father Nattini built St. Mary's Church in Ketchum, converted an old abandoned school in Bellevue into St. Francis Xavier, and was responsible for the construction of St. Peter's Church in Shoshone. Before he left Idaho in 1886 because of his declining health, the popular and energetic priest had made many conversions to the faith and had performed 172 baptisms and at least thirty marriages on the river.[11]

Following Father Nattini's departure, Father Edward Morrissey filled in for nearly a year, and the Belgian-trained Bishop Alphonse J. Glorieux of Boise took charge the last eight months of 1888, during which time he made five missionary trips to Hailey. Even after the Dutch priest, Father Cyril Van der Donckt, began to make regular trips from Pocatello to Wood River in the early 1890s, Bishop Glorieux continued to travel to Hailey intermittently, at least until December 1893 when Father James Thomas was appointed resident pastor there.[12]

Among the fifteen Haileyites organizing a mutual self-improvement society in the fall of 1883 were two ministers, Reverend Pratt and Reverend Osborn.[13] Pratt's denomination is not clear, but Israel Tremain Osborn was an Episcopalian minister who left an indelible imprint on the region. In 1881, after the death of his infant daughter, Osborn left an established parish in Alexandria, Minnesota, and volunteered for missionary work under Bishop Tuttle in Idaho. He was assigned as rector of St. Michaels in Boise, and Osborn first traveled to Wood River in October 1881 when he performed a marriage ceremony for a couple at the bride's home ten miles south of Bellevue.[14]

By late 1882, Osborn had resigned his post at St. Michaels for reasons of "ill health." At the same time Tuttle sought to place a pastor in Wood River, and by coincidence, Osborn had chosen to rehabilitate himself in that region. He had arrived in Hailey on New Year's Day 1883—just in time to perform the Greenhow-Wheat wedding rites. When Tuttle appeared later in the year, he found Osborn "vigorously at work," and his health restored after a strenuous regimen of chopping wood and camp life. Quickly taking charge of the scattered Episcopalian flock in Hailey, where he announced regular Sunday services, Osborn also tended the strays in Bellevue and Ketchum during the week, and later added Bullion.[15]

Osborn also took the lead in the movement to construct a church in Hailey, a structure Tuttle believed would be the only church in town "except a small one built by the Romanists," who were also conducting a campaign for funds to build another in Bellevue. Tuttle himself was impressed enough to pledge $500 to the project. In the interim, other buildings had to make do: Tuttle and Osborn held services together in a theater, once in a dining room, and once in an abandoned restaurant.[16]

During Osborn's first year, Congregational minister George Ritchie had taken the lead in getting the Union Church constructed in Ketchum, but the facilities were shared jointly by the Congregationalists, the Methodists, and the Episcopalians. Eventually, in 1891, it became St. Thomas's Episcopal Church after it was bought by a wealthy Philadelphia woman and presented to the parish in memory of her late husband, himself an Episcopalian priest. (After a new St. Thomas was built in the 1950s, the old building became the home of Louie's Pizza & Italian Restaurant.) St. Paul's Episcopal Church in Bellevue was not completed until the summer of 1889, and Bishop Tuttle held a service in the new building.[17]

But the first Episcopal observances in Hailey, with Osborn in charge, were on January 7, 1883, in the Hailey Theater on Main Street, where a four-voice choir led the congregation. A week later, Osborn held his first "regular" service, this time in the schoolhouse, with standing room only. Thereafter, for several years the Hailey Episcopalians worshipped at the school, at the theater, and later at Chase's Hall.[18]

Meanwhile, the dedication of St. Charles Catholic Church in mid-June of the same year no doubt gave some momentum to the Episcopalian efforts. When Bishop Tuttle and Reverend George H. Davis of St. Michaels in Boise visited in July, they settled upon the name Emmanuel for the congregation and set a goal of raising $2,000 for the building fund.[19]

The church women took the lead with an assortment of

money-raising events. They edited and sold *Vanity Fair,* described by editor Picotte as "a bright, crisp, spicy little sheet, which in turn touted a Ladies Fair to be held in the Hailey Theater July 3 and 4. Decorations were lavish and much was for sale: flowers, dolls, candy, ice cream, lemonade, fancy handiwork (including a fine Japanese quilt made by Mrs. J. K. Morrill, wife of the livery stable owner), wax flowers, ladies slippers, and an embroidered toilet seat. On the first night, patrons heard home-grown poetry, including "The Honest Miner," done in the style of Poe's *The Raven.* Each evening there was music. Those present at the opening night heard three solos by vocalists, one each by a guitarist, a pianist, and a banjo player, plus a piano duet by Alta Greenhow and Sarah Pinney. On the second night, the Ogden Brass Band played a number of selections. Each evening closed with a dance with music by Professor Delius' orchestra. After the ball on July 4, the ladies provided a late supper at Chase's Hall, where Christmas Day church services were held later that year, and where Osborn argued in his sermon that Wood Riverites "devoted too much time to worldly affairs to the utter neglect of religion."[20]

This was the first of numerous fund-raising events: dinners, concerts, masquerade balls, ice cream socials, and special programs of entertainment among them. An evening of "Musical Exercises," for example, starring "the celebrated Smith Family, assisted by well known local talent," made a net profit of $92.05 for the church construction kitty in October 1885. The "Smith Family," were all locals, down to financial manager "Mr. Hosey Aminadab Jones," a.k.a. Land Register Homer Pound.[21]

The fund drive continued on into 1886. In February two dramas, "Miss Chester" and "Lady of Lyons," were presented to raise money, followed with a "grand calico ball" by the young folks. In March, the Emmanuel ladies gave musical and dramatic entertainment at the Opera House, "highlighted with a tambourine drill, doll drill, comedy farce, and some special songs, etc." In May, the Boy's Club and the Young Folks Guild combined to help buy pews for the church. Included was a "Pink Performance," with both the hall and the young ladies decorated in pink. Later the young folks raised additional money at a picnic in Dorsey's Grove, south of Hailey, and the Ladies Guild's "lawn fete" did so well selling ice cream and cake for twenty-five cents that a few days later they were at it again on Croy Street; they made $45 in one day—good but not as lucrative as the "Young Ladies' Soiree" held late in October, which returned a profit of $72.40 for the building fund.[22]

Even before the church was begun, secondary drives were underway to fund the purchase of a bell and an organ. Reverend Osborn contributed $10 and suggested that parishioners each buy a pound of the bell for $.50. By early 1884 a 522-pound bell, cast in Baltimore, was in position at Chase's Hall. It would soon be moved to a tower of its own in front of the hall, awaiting construction of the church itself, and would be used to sound fire alarms, to indicate the noon hour, and for special occasions, as well as summoning the faithful to worship. Theodore Picotte reported a conversation that was supposedly overheard on the street:

"As I heard the bell tolling, last Sunday evening," a citizen remarked to Osborn, "it carried me a-w-a-a-a-y back!"

"I thought it must have carried you somewhere," replied the rector, "as it certainly did not bring you here."[23]

Local performances were often fashion statements. The organ fund drive followed, touched off by an elaborate concert at Ward & Quantrell's Theater on March 13, 1884, which Sarah Pinney opened at the piano "dressed in an elegant white lace skirt and crimson velvet basque with side panels of the same, square neck, décolleté, lace sleeves bouillonne at the shoulders, high coiffure sparkling with diamond dust." When Florence Pound played an instrumental duet with her husband-to-be, David H. Foote, she "wore an ecru bunting skirt, bouffante, with light blue ribbons, and a light brocaded basque, white lace fichu, and low head-dress." Miss Gallagher performed "in a very light brocade, elegantly trimmed with Spanish lace." One of the capstones of the evening was an operetta, *King Alfred,* in which Professor Butler played the title role while clad in "an Oscar Wilde suit, 'hermine' cape, and a Tam O'Shanter with a white feather." At the end, Professor Delius's orchestra held sway, and according to the press, "no such dance music was ever heard in Idaho before." At midnight, the Episcopal ladies served dinner to about sixty people. The net total for the affair of $190.50 went to the organ fund. Two weeks later, without solicitation, Reverend Osborn received the gift of a small Mason & Hamlin cabinet organ from St. Michael's in Boise. A venerable instrument that had come around Cape Horn, Osborn used the organ for years, and he often hauled it by wagon when he conducted services in Ketchum or Bellevue.[24]

In his report of 1884, Bishop Tuttle blamed "the dullness of the times" for the delays in building the church. Emmanuel's cornerstone was laid July 29, 1885, with Bishop Tuttle and Reverend G. H. Davis, now of Ogden, present for the appropriate ceremony, which was an interesting blend of Masonic and church ritual. First a procession marched though town, headed by the Ketchum Brass Band and followed by members of the Hailey Masonic Lodge and the Knights Templar of Salt Lake City in full uniform. At the cornerstone, which came from E. A. White's quarry on Indian Creek, the church choir and the Masons both sang hymns, after which Francis Ensign, stalwart Episcopalian and past grand master of the lodge, conducted the appropriate Masonic rite. He applied the spirit level to the stone and pronounced it square and level; he scattered over it some "corn of nourishment," some "wine of refreshment" and some "oil of joy," and dedicated it and the building-to-be to the worship of God. After that, Tuttle, Davis, and Osborn consecrated both the stone and the church.[25]

The last of the sixty-two thousand bricks from H. Z. Burkhart's kilns had been laid by the end of November. The first service was held in the still uncompleted structure on Christmas Day, 1885. Its total cost, including its ultimate furnishings, came to around four thousand dollars.[26]

Although H. H. Bancroft noted that as of 1883, Methodist, Presbyterian, Episcopal, Congregational, Independent, and Catholic flocks had been organized, not one of the territory's five Baptist, seven Presbyterian, or ten Methodist Churches was in Wood River, according to Comptroller James L. Onderdonk's territorial handbook of 1885. But he was vague and chose to ignore St. Charles Catholic Church by name when he noted that Roman Catholics "have parishes in the chief settlements" and that large numbers of Mormons resided in southeast Idaho. Bellevue had completed a Catholic church in 1884, a structure with walls three bricks thick from local brick kilns. Four years later, parishioners held a dance and dinner to celebrate paying off the debt. Between 1883 and 1892, Bellevue had four churches: Catholic, Episcopal, Baptist, and Presbyterian.[27]

Early Wood River never had a large enough Jewish community to justify the organization of a formal congregation, but the families of merchant S. J. Friedman and his cousin, Simon Moses Friedman, usually joined in the observance of the Sabbath and invited unattached young Jewish men to join them. In September of 1884, about forty people gathered in Hailey's Masonic Hall to celebrate Rosh Hashana, but the Friedmans often traveled to Salt Lake City for the autumn holy days.[28]

As in other mining booms, when the mines and their communities had established themselves, sporadic services by itinerant preachers gave way to more regular religious observances in established church structures ministered by resident clergy. In the process, the fund-raising activities of both youth and women's groups gave an additional and important dimension to cultural and recreational life.

CHAPTER EIGHT NOTES

1. *Hailey Times,* June 18, 1931.

2. Ethelbert Talbot, *My People of the Plains* (New York and London: Harper & Brothers, 1906), p. 117.

3. Daniel Sylvester Tuttle, *Reminiscences of a Missionary Bishop* (New York: T. Whittacker, c. 1906), p. 120; *Spirit of Missions,* XLVI (October, 1881): 458. A general sketch of Tuttle is in *Dictionary of American Biography,* XIX, p. 75. See also Betty Derig, "Pioneer Portraits: Bishop Tuttle," *Idaho Yesterdays,* XII (Winter, 1968–1969): 12–22.

4. Tuttle letter, in *Spirit of Missions,* XLVIII (October, 1883): 441; Betty Derig, p. 21.

5. Talbot, pp. 42, 44, 45–46, 50, 53–54.

6. Ibid., pp. 157–58.

7. Letter from Bishop Tuttle, *Spirit of Missions,* XLVI (September, 1881): 40.

8. Talbot, pp. 58–59, 63.

9. Ibid., pp. 153–56.

10. Mary Brown McGonigal, *Spring of Gladness: Reminiscences of Pioneer Life in the Wood River Valley* (Sun Valley: High Country Lithography, 1976), pp. 33, 131; *Wood River Times* (Hailey), June 26, 1882.

11. Rt. Rev. Cyprian Bradley and Most Rev. E. J. Kelly, *History of the Diocese of Boise* (Boise, n. pub., 1953), I, pp. 164, 169, 171.

12. *Ibid.,* pp. 203, 205, 247–48.

13. *Wood River Times,* October 6, 1883.

14. Born in Oak Hill, New York, in 1847, Osborn had been ordained by Bishop Whipple at Seabury Divinity School in Minnesota in 1875. He married a year later and for the next five years served at Alexandria. See Marilyn Watkinson, *Emmanuel Church, Hailey: The Early Years 1881–1901* (Twin Falls: Professional Print & Copy, 1991), pp. 2–3; *Wood River Times,* January 3, 1883.

15. Watkinson, p. 3; *Spirit of Missions*, XLVII (November and December, 1882): 424; XLVIII (October, November, and December, 1883): 441, 509.

16. *Spirit of Missions*, XLVIII (October, 1883): 441; XLVIII (November and December, 1883): 509; McGonigal, pp. 73–74.

17. Watkinson, pp. 3, 5; Carolyn and Jim Thorburn, eds., *A History of St. Thomas Episcopal Church 1891–1991* (n.p., n.d.), p. 2; *Wood River Times*, June 21, 1889.

18. *Wood River Times*, January 10 and 14, 1883.

19. Watkinson, pp. 8–9.

20. Watkinson, pp. 7–8; *Wood River Times*, December 26, 1883.

21. *Wood River Times*, October 8 and 10, 1885.

22. Watkinson, pp. 43–44.

23. Watkinson, pp. 17–19; *Wood River Times*, December 12, 1883 and February 19, 1884.

24. Watkinson, pp. 20–22; *Wood River Times*, March 15, 1884.

25. Tuttle, "The Eighteenth Annual Report of the Missionary Bishop of Utah and Idaho," *Spirit of Missions*, XLIX (1884): 540; *Wood River Times*, July 29, 1885.

26. Watkinson, p. 30.

27. "The Works of Hubert Howe Bancroft," XXXI (*History of Washington, Idaho, and Montana 1845–1889*) (San Francisco: The History Company, 1890), p. 547; James L. Onderdonk, *Idaho: Facts and Statistics Concerning its Mining, Farming, Stock-raising, Lumbering, and Other Resources and Industries, Together with Notes on the Climate, Scenery, Game, and Mineral Springs* (San Francisco: A. L. Bancroft & Co., 1885), pp. 140–41; McGonigal, pp. 74, 115, 180.

28. Juanita Brooks, *History of the Jews in Utah and Idaho* (Salt Lake City: Western Epics, 1973), p. 127; *Wood River Times*, September 28, 1884.

CHAPTER NINE

KING SILVER IS DEAD: LONG LIVE THE KING

WOOD RIVER MINES produced over two million dollars a year for the three seasons after the railroad came in, with good returns for owners of mines like the Minnie Moore, the Queen of the Hills, the Michigan, or the Overland.[1] A sharp decline began in 1887, and the annual output never approached the maximum reached in 1885, at least until the modern era when the Triumph Mine was developed. Bust was as much a part of the western miner's vocabulary as boom, and those on Wood River were no exceptions.[2]

As early as the latter half of 1884, there were indications of businesses in the doldrums. A year before, the national economy had taken a downturn. Financial uneasiness continued until May 1884, when a panic brought down a welter of banks and brokers, including the brokerage house of Grant & Ward, distinguished by the presence of a former president of the United States.

Despite the fact that its mines were producing well, Wood River reflected some of this uneasiness. Money was tight. The railroad machine shops had suspended operations in Bellevue.

Coffin Brothers, the proprietors of three stores on Wood River, had "made an assignment," the result of outside speculation, and the newly-purchased Minnie Moore started out in fiscal difficulties. "The shadow of hard times is creeping over this region," editor Picotte wrote, but he hastened to note that it was but a temporary matter: Once Republican James G. Blaine were elected president of the United States, capital would again be secure.[3]

In spite of efforts to establish a number of smelters in the area, the treatment of ores remained a problem. The early small plants could not compete with the large ones and quickly went under. Even the most successful, the Philadelphia Mining and Smelting Company's Ketchum operation, was far from perfect and rarely ran at full capacity. To be sure, throughout the mid-1880s it maintained an impressive physical plant, larger than all but a handful of similar smelters in the country. Its lodging house could handle eighty employees of the "small army of men and teams" its operations required: fifty to seventy-five workers directly, plus fifteen charcoal burners under contract, and a substantial number of teamsters hauling ore and supplies. In addition, the company operated a concentrator and four mines, which employed another forty-five men.[4]

Even so, the Philadelphia smelter was seasonal and was limited in the type of ore it could handle. It could make a profit on high silver-low lead, but not on low-grade ores with a variety of impurities. Some experts believed that smelters on the river could not succeed because ore diversity was lacking, and proposed building a large plant at Pocatello, near the junction of the Utah and Northern and Oregon Short Line railroads to draw all types of ores from Idaho, Utah, Montana, and even Colorado and Oregon, but no such enterprise ever developed.[5]

The Ketchum smelter never reached its full potential: Normally it ran only two stacks (sometimes only one) and shut down for the winter in January or February because weather prevented ore-hauling from the mines.[6] There was a certain irony in the way things were done. Wood River mines, including some owned by the Philadelphia company, were shipping ores 1,400 miles to Omaha, paying freight charges of twenty-five dollars a ton and making a profit, while local smelters were lying idle or working at only partial capacity.[7]

In June 1885, the Wood River Mining and Smelting Company, which owned mines, smelter, and sampling works at Muldoon, shut down on orders from the Omaha Smelting Works, which had underwritten part of its operation. Enos Wall was an excellent manager, Picotte thought, but was surrounded by too many hangers-on who "toil not, neither do they spin." Wall stepped down and a new work force was selected, but the Little Wood River smelter handled little ore after that.[8] The *Salt Lake Tribune* pointed to a "stringency in money matters," that caused Wood River to feel a severe depression, although better days were ahead. As the *Tribune* assessed the situation, part of the problem was too many non-producers making an easy living off the miners, and part stemmed from talk that lodes petered out with depth and the impact of a few sales at big prices—both of which prompted owners to try to sell, rather than to work their property. But with capital scarce, good ground lay idle. Depressed lead and silver prices, plus troubles over wages, eventually led to the shutdown of producing mines.[9]

Evidence of economic malaise touching the silver-lead industry was plain where labor was concerned. The early 1880s were years of prosperity for mining and for mining labor throughout much of the West. While the Comstock Lode was on the decline, numerous rich camps were on the rise—Deadwood, Butte, Leadville, Tombstone, and Wood River among them. As experienced mining men left the shadows of Mount Davidson for jobs in the booming new diggings, they brought with them their faith in labor unions and applied them wherever they went. As a result, more than three dozen new miners' unions were organized by the mid-1880s, as the movement spread throughout the mineral West from Bodie to the Black Hills, and from the Arizona deserts to the Montana copper country.[10]

Like workers in all fields, hardrock miners were always concerned about wage levels:

> *When men first started mining,*
> *One prehistoric day,*
> *No doubt there was repining*
> *About the rates of pay.*[11]

By the mid-1880s, such apprehensions proved well-founded. World silver and lead prices began a downward spiral, and in almost all intermountain hardrock camps mine owners waged successful attacks on the prevailing $4.00 a day wage scale. If unions resisted bitterly, sometimes violently, the end result was usually lower pay and often the demise of the unions themselves. At Silver Reef, Utah, miners struck the Stormont early in 1881 to protest wage cuts to $3.50, but after the arrest of twenty-two of their number on charges of riot, the strikers foundered and went back to work at the new scale.[12] In November 1883, under the newly formed San Juan Miners' Association, the mine operators at Telluride, Colorado, jointly reduced wages from $4.00 to $3.50 a day. The resulting strike closed every shipping mine in the district. A compromise at $3.75 eventually failed, and after several months the strikers capitulated. Farther south, in the $4.00 camp of Tombstone, miners vigorously resisted cuts to $3.00 in the spring and summer of 1884. Early in August, about fifty striking miners exchanged gunfire from behind a woodpile with seven guards assigned to protect the hoisting works of the Grand Central mine. Despite strong support and sympathy of many of the townspeople, after months of striking and some violence, the miners gave up, their union broken.[13]

Wood River was not immune to the assault against the $4.00 wage scale. Probably as a result of missionary work by Butte organizers, a miners' union had been organized at Bullion in the summer of 1881 and another was established at Broadford the following year. Both had the support of Picotte, himself a former president of the Mechanics' Union of Lyon County at Silver City, Nevada. In June 1884, Picotte had sounded the alarm of the threat to the union wage level posed by the discharge of hundreds of railroad construction workers once the Oregon Short Line and its Wood River branch were completed.[14] When the new British owners of the Minnie Moore sought to cut operating costs in July of the same year, the recently arrived superintendent, Cecil B. Palmer, believed that cheaper labor was the answer and urged his fellow operators to join with him in reducing wages to $3.50. When a number objected, including Enos Wall and Walter Jenny, Palmer announced the cut unilaterally for the Minnie Moore. Members of the Broadford Miners' Union promptly went out on strike, closing down the property. The other mines refused to follow Palmer's lead, so after only ten days the British company restored the $4.00 level. Picotte congratulated the miners on their triumph and applauded Palmer on his "manly course" in backing down.[15]

Palmer's "manly course" lasted only six months. In mid-January 1885, in conjunction with A. J. Lusk, manager of the Queen of the Hills, Palmer laid off all his wage earners and retained only men doing development work under contract and tributers in the stopes working for a share of the ore they took out. Then he and Lusk announced that the declining price of silver and lead and the high freight rates would not permit the old scale; after January 20, the prevailing wage would be $3.50 per day. When the Broadford Miners' Union called a strike, the Queen of the Hills, which had only wage employees, closed down. But Palmer continued to work the Minnie Moore with contractors and tributers.[16]

The president of the Broadford Miners' Union was Barney McDevitt, a veteran from the $4.00 camps of California, Nevada, and the Southwest, who had left Tombstone after the wage cuts of 1884 to work in the Queen of the Hills.[17] When Lusk signed up a contingent of new contractors to resume work at the Queen, McDevitt denounced the action as part of a union-busting move. The stage was set for a classic owner-miner confrontation—a prelude of the more extreme unrest that was later to come in Butte, Cripple Creek, and the Coeur d'Alenes.[18]

What followed was a 119-day strike, the longest yet in western mines. With the Bullion union strongly supporting their Broadford comrades, McDevitt condemned the use of contractors and announced that no work would resume until the $4.00 wage level was reinstated. But both the Minnie Moore and the Queen of the Hills found plenty of "contractors" at $3.50 a day and for the most part continued to operate. All the while, McDevitt, past president Charles O'Brien, and other zealous union advocates kept the pressure on the scab miners by resorting to intimidation, escorting them out of town, and forcing them to swear on their knees not to return and not to undermine the Miners' Union.[19]

Officials of the two mines (no others were involved), solicited protection from Sheriff Charles Furey, who after a few days arrested McDevitt and eleven others on charges of "unlawful and felonious conspiracy," and provided security for those who signed up to work. After preliminary hearings before the probate judge, McDevitt, O'Brien, and five others were held over for the grand jury, but they were granted bail, part of which was provided by editor Picotte, who fruitlessly called for arbitration. When a crowd of union men prevented scabs from entering the Minnie Moore, sixteen of those interfering were arrested for conspiracy, although at a mass meeting the following evening, the strikers renewed their promise to hold out for $4.00 a day, but pledged to stay within the law in doing so.[20]

Sheriff Furey used posse members from Bellevue and Hailey to escort contractors to work in both mines. To get them to work, the posse members had to help the contractors through a gaunt-let of more than a hundred jeering miners lining the street in Broadford. With financial aid from the Bullion union, Hailey and Bullion merchants, and miners' unions as far away as Bodie and Virginia City, Nevada, the Broadford strikers were confident that their long siege and "moral suasion" would ultimately close down the Minnie Moore and the Queen of the Hills.

But "moral suasion" proved ineffective; more and more "sheepherders and cowboys" went to work underground guarded by three dozen deputies at a cost to Alturas County of $170 a day. By mid-March, seventy-five men were at work in the Minnie Moore and sixty at the Queen. Already, a number of the strikers had departed for greener pastures, including O'Brien. Fights between scabs and strikers led to arrests, and rumors that the miners planned to dynamite Bellevue resulted in the formation of a Committee of Safety, called by some the "stranglers," be-cause they purportedly looked forward to hanging the strike leaders.[21]

Through a massive St. Patrick's Day demonstration, the min-ers made an all-out effort to oust the scabs. Sympathetic labor-ing men poured in from surrounding camps. Fearful that the mines would be seized, managers Lusk and Palmer persuaded the sheriff to add additional guards at the property. Parading through the streets, the assembled miners massed at the union hall to appoint a committee, chaired by McDevitt, to meet with Lusk and Palmer, who at first declined to confer with "such open and notorious violators of the law." But on advice of their attor-neys, they talked with the committee outside the Queen of the Hills works. They accomplished nothing. At this point, accord-ing to Picotte, the cry of "$4.00 a day or blood" arose, the Union flag was unfurled, guns appeared, and the column of miners marched toward the deputies at the Queen, halting only feet away from an open clash, when cooler heads prevailed.[22]

After McDevitt and a handful of union men attempted to

persuade the scabs to quit until the strike ended, the miners headed home exuberantly, feeling on the brink of victory. During the night, Furey telegraphed Acting Governor Curtis and asked for federal troops. In the morning, Curtis and General James S. Brisbin, Commandant of Boise Barracks, arrived in Bellevue—but without military escort. The Bellevue Safety Committee insisted that Curtis proclaim martial law, but he refused. "Martial law or protracted strikes kill a camp for everybody," editor Picotte wrote.[23]

When the governor attempted to set up arbitration, he was rebuffed by Lusk and Palmer, who would brook no compromise; whereupon Curtis and Brisbin departed in disgust, concerned at the "hot blood on both sides." By this time, Bellevue merchants were suffering: Business was at a standstill, and their sympathy with the strikers had clearly waned. Following the governor's departure, the well-armed, deputized "stranglers" resurfaced and escorted the scabs back to the mines, where strikers who tried to stop them were arrested on the spot. The sheriff also detained McDevitt and other union leaders on charges of riot based on the St. Patrick's Day confrontation.[24]

With the Minnie Moore and Queen of the Hills mines now fully manned by $3.50 per day scab labor, editor Picotte urged the union to capitulate, a move that was unpalatable "as a matter of principle" to members who technically continued the strike for two more months, although full-scale mining went on all the while. Finally, on May 19, both unions conceded defeat and abandoned the concept of the $4.00 day. Once the strike was over, other Wood River companies also adopted the $3.50 wage level.[25]

The union's setback led to an exodus of skilled mining men. Some went to the Nevada camps, especially Tuscarora, but many headed for the Montana copper mines where, if the wages were not better, accommodations generally were.

Another consequence of the defeat was the temporary breaking of the Wood River unions. The Broadford Miners' Union dispersed during the summer, and the Bullion Miners' Union went under in October. But before long, the Broadford miners had reorganized under the Knights of Labor and showed that they were still a force to be reckoned with.[26] Throughout the strike, tensions had been high as people used intimidation and confrontation—but limited violence. (Only one man was killed: A young scab accidentally shot a hotel clerk while demonstrating how he would handle any interference by union members.)[27]

Management won this round: There was no question that organized labor had lost the Wood River showdown of 1885. The miners would have to regroup and fight again another day and on different fields. Those fields turned out to be Butte and the Coeur d'Alenes in the 1890s. Broadford expatriates like Charles O'Brien, the former president of the Miners' Union, were among the Butte delegates meeting in 1893 to form the Western Federation of Miners. In fact, two of O'Brien's fellow Wood River strikers, Dan Harrington and Hugh McGee, were convicted of contempt in 1892 for their role in the north Idaho labor troubles.[28]

If Wood River had been "rather dull" economically and had been rocked by the labor disputes in 1885, it was still "one of the prominent camps in Idaho" and new discoveries added to its expectations. Locals argued that lodes actually widened as they deepened, and that legitimate growth was anticipated for 1886.[29] Although such mines as the Idahoan, the Queen of the Hills, and especially the Minnie Moore, "the belle" of the district, were highly publicized, silver mining was in trouble throughout the West. The price of silver steadily depreciated: it went from $1.03125 an ounce in mid-September 1885 to $.91 in August of the following year—the result, Picotte charged, of "the corrupt truckling to the gold-bugs of Wall Street by an incompetent Democratic administration."[30]

Even though rates were now reduced, total labor costs were high. The Philadelphia and Idaho Smelting Company at Ketchum was typical: its wage bill was 55 percent of gross income, and its profits depended upon the prices of lead and silver. Federal statutes of 1879 and 1883 had put import duties on sheet lead and lead ores brought in from outside the country, but the laws allowed gold and silver ores to come in free. In 1886, importation of lead ore and dross shot up 169-fold as smelters in El Paso and Kansas City began to bring in large amounts of duty-free Mexican silver-lead ores. This precipitated a bitter debate until the McKinley Tariff of 1890 put a $.015-per-pound duty on silver and all other ores containing lead.[31]

When their annual contracts with leading Wood River mines expired late in 1886 and early in 1887, the big Omaha and Denver smelters refused to renew them at the old rates. Competing smelters at Ketchum, Salt Lake City, Portland, Reno, and San Francisco opened polite negotiations, but they would not give acceptable prices, not even ones slightly below Omaha rates. So, early in 1887 there were practically no external buyers for Wood River ores.[32]

By the beginning of the next year, the Philadelphia Mining and Smelting Company had undergone what corporate spokesmen called "an amicable reorganization" precipitated by unhappy shareholders. The restructured Philadelphia and Idaho Smelting Company paid wages of $3.00 to $3.50 a day. It ran the Ketchum smelter continuously until 1890, when it shut down until autumn, 1892, then closed for good early in 1893. The company also owned a number of mines, including the North Star on the East Fork, the Silver Star in the Smoky District, and two properties on Boyle Mountain; and even before it halted its smelting activities, the company found it more profitable to mine and ship the ore rather than handle it itself.[33]

In this "period of stagnation," which the *Wood River Times* editor said all mining camps experience from time to time, inhabitants were "thrown upon their own resources for a while." If they rose to the occasion, he counseled, the doldrums period would remain short:

But if the residents sit down to mope and curse the country, and do nothing to develop it, the dull times are prolonged until most of the old residents are compelled to sell out to newer, fresher citizens, after which the region takes a new departure.[34]

A couple of weeks later, Picotte believed the situation at Ketchum was "looking up." One of the four smelting furnaces of the Philadelphia company was working steadily, a second stack was being readied, and there was plenty of ore in the bins. Governor Edward A. Stevenson reported in October that the Philadelphia and Idaho Smelting Company at Ketchum had worked at half capacity, employing fifty-six men at the furnaces, sixty-three in the mines, and an additional seventy-five working on improvements. According to Stevenson, the company produced $421,155 in silver, $185,962 in lead, and $16,033 in gold.[35]

But other producers were in trouble: Within a month a number of them began cutting back and laying off men, sometimes unconnected to silver prices or smelting and shipping rates. For example, the Elkhorn had lost its vein and paid no dividends after 1885. Its story mirrored that of many a Wood River mine that ran out of ore. Owners did limited work, half-heartedly seeking that elusive vein, while catering to individuals or groups who wanted to lease and bond the property for possible sale. Lessees had little luck and buyers were in short supply, even at bargain-basement prices. Still, for years, Isaac Lewis remained sanguine: "I can't help but believe that we have a mine in that hill." Finally on February 18, 1893, after no luck prospecting, Lewis suspended all labor on the Elkhorn, discharged his miners, and blocked up the tunnel. "I am too much crippled in finances to take any more chances," he wrote his partners. "Everything that I have made here, has been 'sunk again in the ground.'"[36] Even after Lewis's death in 1902, lessees vainly worked the property off and on for another fifteen or twenty years. One of them, M. O. Duffy, a former manager of the great Minnie Moore, estimated that half a million dollars had been spent trying to revive the Elkhorn.[37]

Not even such show mines as the Minnie Moore and the Queen of the Hills were exempt. When Superintendent Palmer left for England late in 1885, after the strike had been broken, the Minnie Moore had been in desperate financial straits. With debts estimated at a quarter million dollars, the mine and its works were in the hands of the first mortgagee, with other creditors "left in the lurch." Palmer himself was arrested momentarily at Pendleton, but he was allowed to proceed on home. The debt proved to be lower than originally thought and the controversy with the creditors was satisfactorily adjusted over a period of several years.[38]

Gradually the property came into its own. It was thoroughly explored and yielded much of its total production while in British hands. In 1886 it showed a net profit of $100,000 for the month of October alone, and by the end of the year all its outstanding debts had been paid off. By then, it was regarded as the region's showpiece, even though it was rumored that it might soon be back in American control. For the period of 1886–89, the net smelter return was $1,433,306.13; its operating expenses for the same four years were $784,310.63; new plant costs were $16,454.74; and outlay for new claims was $6,725. The profit was $625,865.76.[39] Between 1883 and 1890, the Minnie Moore reached a depth of 1,100 feet, with an average monthly production of 3,000 tons of ore, of which the total value of lead was $2.6 million and of silver $4 million, or a total of $6.6 million, of which 25 percent was profit to the owners.[40]

Late in 1887, the rumor that the Minnie Moore would shut down in an effort to force lower freight rates became "a reliable report," and about a hundred and fifty men were thrown out of work at Broadford. Seventy-two men were let go at the Queen of the Hills, and about ninety at the Minnie Moore, as the mines went on a winter basis. The Queen retained around fifty employees, and the Minnie Moore kept eighty to do "dead work"—work that was not directly productive, but was necessary for exploration and future production. Moreover, the cost of mining and shipping and the depreciated value of metal gave rise to rumors that owners would reduce wages of those still on the payroll. By mid-December, that had not occurred: rather, lead was up to $5.10 per hundred pounds, and at $.97625 an ounce, silver was as high as it had been in the past two years.[41]

Many thought that the pressure on the railroads was mere pretense, and that the real reason for the layoffs was the desire to reduce wages. This fear was borne out early in 1888, when the Minnie Moore joined its neighbors, the Queen of the Hills and the Relief Mine, in notifying miners that wages would thereafter be set at $3.00 per day. The Ketchum newspaper said the move seemed "like false economy."[42]

At the same time, the *Hailey Daily Inter-Idaho* argued that while the towns didn't look as lively as they were four or five years earlier, they were actually more prosperous. In earlier days, the editor noted, half of the newcomers had no work and no money. "It was simply a stampede that brought them, and many soon departed cursing the country and everybody in it." Men with funds to sustain prospecting had done well. Businesses carried those who were broke, and up through 1882–83 there were many failures.[43]

Pondering the dilemma in which they found themselves, a committee of mine owners called a meeting in James H. Beatty's office in Hailey on the afternoon of November 14, 1887, "to consider the burdens weighing down the mining industry of Wood River, and to elicit ways and means to diminish or eliminate them."[44] Ore producers from several Wood River communities met again in the District Court Room just before Christmas with a more specific aim in mind—to obtain better freight rates. The cost of shipping ore from Hailey to Denver a month later was $17 a ton; to Salt Lake City, $13; to Omaha or Kansas City, $21; but ore-sellers were uniformly charged $20 a ton, regardless of destination.[45]

Some relief came early in 1888 when the Minnie Moore and the Queen of the Hill managed to obtain a "considerable reduction" in freight, handling, and sampling charges. Late in July, mine owners jointly petitioned the Union Pacific Railroad for a uniform rate of $10 a ton on all ores from Wood River to the Missouri River. The response, in the form of new general rates instituted later in the summer, was encouraging: from Hailey to Denver, $10.60 a ton; to Omaha, $12.40; and to Kansas City, $13.40. Wood River's reaction was to ship so much ore that there was a shortage of railroad cars. But soon, the Omaha Smelting Works at Denver and Omaha upped its charges to $28 a ton for both shipping and treatment—an action that was received with bitterness in Wood River, although philosophical folks noted optimistically that silver was also rising in price, and Governor Stevenson believed that the most exorbitant rates had been adjusted with some satisfaction.[46]

During 1888, many of the most important Wood River mines ceased operations. Bust had replaced boom, and many inhabitants left in the spring and winter, although about fifty mines continued to run, "paying a liberal profit," according to the new Governor, George L. Shoup, who, like most local newspaper editors, sought to temper economic reality with optimism.[47] The King of the West closed down in the Smoky District; the Sawtooth country "was almost dormant" except for the Silver King, which shipped ore under a lessee, Major William Hyndman, until a fire in 1892 swept through the shaft, destroying all hoisting, pumping, and circulation works and bringing mining to a halt. Muldoon was in the doldrums with almost no mining activity. A forest fire in 1889 had destroyed the town buildings and the smelter, which had been idle since 1885. Subsequent efforts of Hyndman and of Salt Lake and St. Louis investors to develop new discoveries only sent good money after bad.[48]

Creditors and unpaid miners plastered the Keystone with attachments that forced it to stop work. The Minnie Moore, which had shipped only enough ore to pay expenses in late 1888, ran intermittently in 1889 and 1890. Its work force was laid off for a few days in March 1889 because of a "super-abundance of ore" that filled its dumps. In June 1890 it shut down again after a dispute with the Relief Mine next door.[49]

Located slightly north of the Minnie Moore on the same ledge, the Relief had previously taken out some $1.25 million and paid fifteen consecutive dividends. But with low silver prices, its owners were doing only limited development and exploration work. The controversy between the two companies stemmed from the fact that the Minnie Moore's expensive pumping equipment drained not only its own lower levels but those of the Relief and the nearby Queen of the Hills, neither of which bore any of the cost. With profits negligible and unwilling to drain the adjoining properties free, in 1890 the British owners removed its pumps and allowed the lower parts of the mine to flood.[50]

More than one expert blamed not only low silver prices but the crude mining techniques used. The fluctuations of production in the Mineral Hill and Warm Springs Creek districts did not necessarily correspond to silver and lead price swings; rather, they often reflected the amount of ore in sight at a given time and the nature of the ore shoots, which were relatively small and hard to follow. Underlying contemporary thought was the concept of a "Wood River fault"—the mistaken belief that a major fault cut through the region at a depth of three hundred feet or so. In the early days, underground development had been done mainly horizontally by adits, which made it more difficult to recognize extensions of lodes and limited explorations. Some shoots ran parallel and some were without visible connecting links. Even as late as World War I, when prices and production rose, Wood River had done little in locating virgin ore shoots.[51]

Many properties had no systematic development of ore extraction. Their owners simply "robbed and gouged" the ore bodies, "picking the eyes out" of their mines to remove the richest ore without opening further ground. Thus, when the panic in metal prices came, many companies found themselves with gutted mines and empty treasuries and had no alternative but to suspend operations.[52]

Wood Riverites, T. E. Picotte included, whooped it up for free silver and roundly excoriated Secretary of the Treasury William Windom's decision that effectively allowed Mexican silver-lead ores to enter the country duty free. As the price of lead declined and American smelters refused to pay more for domestic ores, mineowners sought a firm tariff on the lead content of all imported ores. This flood of foreign minerals mined by cheap Mexican labor, they argued, had depressed the price of lead, forced American mines to curtail production, deprived railroads of freight revenue, and thrust labor into unemployment lines.[53]

Coupled with the drive for a stiffer tariff went the call for the injection of a larger amount of silver into the nation's monetary system, a panacea advocated not only by silver miners everywhere, but also by debtors, especially farmers, seeking a cheaper, inflated money. A compromise, the Bland-Allison Act (1878), injected a limited number of silver dollars into the monetary system, and the Sherman Silver Purchase Act of 1890 nearly doubled the Bland-Allison amount, but the remedy was only temporary. From its level of $1.01375 per ounce in May, 1890, silver crept upward to $1.1525 by late September and lead went from $4.0705 to $4.95 per one hundred pounds. Wood River applauded, especially when it was announced that shipping rates to Salt Lake City would take a sharp drop.[54]

But neither half-hearted congressional legislation nor the

new price levels made much difference: Prices were still too low. Ketchum was described as "about as dull just now as any one could well imagine." Its smelter was closed, and even with the momentary price rise of silver, no efforts were made to reopen it. Only a few miners were working and little money circulated. Only when silver was remonetized, its citizens believed, would Ketchum "resume its old and rightful place among the leading silver-producing mining camps in the state."[55] One of the country's foremost mining engineers, William P. Blake, visited Wood River late in 1890 and noted that Bellevue "has just now a half-deserted look." "The fittest have survived," he commented, "and continue to ship ore, but hundreds of claims have been abandoned, or are worked only enough to hold them under the laws."[56]

Instead of climbing further, silver prices began a downward trend in 1891. "This Wood River country is pretty quiet," Isaac Lewis wrote one of his partners in Helena. "A number of good mines are being held for sale. Could produce large outputs, but owners won't operate. A large number of mines & prospects are held by men of no capital to develop with. Most mines are being worked by owners of one or two men, or be Lessees, in parties of two to four men." Even so, Lewis and some other local observers thought they saw better days ahead, and that larger amounts of ore would move later that year, but they admitted that Wood River mines had been "in disgrace" for a number of years.[57]

Perhaps the one bright spot in the summer of 1891 was the visit of "The Little Wizard," financier Jay Gould, who brought a vacationing party to Wood River in his private train. Included were his four children, friends, and an assortment of cooks, porters, private secretaries, and "other attendants." While his daughters, Helen and Anna, heard Bishop Talbot preach at Emmanuel Episcopal Church in Hailey, Gould bathed in the hot springs, visited the Red Elephant mines—where he lunched in the company boardinghouse—and tried the local trout streams. "It is simply delightful!" he said. "The fishing is the finest I ever saw or heard of." So taken was he with the area that he returned the following summer with his family and physician for another vacation.[58]

It is doubtful that Jay Gould shared the locals' monetary beliefs. Like those everywhere in the West who saw their lot tied to the price of silver, Wood Riverites quickly joined the free silver movement by urging the national government to permit the free and unlimited coinage of silver at a ratio of sixteen to one with gold—a move they believed would revitalize the mineral industry and the economy in general. The Ketchum Silver Club, patterned after those of Colorado, was organized in April 1892. Hailey followed with its own organization a few weeks later. With silver constantly sinking in value, the free silver issue dominated saloon conversations and newspaper headlines, although in the election of 1892 Picotte, that staunch Republican, railed at the Populists—that "Ghost Dance party"—and scoffed at their "rutabaga money."[59] Still, the Populists did very well in Alturas County.

In June 1893 the price of silver fell precipitously after the Herschell Committee of the British House of Commons recommended that Her Majesty's mints in India no longer coin silver rupees. Panicked selling on world metal exchanges plunged silver more than 23 percent, from $.81 to $.62 an ounce in only a few hours. Soon it was down to $.5875—with no market in New York "at any price." Industrial chaos followed. Many silver-lead districts, including Coeur d'Alene, suspended operations.[60]

The problems of silver mining and smelting coincided with weaknesses elsewhere in the economy. The failure of two business giants, the Philadelphia and Reading Railroad Company and the National Cordage Company, touched off an ever-widening spiral of financial ruin and national depression. In 1893 alone, over fifteen thousand commercial houses, six hundred banks and other fiscal institutions, and more than fifty railroads had gone under.

The only market left for ore was that already contracted, so Hailey citizens called a mass meeting for July 11 to consider the crisis. The large group in attendance—not unexpectedly—called for free silver immediately, and most of the state's other silver mining towns did likewise.[61]

By September 4, a week before "Silver Day" was observed at the great Chicago Columbian Exposition, a small amount of ore was being shipped. With silver holding steady at just above $.71 and lead at $3.20 per hundred (figures one editor called "Simply Hell!"), depression ruled the river.

There's going to be many a hungry man, many a sad-faced, sick-hearted woman, with helpless, shivering, appealing dear ones, the coming long and dreary winter because of those quotations; and it may be that "The worst is yet to come."[62]

The Minnie Moore had been abandoned, and in 1890 it had been allowed to fill with water. The Queen of the Hills mine, which had closed in 1892, started up pumps in March 1893, in preparation for offering the property on the London market—an effort which had gone on from time to time since 1886. Early in 1892 a British joint-stock company, Queen of the Hills Silver Mines, Ltd., had been registered, and about a year later entered into an agreement with the Bellevue Idaho Mining Company to acquire the Queen of the Hills, plus six other mines and additional properties including "a first class concentrating plant" and "a fine cottage and Office building at Bellevue with sleeping apartment for officers of the Company." The price was £235,000 (£233,000 in shares and £2,000 cash). Seven thousand preferred shares of £1 each were issued, but the company seems not to have done much actual mining in Wood River before it was officially dissolved in 1898. The property itself was not reopened until 1913.[63]

It would take a promoter with a good deal of brass in his

makeup to organize a silver mining company in the 1891–94 era, when previously prosperous operators were cutting back and passing dividends. At Salt Lake City, where a considerable capital for Wood River had been arranged in the past, there was now no activity. At least one Ketchum mining man whined about the "Salt Lake silurians, who will do nothing themselves, nor will they put it in the hands of those who can and will."[64] Yet some properties changed hands, and a few new operations were contemplated. A local group, headed by M. B. Loy, president of the First National Bank of Hailey, acquired the Cyclops Mine, next to the Red Cloud group on Deer Creek, and set out to develop it in August 1891. In the upper Wood River country, James Ben Ali Haggin passed his option on the Solace on to C. J. Johnson, who sold a third interest to stockholders of the Standard Oil Company in the summer of 1892. The Vienna mill started up to work Solace ore, but only on a short-run basis pending a rise in silver prices.[65]

As the price of silver plunged, owners had little choice but to close down or to cut expenses, usually by wage reductions. Seven miles from Hailey, the Red Elephant group laid off twenty-five men—a third of its work force—before Christmas, 1892, although the property had enough ore in sight to warrant a hundred miners—twice as many as it retained. By the following summer, the Red Elephant announced its complete closure, although late 1894 brought a resumption of work, with production of twenty to thirty tons per day. The Pittsburgh-owned Red Cloud Mining Company decided to resume underground operations at reduced wages: In wet places miners received $4.00 a day, and all others got $3.50. By August 1893, the Red Cloud was only working a handful of men.[66]

Some mine managers proposed, and their miners ratified the idea, that a sliding wage scale be established: If silver went to under $.80 an ounce, they would cut $.50 a day "all round." When Congress repealed the Sherman Silver Purchase Act late in 1893 ("The Death of Silver," the *Wood River Times* called it), the price of silver fell sharply. Miners and owners agreed on a survival plan, with wages fixed on the basis of 123 ounces of silver for 30½ days of work of ten hours each. Were silver worth $.85, that would equal $3.50 per day; but with silver at $.62, the wage equivalent would be only $2.57 a day. This sliding scale was accepted by the Hailey Knights of Labor and enforced by the owners, although in the following August, miners at the Red Elephant grumbled that wages were too low and that at $1.00 a day, board was too high. But their bargaining power was low. As editor Picotte put it, "it seems to be a question of either low wages or no wages at all."[67]

The editor of the *Ketchum Keystone* noted in the spring of 1893 that so many wages had been cut and so many mine operations suspended that silver simply was "not in it" for the season. Within a couple of months, the Philadelphia and Idaho Smelting Company closed down its plant and leased both its smelter and its mines, as did the Silver King, farther north at Sawtooth. The Jay Gould, previously a rich producer, went into the hands of lessees, who worked it on a limited basis with some success.[68] Mines like the Star, near Hailey, whose owners had marketed treasury stock early in 1893 to build a concentrating mill, and the War Dance, which had been idle all winter, limped along, extracting enough ore to justify their small crews, but making little profit.[69]

When the Buttercup mine management in Detroit ordered wages slashed one-third, from $3.50 a day to $2.35, the miners rejected the new scale, and the mine closed down and leased its property for the year. At the Queen of the Hills, where water was being pumped out preparatory to operation by the new British company, employees refused to accept a $.75 per day across-the-board cut and were replaced by a new crew at the reduced rates. Soon twenty more were added.[70]

David Falk of Boise, one of the early owners of the ill-fated

Indian Creek smelter, had retreated to the capital city, but still shared ownership of the Star Mine group with John Lemp. In the fall of 1893, the Star Company discharged its employees and Falk and Lemp sold the property to a Salt Lake City outfit, which had difficulty in coming up with the full $110,000 purchase price but were granted a more lenient arrangement to complete the transaction.[71]

The water-filled Minnie Moore, idle for several years, came into the news again early in 1894, when a 9/16 interest was offered for a mere $25,000 by the English syndicate, which had lost heavily in Argentina and was trying to recoup by clearing its decks of non-profitable property. It estimated that pumping out the mine, which was down 900 feet, would cost as much again as the asking price; however, the potential of a property that had already yielded $3.5 million was substantial. But there were no takers; it was late in 1900 before there were serious attempts to work it.[72]

Early in 1893 a Salmon City editor summed it all up: "The Wood River Mining Region is deader than a lime fossil," a charge that made the proprietor of the *Ketchum Keystone* bristle. Even in depression, he countered, Wood River mines turned out far more than those of Salmon. If only Washington would sanction free silver, "thousands of men would pour into this country at once."[73] Alas! Free silver was only a dream; in real life, Wood Riverites had to rely on their own resources.

Many miners left the area, although that didn't necessarily improve their circumstance. Even the gold camps were suffering hard times. One wrote from Cripple Creek, Colorado, that there were about twenty Wood River men there, but only three had jobs, and that "there are more d——d liars to the square inch in Colorado than in the balance of America."[74] A few, like Leopold Cramer of Hailey, marched on Washington in protest with Jacob Coxey's Army.[75]

Many of those who remained at Wood River were out of work. Picotte urged such men to take a lease on some claim for the winter to ensure enough income to feed themselves and to "keep out of mischief in the meantime." "No one is making much nowadays, and wage-earners are not the only sufferers by any means," he said.[76] Some disagreed. They argued that silver was too low for miners even to "make grub at present prices," but many miners took Picotte at his word. At the end of March 1894 it was reported that about twenty men were living at Bullion, all of them making ends meet by working leases. They were marking time. As George Riddle said when he came down to Hailey, "the camp is not dead—only asleep," awaiting an improved silver market, at which point "it will take on new life and boom as it has boomed before."[77]

As they did everywhere in the country, businesses went under. The Bellevue Bank went into liquidation late in 1892, undercut by depressed businesses and the continued closing of mines. The Bellevue lumber and farm implement firm, J. S. Whitten & Co., went "up the spout"; Carothers general merchandise store was "Pushed to the Wall" and was closed by attachment. S. J. Friedman's store—general merchandise and groceries—also failed, and Van Ness's Drugstore was taken over by the sheriff.[78]

The reason for distress, both business and personal, was clear: low silver and lead prices. Silver at $1.00 an ounce would work miracles.

> *How, then, can we defend*
> *The happiness of our homes,*
> *For on silver that surely depends—*
> *It can never be on gold alone.*[79]

The number of delinquent taxpayers went up (and so did the rates of the Alturas Water Company), but the people of Ketchum and Hailey could boast that within their boundaries not a single family "is known to be in want," and that Wood River was in better shape than the large cities of the United States.[80] Of course, if metals were low in price, so were other local products. Hay that had sold for $30 to $40 a ton in 1883 and $18 to $20 a ton in 1886, went for $2.00 a ton in the field in 1893; $2.50 in the stack; and $3.50 to $4.00 delivered in town. Other necessities were correspondingly cheap or available for next to nothing for the fellow who knew how to go about getting them. Hard times gave rise to the new industry of salvaging pieces of coal from along the railroad tracks and some people managed to live off the land. Sage hens and blue grouse were abundant and were hunted tirelessly. The grouse were "big as turkeys" and were offered for sale at $.10 each, with no takers. One enterprising soul confided that food for the summer cost him $2.25: $2.00 for shotgun shells and $.25 for fishhooks. Nobody on Wood River had to go hungry:

> We can freeze the East out, while living high on the best game and the finest fish in the world. To be sure, we may go a little short on clothes. But we can wear buckskin. I'll wear buckskin ten years to get even with the Eastern goldbugs.[81]

The average unemployed miner, especially if he had a family and saw cold weather standing in the wings, probably had less of a utopian view.

With business dull, editor Picotte reasoned that his subscribers would have more time for reading, so he expanded the *Times* by adding fiction as well as news and boilerplate.[82] The Christmas season was an especially hard reminder of economic malaise. In good times, most local businessmen handed out two or three hundred dollars' worth of presents: Every hotel and saloon set out large bowls of eggnog and boxes of Havana cigars for all comers on Christmas morning. But 1893 was an exception: "yesterday there was nothing of the kind," a disappointed Picotte reported. "Or if there was the matter was kept so quietly that very few knew of it."[83]

The next Yuletide saw some improvement, although the Catholic ladies of Bellevue held a pre-Christmas "hard times party" which was well attended by denizens of Hailey and Ketchum as well. Business had picked up some at the end of 1894, and the saloons again quietly dispensed free eggnog and a philosophy of optimism, even though the wholesale price of whisky had gone up $.34 a gallon, which Picotte thought was "an appalling disaster to the rank and file of the Democratic party." Drinkers at the Alturas Hotel were reminded of the good old days "when a two bit piece was the smallest coin in circulation, and about every other man met with expected to soon be a millionaire." If the return of those times was not imminent, a glimmer of recovery was on the horizon. "We are starting—slowly, very slowly, to be sure—on the up grade, and by this time next year we will all be much better off than we are now."[84]

Despite such optimism, Wood River's silver-lead industry did not bounce back quickly. Most of its richest ore deposits were in the Mineral Hill and Warm Springs Creek mining districts. Despite what the local tub-thumpers said, from the beginning probably not more than thirty to forty mines were producing at any one time, and usually fewer than that, but enough to assure profits until about 1887. Just at a time when silver prices were weakening, known ore shoots began to be exhausted at a faster pace than new ones were found, and there was a sharp decline in output. Farther north, the Coeur d'Alenes recuperated more rapidly and rebounded as the silver-lead-zinc producing region par excellence, not only of Idaho, but of the nation.

The crippled state of the industry momentarily turned Wood River attention to gold, and there was some activity along the Snake and in the Camas Gold Belt to the west of Hailey. The future of Idaho silver, in the eyes of perceptive mining experts, would depend upon improved prices and, that failing, new strikes, better management, and economy of production.[85] For Wood River, the silver boom days were over.

CHAPTER NINE NOTES

1. *Mining and Scientific Press* (San Francisco), XLIX (December 13, 1884): 470; *State Preservation Plan, Idaho*, I, p. 53.

2. Joseph B. Umpleby, et al., "Geology and Ore Deposits of the Wood River Region, Idaho" ("With a Description of the Minnie Moore and Nearby Mines," by D. F. Hewett), U.S. Geological Survey *Bulletin* No. 84 (Washington: Government Printing Office, 1930), pp. 83-85.

3. "Praxiteles" to editor (Ketchum, July 7, 1884), *Salt Lake Daily Tribune*, July 12, 1884; "R" to editor (Bellevue, July 22, 1884), *Idaho Tri-Weekly Statesman* (Boise), July 31 and October 9, 1884; *Wood River Times* (Hailey), October 8, 1884.

4. *Mining and Scientific Press*, XLIX (December 20, 1884): 386; L (January 3, 1885): 2; LII (January 23, 1886): 63.

5. *Mining and Scientific Press*, XLIX (October 4, 1884): 217.

6. *Mining and Scientific Press*, XLVII (December 15, 1883): 381; L (January 31, 1885): 76; LI (August 8, 1885): 105.

7. *Mining and Scientific Press*, L (January 31, 1885): 76.

8. *Wood River Times*, July 17, 1885; G. W. Barrett, "Colonel E. A. Wall: Mines, Miners, and Mormons," *Idaho Yesterdays*, XIV (Summer, 1970): 5.

9. *Mining and Scientific Press*, LI (July 25, 1885): 66.

10. Richard E. Lingenfelter, *The Hardrock Miners: A History of the Mining Labor Movement in the American West 1863–1893* (Berkeley, Los Angeles, and London: University of California Press, 1974), p. 128.

11. J. C. Murray, "History," in Eugene Lewis Chicanot, comp. and ed., *Rhymes of the Miner: An Anthology of Canadian Mining Verse* (Gardenvale, Quebec: Federal Publications, Ltd., n.d.), p. 13.

12. Lingenfelter, pp. 160–162.

13. Ibid., pp. 164–68; Eric L. Clements, "Bust and Bust in the Mining West," *Journal of the West*, XXXV (October, 1996): 40.

14. *Wood River Times*, June 21, 1884; Lingenfelter, p. 170.

15. *Wood River Times*, July 21 and 25, 1884; Barrett, "Colonel E. A. Wall," pp. 3–4; George A. McLeod, *History of Alturas and Blaine Counties Idaho* (Hailey: *Hailey Times*, 1938), p. 75–76.

16. *Wood River Times*, January 19 and 20, February 6, 7, 14 and 16, 1885. About the same time, wages at the Vienna and Mountain King mines at Vienna were cut to $3 a day. When the majority of workers announced they would quit, the owners vowed to hire replacements in Salt Lake City. *Mining and Scientific Press*, L (February 21, 1885): 129.

17. Lingenfelter, pp. 169–70.

18. For details of the Broadford strike, see Lingenfelter, pp. 169-77, and also Frank Thomason, "The Bellevue Stranglers," *Idaho Yesterdays*, XIII (Fall, 1949): 26–32.

19. *Wood River Times*, February 6, 10, 12, 16, 18, and 20, 1885.

20. Ibid., February 12, 18, 19, 23, 24, and 25, 1885; *Mining and Scientific Press*, L (March 28, 1885): 204.

21. *Wood River Times*, February 28, March 2, 3, 4, 7, 11, 13, 14, and 18, 1885; *Idaho Tri-Weekly Statesman*, March 7 and 24, 1885.

22. *Wood River Times*, March 16 and 17, 1885; *Idaho Tri-Weekly Statesman*, March 19, 1885.

23. *Wood River Times*, March 18, 19, 20, 26, 27, 28, and 30, 1885; *Idaho Tri-Weekly Statesman*, March 19 and 24, 1885.

24. *Wood River Times*, March 23, 24, 25, 28, and 31, April 2, 1885; *Idaho Tri-Weekly Statesman*, March 24 and April 9, 1885.

25. *Wood River Times*, March 24, April 9, 10, and 11, 1885; *Mining and Scientific Press*, L (May 16, 1885): 321.

26. *Wood River Times*, May 9 and 19, November 2, 1885; Lingenfelter, pp. 176–77.

27. *Wood River Times*, March 24, April 9 and 11, 1885.

28. Lingenfelter, p. 220; Robert Wayne Smith, *The Coeur d'Alene Mining War: A Case Study of an Industrial Dispute* (Corvallis: Oregon State College, 1961), p. 99; Frank Thomason, "The Bellevue Stranglers," *Idaho Yesterdays*, XIII (Fall, 1949): 32.

29. *Mining and Scientific Press*, LII (January 23, 1886): 63.

30. *Mining and Scientific Press*, LIII (October 16, 1886): 246; *Idaho Tri-Weekly Statesman*, December 4, 1886; *Wood River Times*, September 15, 1885; August 9 and 21, 1886.

31. August C. Bolino, *The Role of Mining in the Economic Development of Idaho Territory* (Idaho Bureau of Mines and Geology, Information Circular No. 6, Moscow, August, 1960), pp. 19–21.

32. *Mining and Scientific Press*, LIV (March 19, 1887): 186.

33. McLeod, p. 16; August Constantine Bolino, "An Economic History of Idaho Territory 1863-1890" (Ph.D. dissertation, Saint Louis University, 1957), p. 274; *Engineering and Mining Journal* (New York), XLV (February 25 and March 3, 1888): 149, 167; XLVII (April 20, 1889): 375.

34. *Wood River Times*, September 3, 1887.

35. *Wood River Times*, September 21, 1887; Edward A. Stevenson, "Report of the Governor of Idaho, 1887," in *Report of the Secretary of the Interior, 1887*, p. 816.

36. See Lewis to Hauser, Holter & Hale (Ketchum, September 23, 1889); Lewis to Holter (Ketchum, June 15, 1891 and February 23, 1893), Holter Family Papers, Box 115; Lewis to Hauser, Holter & Hale (Ketchum, September 21, 1891), Hauser Papers, Box 21; Lewis to Hauser (Ketchum, May 16, 1892), Hauser Papers, Box 22; Lewis to Hauser, Holter & Hale (February 4, 1893), Hauser Papers, Box 23, all in Montana Historical Society Archives, Helena.

37. M. O. Duffy to Holter (Hyndman, Idaho, May 20, 1918), Holter Family Papers, Box 115.

38. *Wood River Times*, December 15, 17, and 21, 1885; *Engineering and Mining Journal*, XLI (January 2, 1886): 11.

39. *Engineering and Mining Journal*, XLII (September 18, 1886): 209; XLIII (January 1, 1887): 11; *Wood River Times*, November 6, 1886; Umpleby, et al., pp. 220–21.

40. *Report of the Internal Commerce of the United States for the Year 1890*, Ho. Exec. Doc. No. 6, Pt. II, 51st Cong., 2d Sess. (1890–1891), p. 553; Bolino, *The Role of Mining*, p. 10.

41. *Wood River Times*, September 21; October 13; November 2;

December 17, 1887; *Ketchum Keystone,* October 29, 1887; *Engineering and Mining Journal,* XLIV (December 31, 1887): 491.

42. *Ketchum Keystone* (daily), December 24, 1887 and February 4, 1888.

43. Quoted in *Mining and Scientific Press,* LV (December 31, 1887): 418.

44. *Wood River Times,* November 11, 1887.

45. *Wood River Times,* December 24, 1887 and January 27, 1888; *Engineering and Mining Journal,* XLIV (December 31, 1887): 491.

46. *Wood River Times,* August 31, September 4, 20, and 21, 1888; Edward A. Stevenson, "Report of the Governor of Idaho, 1888," in *Report of the Secretary of the Interior, 1884,* p. 766; *Engineering and Mining Journal,* XLV (January 7, 1888): 24; XLVI (July 28, 1888): 70.

47. George L. Shoup, "Report of the Governor of Idaho, 1889," in *Report of the Secretary of the Interior, 1889,* p. 346; *Wood River Times* (weekly), October 16, 1889.

48. Nancy Miller, "Mining in the Sawtooths," *Idaho Yesterdays,* IX (Spring, 1965): 16; Lewis to E. W. Knight (Ketchum, June 11, 1888), Hauser Papers, Box 17; *Mining and Scientific Press,* LVI (February 4, 1888): 75; LVIII (February 2, 1889): 80; LIX (September 21, 1889): 225; *Engineering and Mining Journal,* XLIV (July 2 and December 31, 1887): 491.

49. *Wood River Times* (weekly), March 13, 1889 and June 11, 1890; *Engineering and Mining Journal,* XLVI (December 15, 1888): 508.

50. *Engineering and Mining Journal,* XLIX (June 21, 1890), pp. 712–13; L (November 29, 1890), p. 631.

51. Clyde P. Ross, *Mining History of South-Central Idaho* (Idaho Bureau of Mines & Geology Pamphlet No. 131, Moscow, July, 1963), pp. 10–12, 25.

52. Robert Bell, *Report of the Mining Districts of Idaho for the Year 1903* (Boise: Statesman Printing Company, 1904), pp. 17–18.

53. *Wood River Times* (weekly), October 9 and 23, 1889; James E. Fell, Jr., *Ores to Metals: The Rocky Mountain Smelting Industry* (Lincoln: University of Nebraska Press, 1979), pp. 193, 195.

54. *Wood River Times* (weekly), May 7, August 6, and September 24, 1890.

55. *Ketchum Keystone,* November 1, 1890.

56. William P. Blake to editor (Bellevue, November 4, 1890), *Engineering and Mining Journal,* L (November 29, 1890): 631.

57. Lewis to Anton Holter (Ketchum, June 15, 1891), Holter Family Papers, Box 115; *Ketchum Keystone,* August 8, 1891.

58. *Wood River Times* (weekly), August 12 and 19, 1891; McLeod, pp. 89–95.

59. *Wood River Times* (weekly), April 13, May 11, and June 1, 1892; *Wood River Times,* October 24 and November 21, 1892.

60. Walter Renton Ingalls, *Lead and Zinc in the United States* (New York: Hill Publishing Co., 1908), p. 34; *Wood River Times,* June 30, 1893 and March 3, 1894.

61. *Wood River Times,* July 7, 12, 18, and 22, 1893.

62. *Wood River Times,* July 5, September 4, October 4 and 17, 1893; *Ketchum Keystone,* October 28, 1893.

63. *Wood River Times,* December 24, 1886; March 8 and May 17, 1893; Queen of the Hills Silver Mines, Ltd., *Memorandum of Agreement and Articles of Association* (March 14, 1892); Agreement of February 25, 1893, between the Bellevue Idaho Mining Company and Queen of the Hills Silver Mines, Ltd.; Queen of the Hills Silver Mines, Ltd., Summary of Capital and Shares, March 31, 1894; Queen of the Hills Silver Mines, Ltd., *Dissolution Notice,* June 17, 1898, all in Companies Registration Office, London; Umpleby, et al., p. 237.

64. *Wood River Times,* December 3, 1892; *Ketchum Keystone,* June 10, 1893.

65. *Engineering and Mining Journal,* LII (August 22, 1891): 233; LIII (June 18, 1892): 648; *Wood River Times,* September 3, 1892.

66. *Wood River Times,* December 19 and 21, 1892; February 19, 1893; January 4, 1894; *Engineering and Mining Journal,* LVI (August 5, 1893): 146; LVIII (December 15, 1894): 586.

67. *Engineering and Mining Journal,* LV (June 10, 1893): 542; *Wood River Times,* May 23 and November 1, 1893; August 16, 1894.

68. *Ketchum Keystone,* March 18, June 10, and July 8, 1893; *Wood River Times,* March 29, 1894.

69. *Engineering and Mining Journal,* LV (January 14 and April 8, 1893): 37, 326; LVI (December 2, 1893): 576.

70. *Wood River Times,* March 8 July 3, 6, and 18, August 10, 1893; *Engineering and Mining Journal,* LVI (August 5, 1893): 146.

71. *Wood River Times,* October 3 and 30, 1893; April 21, 1894.

72. *Wood River Times,* February 19, 1894; McLeod, p. 8.

73. *Ketchum Keystone,* January 11, 1893.

74. *Wood River Times,* March 3 and September 3, 1894.

75. *Wood River Times,* May 13, 1894.

76. *Wood River Times,* November 4, 1893.

77. *Wood River Times,* December 2, 1893; March 28 and 29, 1894.

78. *Wood River Times,* September 24, 1892; May 16, 1893; January 9 and 24, November 6, 1894.

79. "Miner" to editor (March 26, 1894), *Wood River Times,* April 2, 1894.

80. *Wood River Times,* December 12, 1893; January 2 and 18, 1894.

81. Lewis, "Reminiscences," p. 175; *Wood River Times,* October 16, 1893; June 13, August 16, and October 1, 1894.

82. *Wood River Times,* July 29, 1893.

83. *Wood River Times,* December 26, 1893.

84. *Wood River Times,* August 27; December 15 and 26, 1894.

85. *Engineering and Mining Journal,* XLVII (May 18, 1889), p. 463; LVII (January 13, 1894): 26.

EPILOGUE

I F T H E L O W price of silver and the depression of 1893 for-
mally signaled the end of the bonanza days of Wood River, then,
to paraphrase Mark Twain, word of the complete demise of mining was premature and exaggerated. Some mining continued
from time to time, with a slight rally after 1895 followed by an
acute drop to a nadir in 1901, and a gentle improvement for a few
years. In the fall of 1904, one owner noted, "many of the old time
prospects are being revived and some of them are making very
fair showings at a greater depth."[1] That surge tapered off more
gradually until 1911. But occasional discoveries of new ore bodies in old mines brought momentary periods of revival.

During World War I and the early 1920s, production
increased, in part from demand and new or little-developed
deposits of an earlier era. With an occasional exception, most of
the famous old bonanza mines of the early days were quiet,
although a few limped on with brief good runs. The Red
Elephant, for example, produced well in the 1905–8 years. New
owners of the long-idle Minnie Moore pumped out the mine,

and between 1902 and 1906 they took out about $1.1 million in net smelter returns. Despite ongoing water problems, exploration and some mining continued intermittently until the property was again abandoned in 1927 after extensive development had shown the uniqueness of the mine: the Minnie Moore ore bodies had been created prior to others of the region. Wood River veins had been formed at two separate and distinct geologic periods. Although her glory days were over, even as late as 1977, when her dumps were being reprocessed, "the old girl" was still contributing.[2]

In 1917, the River's overall production was up, largely from the Independence Mine located in Warm Springs Creek district on a tributary of Elkhorn Creek, some four miles east of Ketchum. Worked off and on since 1883, the Independence had turned out an estimated $100,000 in 1913, and was the largest producer in the region until its ore bodies were exhausted and it closed down in 1923.[3] Not far from the Independence was the North Star, which first produced in 1883 and by 1915 had turned out an estimated $800,000. But by then, the remaining shoots contained some twenty thousand tons of sphalerite, galena, arsenopyrite, and pyrite in fine-grained refractory combination that could not be treated by existing methods. It was reported that similar ores in the Triumph were amenable to flotation, though to be profitable, lead, zinc, and silver must all be recovered.[4]

The Triumph was probably an extension of the North Star. It was located south of the Independence, six or seven miles northeast of Gimlet, and its surface outcrop was discovered in 1881. But its early yield was limited—it produced 9.7 tons of ore in 1884 and 171 tons in the next ten years. Its owners had declined $40,000 for the property, but for years the mine foundered because of the refractory nature of its ores, a complex mixture of sulfides similar to those of the North Star, but coarser-grained and with lower zinc content. Triumph-type ore was long recognized "as mineralogically and texturally distinct" from other silver-lead vein deposits in the Warm Springs Creek district.[5]

In 1927, selective flotation was successfully applied to the Triumph by a group of Salt Lake entrepreneurs who leased the property from the Haggin-Hearst interests, and production finally become profitable. Even so, the mine closed down for several years in the early 1930s, worked again through World War II, and finally shut down for good in the summer of 1957. Between 1936 and 1945, it turned out about a hundred thousand tons a year and was the second largest silver producer in Idaho. After 1940, the Triumph, the Independence, and the North Star, all combined under the control of a San Francisco conglomerate, took out an estimated $40 million—more than all of Wood River's boom period product combined. Much of the Triumph product was in lead and zinc, and its ore was brought down by aerial tram to the Gimlet railroad siding. Perhaps the measure of the company's success was that in 1993, the Triumph was given the dubious designation as an Environmental Protection Agency Super Fund clean-up site.[6]

High silver prices in 1967 gave a shot in the arm to some of the old properties around Bellevue, which were now revitalized and produced nearly $3.75 million in this and the following year. When this flurry subsided in the spring of 1970, Wood River had turned out more than $62 million, and was not through yet.[7]

Mining was not dead, but it was limited to a few properties, and on a scale that required even more capital than before. Bellevue, Hailey, and Ketchum were no longer the vigorous, pulsating, prosperous mining towns of old. They continued to exist, but often with greatly modified economic bases. Many of the small satellite mining communities failed to survive and became relics of the past. Where saloons and dance halls and restaurants had once rocked with sounds of music and raucous laughter, now only silence prevailed:

The rain, gust-driven, veils the distant pines
Upon the hill,
Yet cannot hide the skeletons of mines
And silent mill;
And through an empty street the cold wind whines
With hag voice shrill.[8]

Before long, not even empty streets existed in some; nature reclaimed its own. Sawtooth City withered and its post office closed its doors in 1890, although a watchman was retained at the Silver King mine for nearly forty years. The postmaster at Bullion also closed up shop in 1890, but the town hung on for several more years. Galena's post office had closed two years earlier; by 1890, the town was deserted. Vienna permanently locked up its postal facilities in 1887. Muldoon retained its post office, and a smattering of its population, with intermittent mining activity over the years, especially from 1908 to 1911. Eventually, most of its mining machinery was shipped to Hailey or Ketchum and only its charcoal kilns remained with sheep grazing among them. So eventually went Carrietown, Doniphan, Gimlet, and the others.[9]

The major Wood River centers lived on. They survived by finding new or broadened sources of livelihood. Roughly half a million acres of Sawtooth National Forest lie in the northern part of the new Blaine County—some of the best stock range for summer and fall grazing of cattle and sheep available in the West. It includes large stands of lodgepole pine, yellow pine, Douglas fir, Alpine fir, and Englemann spruce. Wood River and its tributaries provided excellent trout fishing and a natural winter habitat along Warm Springs Creek for deer, elk, bear, and mountain goats. The hot springs at Hailey, Ketchum, Clarendon, and Easley had long been popular locally, and continued to attract visitors.

For a time, Ketchum served as one of Idaho's most important

sheep shipping points. It also became the forwarding site for mine machinery sent north into the Salmon River area and it became a recreation gateway to a magnificent wilderness array of lakes and streams in central Idaho. Ultimately, winter sports also provided an economic base—for Ketchum particularly—after the Union Pacific railroad accepted the recommendation of Austrian Count Felix Schaffgotsch: In 1936, they built an exclusive ski resort half a mile east of town at Sun Valley, a premier winter playground that became an inspiration to other, now silent, western silver camps—including Alta, Georgetown, and Kellogg.

In time, Ketchum also expanded its "folk industry" to a point where tourism brought in more visitors in the summer than did the ski slopes in the winter. It emerged as an expensive, up-scale community where the affluent built lavish ski lodges or summer homes. Multimillionaire Senator John Heinz of Pennsylvania, for example, imported a fifteenth-century barn from England and had it rebuilt as a spectacular vacation retreat. Real estate values soared. An average house with a decent view might go for half a million dollars; by the 1990s, eight-figure prices were not uncommon. Stock brokers vied with realtors for the business of part-time residents and the growing number of year-round professionals ("fax-muters," someone called them) who worked from this mountain setting. Art galleries outnumbered bars three to one, and local theater groups were active in the summer.[10]

After the boom, Hailey remained the county seat. Its population declined as mining waned, but the town became a market center not only for whatever mining continued, but also for farming, stock, and lumbering. As a shipping point for wheat, oats, and barley, as well as alfalfa, clover, and timothy hay, Hailey became a major supply point for stockmen of the Sawtooth National Forest area. As the sheep industry expanded and spread, the town shipped substantial numbers of sheep and wool clip annually. Likewise, timber and cordwood were important. In recent years, when Ketchum became the focus of the monied elite, Hailey became the family suburb, the affordable bedroom community, for those employed in Ketchum. By the mid-1990s, Hailey too was showing evidence of at least limited up-scale progression of its own as developers, like actor Bruce Willis, underwrote the resurrection of some downtown theater and bar facilities.

Bellevue was the government seat of the old Logan County for several years when Alturas County was reorganized in 1889. But the town lost its position in 1895 when Logan County was abolished, and Hailey became the seat of the new Blaine County. Bellevue continued as a small-scale shipping point and a center for livestock growing and agriculture, which were its primary livelihoods, although it too would eventually serve as a bedroom community for Ketchum.

Old rivalries still persist, but tourist industries have focused some attention on the historic past. As a writer for the *New York Times* wrote of Ketchum recently, perhaps with some exaggeration:

[D]espite a preponderance of $4 million homes, espresso cafes and galleries run by people with European accents, this golden mountain community still prefers to think of itself as somewhat of an Old West geezer in need of a bath and a shot of bourbon.[11]

All of the modern Wood River centers hearken back to the good old days. In Bellevue, visitors can wander through the historic district listed by the National Register of Historic Places— an area bounded by U.S. Highway 93 and Cedar, Fourth, and Oak streets. In Ketchum, guided walking tours are available; tourists can visit Bald Mountain Hot Springs or the Ore Wagon Museum and see relics of the silver boom, including Horace Lewis's giant vehicles. There, too, the Annual Wagon Days celebration held on Labor Day weekend focuses on the rowdiness of the mining era. In Hailey they can still see a number of National

Register sites, including the expensive old Blaine County court-house; Homer Pound's house, where the infant Ezra nearly froze until his mother moved to the hotel; E. J. and Flo Fox's old store building; and the Emmanuel Episcopal Church that Reverend Osborn and the Ladies Guild had worked so hard to finance.

Hailey's Blaine County Historical Museum keeps alive the silver era, including a replica of a mine tunnel. Hailey features its own Days of the West around the Fourth of July, and in mid-August it hosts the Northern Rockies Folk Festival featuring art, music, and the cultural history of the American West.

Wood River was but one of many silver centers, and in its day it was inevitably compared to others, especially Leadville, the Comstock Lode, and the Coeur d'Alenes, although comparative historical studies are lacking.[12] Both Leadville and the Comstock were more compact than Wood River, but far richer. Comstock silver could be treated with simple procedures without smelting, although a good deal of the product was lost. Some Wood River ores were richer than those of the Coeur d'Alenes, but the north Idaho mines were far more extensive and enduring.

Despite claims of the local cheerleaders, even in their best years none of the Wood River towns were very large. There was no counterpart of Virginia City—reputed to have had twenty thousand people in the prime of the Comstock Lode—and no equivalent of Leadville in its heyday with its fourteen or fifteen thousand inhabitants. In his annual report for 1887, Governor Stevenson gave rough population statistics—Hailey, 4,000; Bellevue, 3,000; and Ketchum, 2,000; but all these figures were likely too high. By 1890, Hailey's official count was 1,073; Bellevue, 892; and Ketchum, only 465. Bullion had 119; Galena, 37, Sawtooth, 33; and Muldoon, 64.[13]

Certainly Wood River was no isolated phenomenon in western America. Its rise and fall followed the contours of the classic mining town cycle: rich strikes in isolated areas by roving prospectors; extravagant newspaper and word-of-mouth publicity;

the onrush of thousands, veteran miners and greenhorns alike, all with rosy expectations; a period of sorting out, during which original locators sold their property for a fraction of its worth, and promoters sought to wed mining property and capital, with advantage to themselves. With outside financing came rail connections, smelters, and concentrating mills. Under-ground development brought the transition from camps to towns and in essence the emergence of an industrial economy. When the rich ores began to peter out and the price of silver and lead declined, so too did the fortunes of Wood River. By the end of the 1880s, the original boom was over and the moment of truth was on hand for individual communities.[14]

Wood River exhibited the normal reflexes of western mining regions. If optimism, individualism, and a kind of do-it-yourself-ism were apparent in the raw mining towns, so was cooperation—in laying out mining districts and towns, organizing labor unions and a host of religious, fraternal, and social groups. Nobody was more dependent on a charitable national government than Wood River—in this case, for free mineral land, transportation, and communications. If inhabitants were motivated by a pragmatic optimism, a belief in the inevitability of success, were they any different from residents of small towns elsewhere? Did not the same kind of communities ultimately emerge? Wealth was the hallmark of success. Were the young silver-seekers in Croy's Gulch in 1880 any different in their aspirations from the young homesteaders who pushed out on the prairies of Dakota or Montana, or the young job seekers who left small Illinois towns to seek their fortunes in Chicago in the same year? Intensity might have varied and harsh reality might not have coincided, but the dreams were the same. Once the early phase of the rush was over, was crime really any worse in Hailey than in Ottawa or Mount Vernon? Were not the religious and cultural institutions of Wood River simply those of the hometowns—in New England, the Midwest, or elsewhere—of Wood River's inhabitants? Town rivalries were town rivalries, whether in central Idaho, Ohio, or even Australia, where Sydney and Melbourne went at it hammer and tong. The ethnic mix was probably no more pronounced in bustling Hailey or Ketchum than in other western mining centers, and certainly not as much so as in the steel mills of Pittsburgh or the slaughterhouses of Chicago. America was already a mixed population. Even such unassimilated groups as the Chinese clung to their religion, organized fraternal groups, and marched in Memorial Day and Fourth of July parades, just as their counterparts did in the coal counties of Pennsylvania or West Virginia.

No great technological improvements in mining or smelting came out of Wood River. Underground mining techniques brought from other mineral regions were older, established ones. The smelter at Ketchum was modeled after those developed in Nevada and Colorado. The application of selective flotation to complex Triumph ores came much later than the boom period and at a time when the flotation process was already well established. If Wood River mining and refining were hard on the environment, this was no departure from accepted practices that went back to classical times. The mineral industry had always left the earth ravaged and torn. Mining men at Hailey and Ketchum were applying standards of the late nineteenth century, not those of the end of the twentieth.

Like any concentration of people in a thinly populated territory or state, Wood River did provide a political springboard for a number of its citizens,[15] but it did not produce many bonanza kings who were the counterparts of James G. Fair, James C. Flood, or William Sharon from the Comstock; Marcus Daly or William A. Clark from Butte's copper era; or giants like George Hearst, whose magic touch extended to dozens of mines throughout the West. Money was made, but few great fortunes were amassed here. Of the fifty prominent mine, mill, or smelter owners studied by Richard Peterson in his book on western mining entrepreneurs, only Enos Wall was linked with Wood River.[16] Henry E. Miller got in on the ground floor with the Minnie Moore and did well, certainly, and his house in Bellevue was something of a showpiece. No doubt a number of people made enough to be more than comfortable, but not truly wealthy. Probably much of the real money went out of the territory to Philadelphia, Salt Lake City, New York, and San Francisco to less visible outside capitalists. Isaac Lewis, an example of a moderately successful local mine operator, had a share in the Elkhorn and other mines. In 1892, he listed his worth in all kinds of property (including mines) as $92,457.60, the equivalent of over $1.38 million in 1992 money.[17]

Bust was as much a part of the cycle as boom, and the responses of the Wood River towns to the down side were both typical and atypical of nineteenth-century silver centers.[18] The smaller satellites faded; the larger centers developed other economic bases. The revival of mining at the Independence, the North Star, and the Triumph provided a profitable but limited shot-in-the-arm for Hailey and Ketchum. But this was by no means comparable to the impact of copper, which directly followed silver as Butte's economic mainstay for the better part of a century, or even the long heritage of mineral production, including lead, zinc, copper, iron, manganese, bismuth, and molybdenum that followed Leadville's silver era.

If a few of the rip-roaring camps of the boom eras matured into modern regional centers like Butte, others, gaudily refurbished, capitalized on their past glories. Their mineral exhausted, the Georgetowns, Tombstones, or Virginia Cities no longer measured their wealth in silver bullion, but in the jangle of the cash register as tourists tramp along their wooden sidewalks. The destiny of Ketchum (and to a lesser extent, Hailey), like that of Aspen, Park City, and Telluride, is tied to the annual snowfall level and the daily traffic on the ski lifts and to the summer tourist trade. But most of the once bustling camps are quiet.

"Dead Towns," John Muir had called them when he visited Nevada in 1879. "Coyotes now wander unmolested through the brushy streets, and of all the busy throng that so lavishly spent their time and money here only one remains—a lone bachelor with one suspender."[19] Some settlements left crumbling ruins, but many left no physical legacy at all—and no bachelor with one suspender. Sawtooth City, Muldoon, Bullion, and the other small Wood River boom camps are in the same category as once-flourishing and now defunct towns like Caribou in Colorado, Swansea in Nevada, Elkhorn in Montana, and Mineral Park in Arizona—just a few of the names dotting the history of the mineral West.

But such ghost towns are not necessarily symbols of the failure of capitalism or of the westering experience. Those people who flocked into boom camps knew full well the transitory nature of such places; they knew that even successful mines were wasting assets, that bonanzas did not continue forever. Towns existed as long as they had a purpose to serve. When metal production was no longer profitable, that *raison d'être* ceased to exist and residents drifted off, perhaps to repeat the experience elsewhere.[20] It was part of the experience of being a miner.

EPILOGUE NOTES

1. Isaac I. Lewis to Holter (Ketchum, September 26, 1904), Holter Family Papers, Montana Historical Society Archives, Helena, Box 115.

2. D. F. Hewett, "Geology of the Minnie Moore and Nearby Mines" in Joseph Umpleby, et al., "Geology and Ore Deposits of the Wood River Region, Idaho," U.S. Geological Survey *Bulletin* No. 814 (Washington: Government Printing Office, 1930), pp. 221–22; Stewart Campbell, "A Geologic Error Regarding the Wood River District," *Engineering and Mining Journal* (New York), CXXVI (August 25, 1928):

287; Merle W. Wells, *Gold Camps and Silver Cities: Nineteenth Century Mining in Central and South Idaho*, 2d ed. (Moscow: Idaho Bureau of Mines & Geology *Bulletin* No. 22, 1983), p. 119.

3. Umpleby, et al., pp. 82, 84–85, 174–75.

4. Ibid., p. 86.

5. Ibid., pp. 182–83; Richard F. Sanford and Joseph L. Wooden, "Sources of Lead in Ore Deposits of Central Idaho," USGS *Bulletin* 2064–N (1995), N1–N2.

6. *Engineering and Mining Journal*, CXXIV (September 10, 1927): 425; CXXXXII (June, 1941): 74; Robert J. W. Turner and Bruce R. Otto, "Structural and Stratigraphic Setting of the Triumph Stratiform Zinc-Lead-Silver Deposit, Demonian Milligen Formation, Central Idaho," USGS *Bulletin* 2064–E (1995), E2; *State Preservation Plan, Idaho*, I (Boise: Idaho State Historical Society, 1974), p. 53; Paul Karl Link and E. Chilton Phoenix, *Rocks, Rails & Trails* (Pocatello: Idaho State University Press, 1994), p. 170.

7. Wells, p. 119. Early records were haphazard and incomplete. Large amounts of ores went to smelters outside the territory making tracing impossible. The most valuable source for the early years are records of the Hailey Smelting works, made available to Umpleby by E. Daft, ore buyer for the American Smelting & Refining Company, and of the Ketchum smelter, the latter in the hands of Alonzo Price at the time of Umpleby's survey, but both are fragmentary. Ore shipments that did not go through the Hailey Sampling Works were not recorded and numerous consignments entered only in the name of individuals could not be credited to specific mines. The U.S. Geological Survey began gathering production data on Wood River in 1902, but it took time for even that to become complete. See *Mineral Resources of the United States, Calendar Year 1886* (Washington: Government Printing Office, 1887), p. 146; *Mineral Resources of the United States, Calendar Year 1887* (Washington: Government Printing Office, 1888), p. 107; Umpleby, et al., pp. 85–86.

8. Arthur Chapman, "In a Deserted Mining Camp," in *Out Where the West Begins* (Boston: Houghton Mifflin Co., 1917), p. 53.

9. Lalia Boone, *Idaho Place Names* (Moscow: University of Idaho Press, 1988), pp. 149, 265, 386; Donald C. Miller, *Ghost Towns of Idaho*

(Boulder: Pruett Publishing Co., 1976), pp. 3, 4; Wayne C. Sparling, *Southern Idaho Ghost Towns* (Caldwell: Caxton Printers, 1974), p. 79; Vardis Fisher, *The Idaho Encyclopedia* (Caldwell: Caxton Printers, 1938), pp. 100, 101, 102, 104, 108, 111, 113.

10. Esquire, CXIV (December, 1990): 102; *Architectural Digest*, L (June, 1993): 128-35; *Washington Post*, April 1, 1996; *The New York Times*, August 30, 1990.

11. *The New York Times*, August 30, 1990.

12. Among the excellent histories of silver mining towns or districts are: W. Turrentine Jackson, *Treasure Hill: Portrait of a Silver Mining Camp* (Tucson: University of Arizona Press, 1963); Malcolm J. Rohrbough, *Aspen: The History of a Silver-Mining Town, 1879–1893* (New York & Oxford: Oxford University Press, 1986); Don L. and Jean Harvey Griswold, *The Carbonate Camp Called Leadville* (Denver: University of Denver Press, 1951); Duane A. Smith, *Silver Saga: The Story of Caribou, Colorado* (Boulder: Pruett Publishing Company, 1974); James W. Hulse, *Lincoln County, Nevada: 1864–1909* (Reno: University of Nevada Press, 1971); Grant H. Smith, *The History of the Comstock Lode* (University of Nevada Bulletin, Vol. 37, No. 3, Geology and Mining Series 37, Reno, 1943). For a perceptive comparative study of two Arizona mining towns, one silver (Tombstone) and one copper center (Jerome) of different eras, see Eric L. Clements, "Bust and Bust in the Mining West," *Journal of the West*, XXXV (October, 1996): 40–53.

13. Edward A. Stevenson, "Report of the Governor of Idaho, 1887," in *Report of the Secretary of the Interior, 1887*, p. 816; *Report of the Population of the United States at the Eleventh Census: 1890* (Washington: Government Printing Office, 1895), Pt. I, p. 99.

14. See Rodman Wilson Paul, "Colorado as a Pioneer of Science in the Mining West," *The Mississippi Valley Historical Review*, XLVII (June, 1960): 35–36.

15. Some examples include James H. Hawley, U.S. district attorney in Hailey in 1886, who ultimately became governor of the state; English-born Frank R. Gooding, who began his Idaho career in Ketchum in 1881, as mail carrier and then firewood and charcoal contractor, and eventually became Governor and United States Senator; James Gunn, an Irishman and Civil War veteran, who edited a Hailey

newspaper in the early 1880s, and eventually sat in the first Idaho state legislature and in the 55th Congress. Isaac Newton Sullivan of Hailey served over twenty-six years on the Idaho Supreme Court and was its first Chief Justice. Charles O. Stockslager in 1888 became Receiver of the U.S. Land Office in Hailey and went on to spend fourteen years as district judge and six years on the Idaho Supreme Court. James H. Beatty, also of Hailey, was one of the territory's last justices, then he served seventeen years as U.S. District Judge in the state. Hailey's George H. Roberts, who had once been Attorney General of Nebraska, was elected to the same post in the new state of Idaho. Isaac Garrett of Hailey, along with A. J. Pinkham and George J. Lewis, both of Ketchum, all served terms as Secretary of State of Idaho. See *Biographical Directory of the American Congress 1774–1949*, pp. 1220–1221, 1244; "The Works of Hubert Howe Bancroft," XXXI (*History of Washington, Idaho, and Montana 1845–1889*) (San Francisco: The History Company, 1890), p. 583; George A. McLeod, *History of Alturas and Blaine Counties Idaho* (Hailey: Hailey Times, 1938 pp. 116–118.

16. Richard H. Peterson, *The Bonanza Kings: The Social Origins and Business Behavior of Western Mining Entrepreneurs, 1870–1900* (Lincoln: University of Nebraska Press, 1977), pp. 19, 78, 81, 108.

17. Isaac I. Lewis, "Reminiscences," (Ketchum, March 28, 1892), typescript, pp. 197, 199, American Heritage Center, University of Wyoming. Calculated per John J. McCusker, *How Much is That in Real Money? A Historical Price Index for Use as a Deflator of Money Values in the Economy of the United States* (Worcester: American Antiquarian Society, 1992), pp. 329, 332.

18. The bust aspects of mining have not been studied in much detail. For a few exceptions see Clements, "Bust and Bust in the Mining West"; Hulse, *Lincoln County, Nevada: 1864–1909*; Michael A. Amundson, "Home on the Range No More: The Boom and Bust of a Wyoming Uranium Mining Town, 1957–1988," *Western Historical Quarterly*, XXVI (Winter, 1995): 483–505; and Andrew Gulliford, *Boomtown Blues: Colorado Oil Shale, 1885–1985* (Niwot: University Press of Colorado, 1989).

19. *Evening Bulletin* (San Francisco), January 15, 1879.

20. Clements, p. 49–50.

BIBLIOGRAPHICAL STATEMENT

ALTHOUGH WOOD RIVER does not figure prominently in most histories of Idaho, a number have been helpful in providing general background, especially the joint work of Merrill D. Beal and Merle W. Wells and the recent books by Carlos A. Schwantes and Leonard J. Arrington. At a more local level, George A. McLeod, *History of Alturas and Blaine Counties Idaho* (Hailey: *Hailey Times*, 1938) has been a fundamental source. Also useful is a promotional volume put out by the Territorial Comptroller: James L. Onderdonk, *Idaho: Facts and Statistics Concerning its Mining, Farming, Stock-raising, Lumbering, and Other Resources and Industries, Together with Notes on the Climate, Scenery, Game, and Mineral Springs* (San Francisco: A. L. Bancroft & Co., 1885).

Newspaper accounts have been of prime importance, especially those in the *Idaho Tri-Weekly Statesman* (Boise); the *Salt Lake Daily Tribune*; the *Wood River Times* (Hailey), both daily and weekly editions; and the *Ketchum Keystone*. In like fashion, periodical literature has been vital: *Idaho Yesterdays*, the publication of the Idaho Historical Society, has illuminated many aspects of the story. Also essential has been use of the two major mining periodicals of the day, *Mining and Scientific Press* (San Francisco) and the *Engineering and Mining Journal* (New York). The Episcopal publication, *The Spirit of Missions*, has been invaluable in describing early religious activity in the area. Waller B. Wigginton, "The Pounds at Hailey," *Rendezvous*, IV (Spring, 1969, pp. 31–68), paints an accurate and detailed group portrait of one of Hailey's first families, in the process providing an antidote for the jaundiced impressions left by Ezra Pound in his strange little book, *Indiscretions; or, Une Revue de Deux Mondes* (Paris: Three Mountains Press, 1923). Of a number of reminiscences that have been used, two have proved invaluable. One, by a perceptive woman who spent considerable time in Wood River, is Carrie Adell Strahorn, *Fifteen Thousand Miles by Stage* (New York & London: G. P. Putnam's Sons, 1911); the other is unpublished, a very detailed description of the life of one of Ketchum's leading citizens during the boom, Isaac I. Lewis, "Reminiscences," (Ketchum, March 28, 1892), located in the Western Heritage Center, University of Wyoming, Laramie.

Lewis's account is augmented by several hundred of his letters written to his partners in Montana and now found in the Samuel T. Hauser Papers at the Montana Historical Society Archives in Helena— a gem of a collection which adds another dimension to the understanding of mine operation and manipulation in boom time Wood River.

A variety of official Idaho state documents have added much to this study. These range from the legislative "Journals" and "General Laws of the Territory of Idaho," passed at different sessions, to the "Idaho Reports," which provide decisions of territorial appeals and supreme courts. Other pertinent state-sponsored publications include a number of specialized studies produced by the Idaho Bureau of Mines and Geology in Moscow, of which the most important has been Bulletin No. 22, Merle W. Wells, *Gold Camps & Silver Cities: Nineteenth Century Mining in Central and Southern Idaho* (2d edition, 1983), a fine historical assessment of the early mining era.

Federal documents have been widely consulted and run the gamut from annual reports of the directors of the Mint and of the territorial governors (written to the Secretary of the Interior) to the rich output of the United States Geological Survey, especially the series *Mineral Resources of the United States* and a number of specific studies on Wood River and kindred areas. Of special significance is Joseph B.

Umpleby, Lewis G. Westgate, and Clyde B. Ross, *Geology and Ore Deposits of the Wood River Region, Idaho,* United States Geological Survey *Bulletin* 814 (Washington: Government Printing Office, 1930).

INDEX

Index

Index